# Flying for Peanuts

# Flying for Peanuts

## Tough Deals, Steep Bargains, and Revolution in the Skies

### Frank Lorenzo

Skyhorse Publishing

Skyhorse Publishing books may be purchased in bulk at special discounts for sales promotion, corporate gifts, fund-raising, or educational purposes. Special editions can also be created to specifications. For details, contact the Special Sales Department, Skyhorse Publishing, 307 West 36th Street, 11th Floor, New York, NY 10018 or info@skyhorsepublishing.com.

Skyhorse® and Skyhorse Publishing® are registered trademarks of Skyhorse Publishing, Inc.®, a Delaware corporation.

Visit our website at www.skyhorsepublishing.com.

10 9 8 7 6 5 4 3 2 1

Library of Congress Cataloging-in-Publication Data is available on file.

Cover design by Michelle Manley
Cover photo credit: George W. Hamlin

ISBN: 978-1-5107-8166-5
Ebook ISBN: 978-1-5107-8173-3

Printed in the United States of America

*I dedicate this book to my wonderful wife, Sharon; and our four children, Nicole, Mercedes, Carolina, and Timon. Thank you for your support during our both challenging and great times together.*

*This book is also dedicated to the great team of employees I was privileged to work with at the several airlines we controlled. Thank you for your passion and commitment.*

# CONTENTS

*Prelude*                                                                    *ix*

**Chapter 1:** The Making of an Entrepreneur: 1940–1963          1
**Chapter 2:** Early Days: 1963–1970                                        25
**Chapter 3:** Milestones: 1971–1975                                       53
**Chapter 4:** Changes in the Air: 1975–1978                              87
**Chapter 5:** The Pursuit of National Airlines: 1978–1979       107
**Chapter 6:** The Birth of New York Air: 1979–1981               131
**Chapter 7:** The Continental Acquisition: 1979–1983            157
**Chapter 8:** The New Continental: 1983–1984                      191
**Chapter 9:** Seeking Critical Mass: 1985                            221
**Chapter 10:** Eastern Airlines: 1985–1990                          243
**Chapter 11:** The Shuttle Sale: 1988–1990                         275
**Chapter 12:** Making Continental Stronger 1986–1990          301
**Chapter 13:** Leaving Continental: 1990                            331

*Postscript*                                                               *355*
*Acknowledgments*                                                     *365*

# PRELUDE

OVER THE COURSE OF YOUR LIFE, YOU meet thousands of people. Obviously, some are more memorable than others. Some have a great impact on you. Some pass you like ships in the night. During my twenty-five years in the airline industry, including nearly twenty as the head of Texas Air Corporation, which eventually took over Continental Airlines, I met, worked with, and competed against some of the giants of business and politics. There was the legendary Captain Eddie Rickenbacker, the World War I ace, who became the principal owner of Eastern Airlines. There were his successors, including Colonel Frank Borman, the Apollo 8 commander who with his crew became one of the first astronauts to circle the moon. There was Brigadier General William Seawall, CEO of Pan Am. There was the renowned Robert Crandall, CEO of American Airlines, who had an outsize influence on commercial aviation in the United States. This list goes on. Some have died; almost all have retired; only a few are still active.

The most recognizable individual with whom my story intertwines is a person who grew up less than five miles from where I did, in Queens, New York. He and I could not have been more different. He grew up in Jamaica Estates, an affluent suburban neighborhood, the son of a successful real estate builder and developer. I grew up in Rego Park, a middle-income suburb, the son of Spanish immigrants, my father a onetime hotel dishwasher and later club bartender who, with my beautician mother, founded and owned a small beauty parlor in Manhattan.

The man from Jamaica Estates would go into his father's successful real estate business after college and lead the development of a number of large building projects for the family company, while I would strike out on my own, using my savings of $6,000 as a launchpad. He—Donald John Trump—would become the forty-fifth president of the United States. I would go on to build a large airline organization—at one time the largest in the free world—while serving as chief executive officer of its principal airline holding, Continental Airlines, as well as the group known as Texas Air Corporation. The dichotomy between the two of us couldn't be starker. Yet eventually our paths converged, leading us to negotiate one of the highest-profile deals either of us had ever put together.

My path crossed with another familiar name in business circles who is still active today: Carl Icahn. One of the most famous corporate raiders of the 1980s and 1990s, Icahn, like Trump, was a tough negotiator and a smart and successful businessman. He beat us out of acquiring TWA, after we had a purchase contract with the airline, in 1985.

Regarding Frank Borman—well, there were times when I had my doubts about his sincerity, principally when we were negotiating a takeover. However, I can say that he was one of the most honorable men I've ever known. A true pioneer, he was a no-nonsense leader in the space program and at Eastern. He did make some decisions that proved to be bad mistakes, but who among us hasn't?

Jay Pritzker, founder of the empire that eventually became known as Hyatt Hotels Corporation, was another well-known person with whom I had business dealings. Unlike Trump and Icahn, who saw airlines as a means to an end, Pritzker had a true affinity for the industry and maintained a long-term view of the business. And unlike Trump and Icahn, for whom gaudy displays of wealth were common, Jay was known to stay in hotel rooms with his brother and father in order to save money. He was also a director of Continental Airlines who became concerned about the carrier's health during the tumultuous transition from regulation to deregulation. It was Jay who suggested to me, at one of Continental's annual get-togethers, that Continental needed to get a group of guys like ours to make a bid for the ailing airline. We did so in 1981.

There are many more people whom I dealt with early in my airline career and who circled back to me later in important ways. You'll read about them in this book, although they will be among the many unsung heroes that made it all happen. You'll also read about my family history, my youthful entrepreneurship, my initial plan to go into the banjo bar business, the aviation advisory firm I founded with a classmate on a shoestring (our "office" was located in a public library equipped with a phone booth), and many of my other successes and failures. In addition, you'll read about the strategy I developed to deal with the federal government's policy toward airlines, which completely wrecked the economics of our business in an upheaval similar to the one companies are experiencing today as a result of technology and other factors. *Flying for Peanuts* tells the story of all this and more.

Also in the pages ahead, you'll see how fate, circumstance, and an appetite for adventure often converged and led me to the next level up. I was always a risk-taker, following my intuition and never taking no for an answer. As you'll see, the easy or conventional way was not in my DNA. If you told me no, I would find a yes. Some might even have called me impulsive at times—certainly headstrong. In the press, I've even been called ruthless. But I don't think that is fair or accurate. I was strategic and calculating in my business dealings, whether with other airline executives or with the unions. I held my cards close, waiting for what I felt was a good opportunity to buy or sell an airline. Timing is everything. You'll see how and why I did the deals the way I did, and that calculated risk-taking and correct analysis of opportunity are the keys to success.

While my dream was to lead, first in the airline industry and then in investing, I hope my shared life experience will give you the motivation to fulfill your own dreams, whatever they may be. I believe that each of us can soar into the sky, so to speak, aiming to be the best in whatever we choose to do.

# CHAPTER ONE

# The Making of an Entrepreneur

*From Queens to Cambridge*
*1940–1963*

ARE PEOPLE really captains of their own fate? Or does fate cast a mold for us, one that we can modify a bit, add color and polish to, but never completely reshape?

I suspect that who I am, the essence of myself, was at least partially formed by forces beyond my control. And I suspect that my journey into the business of starting and acquiring airlines was at least partially determined by the road map that heredity and my parents inadvertently created for me.

Both of my parents arrived on American shores from Spain, after taking separate voyages one month apart. They traveled across the Atlantic in steerage, over rough seas, eating little, sleeping in dorm-style bunks, and using a hole in the floor as a toilet.

My mother, Anita Trinidad Paulina Mateos Gandara, arrived at Ellis Island in June 1920. She was eight years old and made the crossing with her mother and six-year-old brother, hoping to reunite with her father, who had settled in West Orange, New Jersey, two years earlier.

My father, Olegario Manuel Lorenzo y Nuñez, was seventeen years

1

old when he crossed over. He had made the trip a month earlier, in May, accompanied by an uncle and a cousin, and soon the three of them found an apartment in Manhattan. Coincidentally, my father's passage was sponsored by my mother's family. Despite this early connection, because of the age difference, my parents never met until after they had both arrived in the new country.

Their journeys—uncomfortable, uncertain, yet hopeful and not a little daring—began in the rural northwestern Spanish province of Galicia. Life was hard in Galicia in 1920; it is still a rugged life today. The wet and cool climate, combined with the mountainous terrain, has always made farming very difficult—nothing like the sunny south of Spain. Perhaps as a result, the locals developed a hardy temperament. Galicians, known as *gallegos*, are considered very stubborn, very committed, and very loyal. *Gallego* means "dragon" in Spanish, and inside every Galician, it is said, there beats the heart of a dragon. People who know me, and who know the region and the language, have often said I have a lot of *gallego* in me. If this is true, then maybe I have Galicia to thank—or blame.

My parents grew up in the impoverished village of Caldelas de Tuy, right on the Portuguese border and the Minho River. In the early 1900s, Caldelas was known for its hot springs and baths, and its hotels catered to out-of-towners seeking mineral treatments prescribed by their doctors. My mother's father first came to Caldelas for such treatments from the similarly impoverished Estremadura region; he never left. He had had some early entrepreneurial success in the chocolate business and later studied accounting. But after the voyage to America, he never managed to transfer those skills to comparable employment in the new country and worked as a laborer. Nevertheless, he began his adult life as an entrepreneur.

My father came from a rural peasant family of fisherman and farmers, and they all struggled from catch to crop. They were never hungry, but they were never quite full, either, and nothing was easy. As a young man, my father was no stranger to hard work, but he dreamed of a land where all his hard work might be rewarded. He was a very dashing guy, a conqueror with an entrepreneurial soul that was destined to find its home in America.

My father made a clean break when he left Spain. By changing his birth date in the local church record, he made himself just short of military age and was therefore allowed to leave the country. He rarely talked about his past or his homeland once he arrived in America. As a child, I don't remember my father or mother ever trying to instill a sense of family history or cultural pride in any of their children. And so I grew up thinking that Spain was a poverty-stricken place, lacking in economic security and comforts—although of course those were the difficult Franco years after the revolution, and I'm sure that colored my parents' thinking. Over time, I've replaced those images of Spain with a more up-to-date, certainly truer picture and have developed a tremendous respect for the country and its people. I return at every opportunity, and I am continually charmed by the sensitivities and ambitions of the people there and embrace the culture of the region with the pride of a native.

In the early 1920s, my father began calling himself Larry. He found work waiting tables at places like the Williams Club and the Princeton Club. At night, he played saxophone in the speakeasies and clubs that thrived during the Prohibition years. He was good-looking, with a thick head of hair he would keep throughout his life, and he was always careful about his appearance. He was not tall or otherwise imposing, but he cut a memorable figure. Despite his fearless sense of adventure and sometimes swashbuckling demeanor, he was somewhat shy.

My mother, who went by the name Ana once she arrived in America, settled with her family in New Jersey near her father's job at the Edison laboratory. When the laboratory closed in 1923, the family moved to an apartment on East 43rd Street, the same building where my father and his family had an apartment, two flights up. The closure of that Edison laboratory is probably the reason that I grew up in New York. Had it remained open, my mother's family certainly would never have moved to the city.

By the time my mother was sixteen, she was waiting tables at the

3

Biltmore Hotel and had become a beautiful young woman. She had long brown hair and fine features; in the photos I've seen of her in her youth, she seemed to favor the smart fashions of the day. She was also ambitious and was going to school to become a beautician. After she passed away, we found paperwork from a manicurists' school she had enrolled in when she was fourteen and a certificate from that same school when she graduated at the age of sixteen. People started really young then and displayed their entrepreneurial leaning early.

My father, nine years her senior, began to take notice. He was very proper in his pursuit but also very persistent. He wrote my mother a note, dated January 25, 1928, in which he stated his intentions in formal English: "I have always been very interested in you and would like to speak with you," he declared in his finest handwriting. A week later, he wrote again to state that he was "waiting patiently" for a reply.

My mother, who kept both letters, showed the correspondence to her father, who wasn't pleased. The nine-year age difference troubled him, even though he and his wife, my grandmother, were also separated by a nine-year age gap. But Mom was taken by Dad's dashing appearance and kind manner. She was hopeful that her father would soon give in, but she was not willing to go against his wishes.

My father's *gallego* resolve ultimately wore my grandfather down, and my parents were allowed to pursue their courtship. They were married in the spring of 1929 at the Church of Saint Agnes, around the corner from their apartment building. Two days before their first Christmas together, my mother gave birth to a baby boy named Olegario. He was named after my father, and like his father, he became known as Larry. Six years later, she gave birth to another boy, Valentin, who, like his uncle and grandfather before him, went by the name Val.

Around the time of Val's birth, during the Depression, my parents took their first step as American entrepreneurs and opened a beauty shop in midtown Manhattan. They had each completed their separate stints in beauty school and had saved enough money by 1937 to lease a storefront on East 34th Street between Lexington and Park Avenues. They called their shop the Larian Beauty Salon, after Larry and Ana, and with the shop's opening the two of them began a stretch of long days and six-day weeks that would last for nearly forty years.

For immigrants who had arrived nearly penniless, they did well. At its busiest, the shop had eight people on its payroll. My father commanded the front, concentrating on the business end but also doing haircuts and permanent waves. My mother was the hands-on beautician, tending personally to her loyal customers. Both my parents worked hard and took tremendous pride in their business. They provided a service, contributed to the community, and called their own shots. Eighteen years after their uncertain voyages over the sea, they were living their American dream. And perhaps, in ways that I hadn't given much thought to until now, their move from wage earners to business builders had, by example, cleared a path for me to follow.

My arrival in this world, on Sunday morning, May 19, 1940, was a difficult and precarious one. My mother battled through sixteen hours of labor in our apartment on East 33rd Street, with my father and a very competent midwife named Stella Tofani at her bedside. My mother's suffering was so severe that Mrs. Tofani was ready to summon a doctor when I finally emerged with the umbilical cord twisted around my neck and the amniotic sac still clinging to my tiny body. This last detail, Mrs. Tofani declared, was a sign that I would always be shielded from bad luck. I was born at home rather than in a hospital because my mother was concerned about a couple of widely publicized cases of misidentified children at hospitals.

I was baptized Francisco Anthony Lorenzo, but everyone called me Paquito. Paco is a fairly common Spanish nickname for Francisco. The added diminutive translated to "little Paco." Eventually, it was shortened to Quito until I finally outgrew that in my teens and settled into Francisco and later Frank.

Within a year of my birth, my parents gave up their crowded two-bedroom, $45-a-month apartment and moved with their three boys to a new two-story brick house they had built on a double lot on Dieterle Crescent in the Queens neighborhood of Rego Park. The house cost $16,000 ($338,000 in 2024 dollars), which was a lot of money in

My mother with midwife Mrs. Tofani, and me as infant at our Rego Park home (1940).

1941, and they took out a mortgage for $4,000 (equivalent to roughly $84,000 in 2024). My parents were not comfortable living in debt, so they rushed to pay off their loan as quickly as possible. "At that time," my mother recalled, "until we had paid off our mortgage, we couldn't sleep well." They paid off the loan in two years. My mother continued to live in that house until she suffered a bad stroke and passed away in 2008. Maybe my parents' feelings rubbed off on me, since I hold a similar attitude toward personal debt.

Our house was directly beneath an approach pattern to LaGuardia Airport, which had opened in 1938. The planes never bothered me. They were just there, like the furniture. My father used to stand outside, and when a plane flew overhead, he would smile and shout, "What noise?" I still have childhood memories of being in our backyard, watching the planes pass overhead, and imagining long flights to exotic destinations.

We lived comfortably, and my parents were careful with their money, so there was always enough for piano lessons, baseball gloves, decent clothes, and family vacations. Looking back, though, I realize that my parents were stricter with money than was probably necessary, but that was just the way things were back then, particularly among immigrant families and through the Depression. Business was good at the beauty parlor. The war economy meant that women were joining the workforce in droves, and they wanted to look good for their job interviews and for nights on the town after work—all trends that my parents foresaw.

The high volume of customers led to a continual debate between my parents about prices: my mother wanted to raise them in order to increase the business's modest profits and modernize the shop, while my father was concerned about scaring off their loyal patrons. Over time, they settled on a middle ground, raising prices a little and modernizing a little. There were many times in my airline days when I was seated across a conference table debating fares with my colleagues and my thoughts would wander back to these kitchen-table discussions between Mom and Dad.

I can't remember a time when I didn't have an after-school,

weekend, or summer job. I liked putting in a full day's work and doing my job well. Really. I also liked making money, saving it, and watching it grow. My mother remembered that when I was a small boy, around ten or eleven years old, I would loan money from my piggy bank to my older brothers, who never seemed to have enough.

Often, entrepreneurs not only have role models like my parents but also start young. In fact, I hit on one of my first entrepreneurial schemes in the summer of 1952 with my brother Val. There was a wave of post-war home building in our neighborhood, and we quickly noticed that there were a lot of thirsty construction workers toiling in the hot sun. We loaded up my little red wagon with ten-cent sodas at the Woodhaven Boulevard A&P and carted our inventory to home-building sites in the area, selling those sodas for a quarter apiece. Never again in my business career would I enjoy such substantial profit margins!

As I grew up, my interests expanded to include baseball, photography, and collecting trading cards. Many nice-weather Sunday mornings were spent ditching Mass with my brothers and picking up a game of baseball in the schoolyard with some of the other neighborhood kids. We made a funny picture, I'm sure, all of us dressed in starched white shirts and pressed pants, careful not to slide or dive for a ball in our good clothes. Of course, with everyone dressed for church, no one was at a significant disadvantage.

It didn't take much to keep me out of church, despite my parents' best efforts to keep me in the fold. I was raised a Roman Catholic, but beyond the benchmark rituals of baptism, First Communion, and Confirmation, my church attendance fell off after I went to high school. I also was never a great fan of the formality of my religion or its constraints. However, my parentally instilled work ethic took hold early and, I like to think, never left.

My interest in photography began when I was very young, and it remains a hobby today. It also helped me launch another of my youthful enterprises. When I was around thirteen, I used some of my savings to buy a secondhand Argus C3 camera, one of the first 35mm cameras with a coupled range finder. Before long, I even set up a darkroom under the basement stairs in our house. One time I persuaded my friend Albert Wertheim and his parents to let me take pictures of his bar mitzvah. I did the job on spec, and after learning that everyone was pleased with the results, I presented the Wertheims with a bill for around $60, which wasn't peanuts. I sweated over whether Albert's parents would agree to pay a kid so much money for the photos. But they paid, although I heard a comment or two about the fact that I was not very shy about billing.

Like my brothers before me, I pitched in at the beauty parlor on occasional Saturdays. Initially, my job was to use a special magnet to remove pins from the hair of ladies who had had a finger wave, which was very popular in those days. But I soon talked myself into a promotion and wound up working at the cash register and running the front desk. I was never crazy about working at the shop and remember marveling at my father's patience with the women he occasionally described as "squawking hens."

I was actually a pretty good student, even if I sometimes joined a few friends in skipping school to spend the day in Times Square. At Stephen A. Halsey Junior High School, I was placed in a so-called special progress group, which compressed the seventh-, eighth-, and ninth-grade curricula into two years and put me a full school year ahead of my peers. I went on to Forest Hills High School, where I managed to make the honor society, then called Arista, nearly every term—and still found time for baseball, after-school jobs, and my share of goofing off.

Perhaps my most abiding interest in those years was airlines. I was fascinated by them. Maybe it had to do with the proximity of our house to LaGuardia. I followed news of the airline industry the way other kids looked at box scores (although I kept up with those, too). I sent away for the annual reports of some of the commercial aviation giants and even used some of the savings from my after-school jobs to purchase stock in Trans World Airlines, better known as TWA—destined to be my first employer out of business school.

Despite my intense interest in commercial flight, I never actually flew in an airplane until I was fifteen. During the summer of 1955, my parents decided we would all fly to Europe to visit my brother Val, who was stationed in Germany with the army. After persuading my parents to let me make the travel plans, I completed several after-school treks to LaGuardia, where I could discuss the details of the trip with the ticket agents there. I had very definite opinions about the various airlines when I was a kid. I had decided that TWA was my favorite (largely, I suspect, because I had heard so much about Howard Hughes, who controlled TWA then), so I planned the entire trip around TWA schedules. I could have used the phone, but it was more exciting to go out to the airport, and ticket agents were one of the main ways you purchased passage in those days.

That first flight from LaGuardia, on August 7, 1955, remains a vivid memory. I can still picture the long walk we made out of the terminal, stepping past a fence and onto the tarmac, climbing the stairs, and boarding one of TWA's Lockheed L-049 Constellation propeller airplanes. I was struck by its splendor. My heart raced.

I sat on the aisle, snapped pictures of everything, and even took notes. I wanted to remember it all. I was also amazed at the incredibly short interval between sunset and sunrise: when you're traveling east, especially in the summer, the sun sets on one side of the plane and quickly rises on the other. I hopped back and forth between windows, astonished at the spectacle. The engine noise, which didn't bother me at all when we were up in the air, buzzed in my ears for hours after landing. One thing I thought was very curious was the fire coming out the sides of the piston engines. I found it a bit scary until it was explained to me.

The first leg of our trip took us to Gander, Newfoundland, for a fuel stop. In those days, aircraft usually couldn't make it across the Atlantic without refueling. Then it was on to London for a few days. Our next flight was to Frankfurt, where we stayed a day and then took the train to Idar-Oberstein, near the French border, where Val was stationed. After we got there, Val went on leave and accompanied us to Amsterdam, which I found a most interesting city. One evening when our parents were briefly not with us, my brother showed me a bar where women were sitting in the front—on display, so to speak—a very new concept for a fifteen-year-old.

After my brother went back to his base, we traveled on to Zurich, Rome, Capri, Madrid, and Galicia before flying home out of Lisbon.

I had booked us into first-class hotels at each stop on our itinerary: the Frankfurter Hof in Frankfurt, the Dolder Grand in Zurich, the Excelsior in Rome, and the Castellana Hilton in Madrid. We also ate in all the best restaurants. Prices were reasonable in those days: business and tourist travel was still so light in postwar Europe that even the most elegant accommodations were affordable.

In Galicia, however, in my parents' hometown, we stayed for free at the Universal Hotel, a small run-down place my parents had purchased years earlier from my mother's aunt, who was retiring without an heir. It had been a popular resort at the turn of the century, but now it was losing money (and would continue to do so until my parents sold it, for very little, in the 1970s). There was some sadness to this homecoming. My parents enjoyed seeing old friends and family, but I think my father finally recognized that this was a world he had left for good. I enjoyed meeting a few relatives—aunts, uncles, and cousins— and in the process I got a feel for the life and rugged culture of Galicia. I have returned many times since.

When we got back, I framed the commemorative certificate that TWA issued to overseas travelers at the time, which proclaimed that "Francisco Lorenzo hath flown the Aerial Course by TWA Skyliner over Oceanus Atlanticus." The framed certificate remained on my old bedroom wall in our house in Rego Park for fifty-three years, until my mother's passing.

---

I received very little guidance from my parents when it came time for college, but my father assured me that cost would not be a factor in my choice of where to go. He was a proud man, and he'd worked hard to make sure his sons had the educational opportunities that had been unavailable to him. My father also had some very firm ideas about scholarships and financial aid. I might well have qualified for some

## TRANS WORLD AIRLINES, Inc.

Industrial Relations Dept.
P. O. Box 637
New York Airport Station
Flushing 71, New York
March 14, 1956

Mr. Frank Lorenzo
63-44 Dieterle Cres.
Rego Park 74, N. Y.

Dear Mr. Lorenzo:
Thank you for your recent letter in which you expressed an interest in becoming associated with our company on a temporary basis.

We are sorry to inform you that due to the highly specialized work required in commercial aviation, and the amount of time required in training new employees, consideration cannot be given to temporary assignments. All assignments are made on a permanent basis.

Your interest in Trans World Airlines is sincerely appreciated.

Very truly yours,

TRANS WORLD AIRLINES, INC.

*Elizabeth Leloche*

Personnel Representative
Atlantic Region

U.S.A. · EUROPE · AFRICA · ASIA

Letters from TWA on employment when sixteen and eighteen (1956 and 1958).

## TRANS WORLD AIRLINES, INC.

Industrial Relations Dept.
P. O. Box 637
New York Airport Station
Flushing 71, New York
January 15, 1958

Dear Mr. Lorenzo:

Your application is in our active files.

At the present time we have several vacancies that may be of
interest to you, and would therefore appreciate your reporting
to this office, Room 219, Hangar 4, LaGuardia Field for a
personal interview at the earliest possible date. Interviews
are conducted daily, Monday through Friday, between the hours
of 9:00 a.m. and 1:00 p.m.

Unless we hear from you within seven days from the date appear-
ing on this letter we will assume you are no longer interested
and your application will be removed from our files.

Very truly yours,

TRANS WORLD AIRLINES, INC.,

*John A. Banes*

Personnel Representative
Atlantic Region

U.S.A. · EUROPE · AFRICA · ASIA

scholarships, but I never applied for any of them. In Dad's proud mind, scholarships were like welfare. I guess times have changed.

If I had any career plans at all, I suppose I thought about becoming an engineer. But I also realized that I wanted a broad liberal arts education, whereas most undergraduate engineering schools demanded very narrow courses of study. So I applied to an eclectic batch of schools and finally settled on Columbia College, part of Columbia University, in New York. I still remember vividly my interview at Columbia, where I was told that the school focused on building the "whole man" (women wouldn't be admitted until 1983) and offered a broad array of courses, including its "core" curriculum, which impressed a sixteen-year-old immigrant's son.

But my hopes for living away from home for the first time were dashed by an on-campus housing shortage at Columbia. Entering freshmen from the New York area were required to live at home for the first year. Fortunately, it wasn't long before I found a way around this problem. A new friend from Philadelphia, Charlie Blessing, offered me the spare bed in his Hartley Hall dorm room, left vacant by a no-show student. I started camping out there informally several nights a week and finally was given the room by the dean's office.

Gradually, as I officially settled into my room at Hartley Hall, I also settled into a routine. In addition to my studies, I busied myself with crew, although I was never better than a mediocre oarsman and was never thrilled with the long hours of training—or with training in the cold. I gave up crew after my sophomore year because I had so much else going on. I'd gotten involved in the campus radio station, WKCR, first as publicity director and later as host of my own nightly rock-and-roll show. I was also secretary and later president of the undergraduate dormitory council, the student disciplinary committee. I pledged the Sigma Chi fraternity during freshman year and eventually became vice president of our chapter.

I also found some time to attend classes and to study. Not a lot, but some. My grades were just okay. I was nowhere near the top of my class, as I had been in high school. Granted, I didn't devote as much

Chatting it up with Columbia Dean John Palfrey at a rowing team reception (1958).

time to my coursework as I might have, but school had always come easily to me, and I figured I'd squeak by. There was too much else to do. I pulled mostly Bs and C pluses, with an occasional A. There were a couple of Ds in there, too, and an F in calculus—it wasn't for me.

The most memorable incident of my undergraduate career,

however, is one I would just as soon forget. During the second half of my sophomore year, several of us became active in student government and were all helping our friends in the annual cycle of student elections. One of my closest Sigma Chi buddies, Vin Chiarello, was on the ballot for president of the student council, and a bunch of us worked on his campaign. As the election approached, we heard whispers that Vin's opponent was involved with the guys in the computer room, who counted the ballots, in "swaying" the election. As head of the disciplinary committee, I should have been committed to blowing the whistle on them. But we foolishly chose the low road right along with them. We set up our own scheme, enabling Vin's friends to vote twice on his behalf—and got caught.

To make it worse, because I was the ranking member of the dorm council, my behavior should have been above reproach. I was publicly embarrassed and forced to resign. I felt like I'd let down everyone at the school, even the institution itself. There was no disciplinary action taken against any of us, but the barrage of negative publicity was punishment enough. News of the election cheating even reached my parents through the *New York Times*.

The double-voting scandal had a profound effect on me. I vowed to never again be dishonest. While I have since suffered more than my share of difficult press, I have never again lost sleep over my own integrity. It took a teenager's misstep to set me on a very clear path.

It may seem ironic, but during my time in college I became a card-carrying member of the International Brotherhood of Teamsters. For several summers and over a number of winter breaks, I worked as an assistant truck driver and later as a truck driver and deliveryman for Coca-Cola, operating out of the bottling plant in Astoria, Queens. I began by helping offload the trucks and making deliveries to local supermarkets, delicatessens, and bars. I started at $125 a week plus a modest commission. Later, as a driver on my own, I worked almost entirely on commission, which I enjoyed much more.

This job gave me my first taste of unions, which made an impression that lasted throughout my business career. Teamster membership was a condition of my employment, although I rapidly discovered that my best interests didn't always coincide with the union's. There were many ridiculous, almost arbitrary restrictions placed on our jobs, and most of them seemed to keep me from making as much money as I might have. For example, I was only allowed to handle the bottles when I was out on my route. Inside the plant, only loaders could touch the soda bottles. Some mornings, when I saw broken or empty bottles in the cases already loaded on my truck, I'd have to wait as long as fifteen minutes for a loader to replace them, delaying my departure— much to my annoyance. Naturally, the union rules were there to ensure the security of the loaders' work.

However, I didn't always follow the work rules to the letter. I used to spend my lunch hour visiting the stores on my route, inspecting the Coke displays, making sure they were neat and the prices clearly marked, which would help sales and me. Every now and then, someone would spot me and file a grievance, since we were not allowed to work during the lunch hour. On occasional Sundays, I'd check some of our large accounts to see how their inventory was holding up over the weekend and who might need a bigger delivery on Monday morning. This, too, was against the rules, but I kept at it because it made my job easier and more lucrative during the regular workweek. As time went on, I began to realize that these rules had been instituted for the benefit of the older, year-round driver-salesmen who were eager to see their relaxed standards of productivity maintained by seasonal hands, usually college guys hired during summer months or around Christmas, the company's two busiest seasons.

There was continual tension between labor and management, so much so that some of the full-time guys took pleasure in effectively stealing Coke from our customers. They worked out these little schemes over the years, and they'd show them off with great pride to the temporary college kids whom they trusted, as if they were hard-earned tricks of the trade. One of their favorite scams, I learned, was to walk in the front door of a supermarket with several cases of soda on a hand truck, then wheel the merchandise right on out the back door and around again to the front. The store manager monitoring the delivery counted the cases twice, and the drivers double-billed and pocketed the extra.

I tried to empathize with the guys on my shift. I really did. They were just doing their jobs the way they were told to and looking to get away with whatever they could. I realized that the union wasn't there to protect us seasonal kids, although we paid the same dues; it was there for the lifers, the older guys who had to lift cases all year. They didn't need a bunch of enterprising college kids showing them up each summer and Christmas. To them, the restrictive work rules made sense. They made the job more human, more bearable.

---

One of my professors at Columbia was the well-respected Richard Neustadt, who went on after my college days to become dean of Harvard's Graduate School of Public Administration. In my junior year, he split his time between New York and Washington, DC, where he served as an adviser to president-elect John F. Kennedy as he prepared for assuming the presidency. It was during this period that I took his fascinating course in political science and enjoyed it a great deal, despite his occasional absences. One evening, he happened to be dining with his family at the men's faculty club, where I was waiting tables. Around the same time, there had been some new unpleasant publicity surrounding the then year-old student election scandal. This second splash of attention had caught me by surprise, and my professor assumed I was taking it hard.

"Mr. Lorenzo," he said as I approached his table, "I see they're still giving you a tough time. You look depressed."

"Yes, sir," I said, "although I'm getting used to it by now." What was really bothering me, and what I wasn't used to, was my lack of direction beyond Columbia, and I thought I'd take the opportunity to ask the professor his opinion of my plans. "Actually, sir," I allowed, "it's more than just the campus newspaper stuff. The truth is I'm worried that this student election business will keep me out of a good graduate school."

Neustadt assured me that this was nonsense and invited me to his office later in the week to discuss the matter further. When I took him up on his offer and restated the case against myself during our meeting, he boosted my spirits by saying, "I think you'll do great."

"I was wondering about Harvard Business School," I then told him, half expecting him to take me down a notch. He asked me about my interest in Columbia's own business school, but I explained that I had lived in New York City all my life and that in addition to its being a great school, Harvard's location in Boston would be a good change for me.

Neustadt understood and offered to write a recommendation on my behalf. I was delighted and left his office with my heart set on Harvard, despite my mediocre grades, and buried myself in preparation for the Graduate Record Exams. Ultimately, I scored well above average on the math portion of the exams and well below average on the verbal portion, so I feared that my only strength would be Professor Neustadt's recommendation.

However, I didn't want to rely solely on a recommendation, even a great one, so I requested an interview at the school. But the Harvard admissions people were very reluctant to grant me one because personal interviews weren't part of the admissions process in those days. Still, I believed that the only way I could get the university to look past my lackluster academic record was to have a face-to-face meeting. Fortunately, the admissions people agreed, and, although I had made numerous fallback plans, including joining the Marines, I was accepted to the class of 1963.

At first, I was very intimidated by Harvard and the environment at the business school. I was only twenty-one, young for any graduate school but especially for HBS. Almost all my classmates had two or three years of full-time career-oriented work experience under their belts. Quite a few still had silver spoons in their mouths, and many had gone to boarding school. They all seemed older, smarter, more sophisticated—particularly, I suppose, to a son of immigrants.

Right away, I knew that staying in the program would be one of the toughest challenges I would ever face. Professors at HBS teach by example, through the case method. Each night, we were given two or three cases to study, each detailing a particular crisis or dilemma facing the management team at a real corporation. These cases were prepared with the cooperation of the companies under review, whose executives would often visit our classes and offer analysis and insight from an insider's perspective. Our nightly reading usually ran between thirty and fifty pages, complete with facts and statistics. We were expected to arrive in class prepared to discuss the material from all angles, although we examined most cases from the president's viewpoint. We learned by second-guessing some of the country's most respected economists and business leaders and used to joke that Harvard didn't train too many middle managers, which was essentially true. It was a school for "big bosses," and the case discussions almost always focused on what the top executive should do in a given situation.

My first class was a required course in production management, and our inaugural case was an analysis of the way in which a company called Dominion Engineering had managed a specific crisis. Dominion Engineering was a well-known example at Harvard at the time, and its lead-off spot in the first-term curriculum no doubt contributed to its legendary status. I had worked through most of the material the night before. Sort of. Truth is, I didn't quite follow it and thought I could wing it through a brief discussion in the unlikely event I was called on. With ninety or so people in the class, I thought my chances of escaping the professor's notice were pretty good.

My production professor was a young guy named Jim McKenney, and he must have had a sixth sense for students like me. Jim went on to become Harvard's guru on information and data processing and one of the country's leading experts on computer systems, but at the time he was just starting out. (Years later, I asked him to join the board of Texas Air Corporation's data processing subsidiary.) He must have seen me nervously shifting in my seat and recognized it as a sign of unpreparedness. Of course, he called on me immediately. They do that at Harvard, I quickly learned.

"Mr. Lorenzo," the professor said, "what do you think about the way the president attacked this problem?"

I stammered something incoherent, certain the room was about to erupt in derisive laughter. Of course, as the term wore on, a great many of my colleagues uttered similarly incoherent responses to comparable questions, but I was the first guy in our section to suffer such indignity. Although I wouldn't be the last, I didn't appreciate it.

It was an unnerving experience, to be caught unprepared like that in my very first class, and I left the room feeling shaken. How could I compete with these whiz kids? Who was I trying to fool? By the second day of classes, I decided Harvard wasn't for me. I didn't think I could hack it, and it made perfect sense to cut my losses while they were still short.

I went to see the dean of students and told him that I wanted to drop out and likely enlist in the Marines. I told him that I was in over my head. He listened with patience and compassion and then laid out my options, just as he must have done for hundreds of overwhelmed students before me. I could pick up and go immediately, he said, or I could request a leave of absence. The leave was the only way to secure a space for me at the school in the future should I elect to return. The only requirement in granting a leave, the dean said, was that I visit the school's psychological counselor.

I hadn't thought things through that far. I just wanted out. But I figured it was silly to have struggled as I had to gain admission to an MBA program like Harvard's, only to run away from it after a single day. I decided to keep my options open and visit the school's resident counselor, who told me that to be satisfactorily discharged by him for a leave of absence, I would have to remain for two weeks of classes in order to get a full picture of the school.

So I stayed, and the psychologist held my hand through the intimidating first couple of weeks. By the second week, I was more comfortable in my classes and decided to stay. I have been forever grateful to the school for cleverly protracting my leave-taking and getting me to give the program and myself a second chance.

Harvard Business School divided its students into seven sections, each with around ninety students. All my first-year classes were with the same group of men, in section G. (Women gained entrance to HBS in my second year.) We studied together, ate together, and roomed together. In the second year, we all went our separate ways in a variety of elective courses. Once I got to know my classmates, I realized that my initial doubts and fears were epidemic: these guys shared the same worries, and none of them was as perfect as I'd thought. Still, many went on to significant accomplishments—Reuben Mark as the head of Colgate-Palmolive, Vernon Loucks as the head of Baxter Travenol, Bill Agee as the head of Bendix, and so on.

There was also my very good friend Jack Heinz, who went into politics and became a US senator from Pennsylvania. He died, very sadly, in an aviation accident in 1991. Jack and I spent a lot of time together and remained friends for nearly thirty years. We even had plans to build houses on neighboring lots in Sun Valley, Idaho, a project that was organized by Jack.

Between my first and second years at HBS, I took a summer job as a financial analyst for Kaiser Aluminum in Oakland, California. My first assignment was to evaluate whether Kaiser should lease or buy its company cars. I was also asked to study whether it made economic sense for it to continue in the production of certain types of aluminum.

It was a terrific summer and the beginning of a long love affair with the Bay Area. It was also my first sweet taste of the white-collar lifestyle and its attendant perks: a good salary, a modest expense account, and shared use of a company car. These, I learned, were all things I could get used to.

---

The most valuable lesson I learned that summer, however, was that I was bored by aluminum. I enjoyed my job, but the appeal of the company's product quickly wore thin, and I promised myself that the first real job I took after graduate school would be with a company whose products I could get excited about. I wasn't totally sure what that would be, but I knew that aluminum just didn't turn me on—except when it became part of a plane.

The only major airline to recruit on campus in 1963 was TWA. The company was looking for a couple of business-school graduates to help swell the ranks in finance and marketing. Unfortunately, the recruiters weren't looking for me. Or if they were, they didn't recognize it at first. I had an apparently successful initial interview on campus, then a round of follow-up interviews at TWA headquarters in New York, after which I thought I had a good shot at the job.

TWA was going through an unusual period at the time. Control had been wrested from Howard Hughes after a protracted legal battle, and the new president, Charles Tillinghast, and most of the senior management were still fairly new to the company. Many of them had never worked in the airline industry prior to their appointments. I made the rounds of these freshly minted airline executives, and I took every opportunity to impress them with my working knowledge of the company and its problems. I also volunteered a few suggestions while I was at it. I think I knew more about TWA than some of these executives, and I learned later that I probably rubbed a few of them the wrong way—enough, anyway, to turn me down.

My style in those days was to say whatever was on my mind. I usually never thought about the consequences. If I had an opinion, I gave voice to it, even if I was a little abrupt. My style hasn't changed all that much over the years, although now I think I can better anticipate the fallout.

A few weeks after my New York interviews, I received a letter from the controller, Pat O'Crowley, stating that TWA had no suitable openings for me at that time. He thanked me for my interest and wished me luck in my job search. I couldn't understand the rejection and wouldn't accept it. I was clearly qualified for TWA's rookie-level analyst job, and I knew that the starting salary wasn't competitive enough to attract more than a handful of other applicants from Harvard. So I sent a letter back, politely expressing my disappointment and asking that my application be reconsidered. In the letter, I told O'Crowley that the company was making a mistake by not hiring me and that I would make a great addition to the staff. I had nothing to lose—after all, I had already been turned down.

Looking back, I realize I had a lot of chutzpah for a twenty-two-year-old kid. But a few weeks later, O'Crowley sent me a letter and offered me a job. I was thrilled, but I didn't move too quickly to accept the position. I had some other leads to explore—or at least that's the way I played it. Mostly, I wanted time to take a closer look at TWA, to accurately assess the company's outlook for success and mine along with it. I was so bent on making a reasonable review of the TWA operation that I even made an unannounced visit to the company's Kansas City hub on a return stopover from a West Coast job interview with Boeing. I walked into TWA's main offices and asked to be shown around. Of course, no one in Kansas City had any idea who I was, but I asked them to call New York and clear it with O'Crowley's office.

While a bit brassy, my impromptu Kansas City visit turned out to be a sound move. It helped me understand the company and supported my decision to take the job. It also gave me great respect for Kansas City's function as an operational center and pulsebeat—a far cry from the executive offices in New York, where my job would be based. Still, the New York offices were pleasant and informal, and everyone seemed to enjoy their jobs. Despite the fact that it was a big company, with operating revenues of more than $400 million, it seemed like a small-company environment I could grow in. And it was in airlines.

CHAPTER TWO

# Early Days

*Choosing a Path*
*1963–1970*

**W**HEN I arrived at the New York offices of TWA at 380 Madison Avenue in June 1963, I discovered that there was no place for me to sit. The company was expanding so rapidly that it had outgrown its office space, so I began my tenure there hopping from one office to another, keeping desk chairs warm for traveling executives. I wasn't thrilled with this arrangement, but I was able to turn it my advantage. My assignments to offices normally occupied by senior managers gave me valuable insights into the company's high-level maneuverings.

For example, one day I was assigned to a senior vice president's office right across from the office of Charles Tillinghast, the CEO. That happened to be the very day that Floyd Hall, TWA's senior vice president and general manager, chose to walk in, offer his resignation, and announce his intention to join Eastern Airlines as president. From the other side of the closed door came a very heated exchange. Until that moment, I'd seen Tillinghast as a relaxed, easygoing man, but he was not happy with Hall's departure to a major competitor. The up-close glimpse of my boss with his guard down and his dander up was enlightening, and it left me better prepared to deal with him on other matters in the future—particularly since one of my later assignments was to write the president's quarterly report to shareholders. It also briefed me for my future dealings with Hall when our paths would cross again.

My first assignment at TWA was to assess the paper flow throughout the company. Memos and reports were being generated by various departments at cross-purposes, often presenting the same information in different ways and circulating it to the same people. It fell to me to recommend ways to trim the excess.

The project provided a wonderful overview of TWA and gave me license to examine all aspects of the company's business. It also involved traveling to the company's operational base, in Kansas City, and I took that privilege very seriously. In those days, TWA was a fragmented organization, broken mainly into the operating fiefdom, largely in Kansas City, and the marketing and finance fiefdoms, in New York. There were other fiefdoms as well. Each tended to generate and husband its own reports. Naturally, there was a lot of duplication, so I bounced back and forth among the various divisions and produced a system that essentially informed one division what the other was doing, thereby eliminating a mountain of superfluous paperwork.

I was astonished by the management lapses at TWA. Another early assignment offered a disturbing example. I was asked to evaluate the profitability of our separate fleet of cargo jets. To me, the only logical way to appraise the viability of those planes was to also look at the cargo we were flying on our passenger fleet. This was difficult, predictably, because passenger baggage was mixed with freight in the bellies of our commercial planes. The dilemma, as I saw it, was that the cargo guys would load as much freight as possible onto their all-cargo jets so they'd go out full, while the passenger planes often went out with belly room to spare, which could well have carried freight. As in any bureaucracy, the higher-ups—in our case, those in cargo—had to justify their jobs in order to keep them, but the historical way of evaluating the operation just didn't make sense. Over time, TWA eliminated a separate cargo fleet, in line with my group's recommendations.

There were other instances of mismanagement and bad judgment, as I saw it. For example, TWA's marketing department once had the bright idea to outfit flight attendants, who at that time were all female, in paper dresses for a promotion. In the regulated environment of those days, management would try all kinds of ways to differentiate the product, because it was the only way to stand out. You couldn't touch fares, which would have been the most important benefit we could have given to the consumer, but we could fancy up the service, which evidently was the impulse behind this particular piece of silliness. So the company commissioned some designers to turn out a few snazzy, brightly colored paper outfits for our attendants. The only problem was that there was no give to the paper material. This is not a good thing on airplanes, because the human body expands at high altitudes. Most of the time, underneath fabric, the slight transformation goes unnoticed. But not with our paper dresses. They tended to split right down the middle, which probably made the gimmick more popular than intended.

The best thing about working for TWA in those days was the non-revenue pass, which allowed employees to travel for free anywhere on the company's route system, provided there was an empty seat. Most carriers offer this perk to all their employees, from top to bottom, and I've always thought it was one of the most attractive benefits of an airline career—a great morale builder.

Like many new airline employees, I used my free passes frequently. Most weekends, I'd go to Idlewild (soon to be rechristened John F. Kennedy International Airport) and head for parts unknown, often with my Harvard pal and TWA office mate, Mike Newman. We studied the reservations sheets to see which flights looked undersold; the more empty seats there were, the more likely we'd get where we wanted to go and back, since we flew standby. We never really knew where we'd wind up.

Sometimes, on the subway to the beautiful Eero Saarinen–designed TWA terminal on a Friday afternoon, we'd decide we were in the mood for London, or maybe a particular Paris bistro. Other times we'd flip a coin. And sometimes we'd follow some pretty flight attendants to Frankfurt or Madrid on the off chance they might be free for dinner. One time, while my parents were vacationing in Greece, Mike and I flew to Athens and surprised them in the lobby of their hotel, the Grande Bretagne.

The European jaunts worked particularly well because we were usually able to catch a flight on Friday evening after work, arrive on Saturday morning, then return on Sunday. With the time change, we would be back in New York by early evening. The trips out to California were always a little chancier because the time zones were working against us. Our favorite itinerary that first winter was to fly standby to San Francisco on a Friday afternoon, where we'd meet up with some of my friends from my summer job at Kaiser Aluminum, then drive up to Lake Tahoe for two days of skiing. Sundays on the slopes were cut short in order to get back to San Francisco in time to catch the overnight red-eye home to New York. We'd land at Idlewild at 6:00 a.m. or so, if

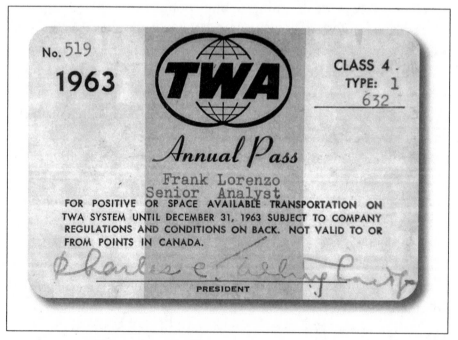

The cherished TWA annual Pass (1963).

the plane was on time. Then we would race home for a shower and a change of clothes and stumble into the office before nine as if it were nothing at all.

The weekend globe-trotting got old after a while—and more than a little wearying. We were forced to cut back before our bodies gave out, but the idea of picking up and jetting to some far-off place never lost its special thrill. I continued to enjoy extensive travel throughout my airline career and in the years afterward.

---

One issue I needed to contend with early in my TWA career was military service, mandatory in those days. I had prepared for this by pursuing a direct commission as a lieutenant in the army, which required a two-year commitment. However, after getting enmeshed in my career at TWA, and after I had received the direct commission, I decided that I didn't want to accept it and break away for two years and instead would enlist in the army reserves, which would take me away for only six months. After this I would be obligated to serve one night a week and a weekend each month at the Park Avenue Armory as well as two weeks each summer for the following six years at Camp Drum, in northern New York State.

I left TWA to begin my army training at Fort Dix, New Jersey, in May 1964. Six months away would be no piece of cake, but at age twenty-four, with a career on the rise, I decided it was the best option. The likelihood of my being sent overseas was slim; American involvement in the Vietnam War was still pretty modest then. I was prepared to go, but I didn't like the idea of fighting in general or fighting this war in particular. As a foot soldier, I had a tough time believing this was a war we could win. I was as patriotic as the next guy, but I just didn't like our chances. In addition, I had lost too many friends to that war—including my closest fraternity buddy, Vin Chiarello, killed in a DC-3 flight near Hanoi during a US intelligence operation.

Those six months turned almost all my routines upside down and left me looking at almost everything in new ways. I was surprised to discover that I was a very flexible person, which I didn't know at the time and which my critics will line up to argue is no longer the case. I had some trouble dealing with the rows of open toilets in the latrine, but I even got used to those in time. In all, the army helped instill a certain discipline in my daily life, making me far more conscious about diet and exercise and the limits I could place on my body. I used to look forward to the drills that other soldiers dreaded. On our long forced marches, loaded down with full packs, I distracted myself from the pain by planning my next stock move or charting my future course at TWA.

But nothing in the army reserves prepared me for what I found when I returned to the office. Fort Dix had taken me out of the loop during a pivotal time of reorganization at the company. For one thing, the executive headquarters had moved from the two and a half floors where I started to more than a dozen floors in the Burroughs Building at 605 Third Avenue. Suddenly we were in a vast corporate space, with a bureaucracy to match. The old TWA was small and personal; the new TWA was a slow-footed giant.

Even the focus of my job had changed, and I soon felt like a highly paid bean counter. Most of my time was devoted to a complicated lawsuit that TWA had brought against Howard Hughes, its majority shareholder, whose shares were locked up in a voting trust held by the airline's creditors. The company was alleging gross mismanagement during the last ten years of his TWA stewardship. I had a tough time with this case, not just because it was up to me to calculate all the alleged damages, some of them pretty far-fetched, but also—and chiefly—because I felt warmly toward a man who had done as much as Charles Lindbergh to fuel the American public's fascination with commercial aviation.

Before he became the eccentric billionaire and recluse he is remembered as today, Hughes was a pioneer. His love of flying was infectious, and in 1939, through his Hughes Tool Company, he used some of his vast resources to purchase large blocks of TWA stock. Five years later, he set a new transcontinental speed record by flying a TWA Lockheed Constellation from Burbank, California, to Washington, DC, in seven hours, which effectively opened the doors to nonstop flights across the United States. To a small boy growing up beneath the approach path to LaGuardia, Hughes was a true hero.

At TWA, however, veterans traded horror stories about Hughes managing their public company as his personal asset. One old-timer, Joe Stellabotte, who oversaw aircraft scheduling, told of the time Hughes took one of the newly delivered Lockheed 1649A StarStream Super Constellation aircraft to the Bahamas to "test it out," despite the fact that the plane had already been certified for passenger use. According to Joe, the scheduling guys had to cancel flights and leave TWA passengers stranded just to accommodate Hughes, who reportedly didn't like Bahamas hotels and slept in the plane during his extended stay on the islands.

The ultimate downfall of Howard Hughes at TWA can be traced to his purchase in the late 1950s of a fleet of four-engine Convair 880s, which he particularly liked, a decision that would ultimately cost him control of the company. The Convair jets were built like tanks, and like tanks, they guzzled fuel. They were just too heavy to fly effciently. They also carried far fewer passengers than the Boeing 707s that American— and, later, TWA—ordered and the Douglas DC-8s that United ordered.

But Hughes dawdled in placing orders for the 707s and 880s. He was accustomed to ordering planes through his Hughes Tool Company for tax reasons, assigning them to TWA after delivery. But Hughes Tool Company was going through a rare period of cash-flow shortages, and he couldn't pay cash for the airplanes, which he preferred to do because he didn't want to borrow the vast sums required for jets. So he waited, hoping things would turn around. When they didn't, he ordered the planes anyway but had to scramble to arrange financing. Several banks and insurance companies demanded that Hughes's TWA stock, which amounted to 78 percent of the outstanding shares, be placed into a voting trust as a condition of the financing, although Hughes would still own the shares. Faced with a deadline and no alternatives, Hughes finally buckled and pledged the stock, losing control of TWA. But the delay in ordering and taking delivery of the planes cost TWA dearly, and the company sued its now absentee owner.

To this day, I think of Hughes in heroic terms, as a father figure to a fledgling industry, yet I can't shed the image of him as an aloof, bitter man, out of touch with the realities of the marketplace.

After a while, I began to look at the Hughes lawsuit as a waste of my time, although it made sense from a corporate and creditor perspective. Eventually, TWA was awarded more than $137 million in treble damages. Hughes appealed, and while this wound its way through the courts, he surprised everyone in 1966 by selling his TWA holdings in a giant stock offering for $546.5 million (about $5.2 billion in 2024 dollars).[1]

But I was bored and frustrated by my role in the litigation process and started to dislike going to work each day. By then I was twenty-five years old, full of ideas and energy, and there were better things for me to do than beat an old man's reputation into the ground. I wanted to roll up my sleeves and plunge into something more exciting and rewarding.

---

As my dissatisfaction grew at TWA, I tried to step back and assess the career path I had chosen. My strengths, I had begun to realize, were in marketing and finance, but I was far too junior to make any significant contributions in these areas. Most troubling was the fact that commercial aviation was still a regulated business, and the various government-imposed restrictions were almost always at odds with my spirit of enterprise.

---

[1]    Hughes never lost his love for airlines. In 1962, while barred by the banks from running TWA, Hughes purchased control of Northeast Airlines from the Atlas Corporation, which had owned Northeast since 1938. He sold his 55 percent interest in the airline in 1964. In 1970, he bought the regional airline Air West and renamed it Hughes Airwest. In 1980, Republic Airlines purchased Airwest from Hughes. Hughes died in 1976, a recluse.

As I saw it, I had two options: I could take a job at another airline, which would at least free me from the tangle of the Hughes Tool Company lawsuit and might offer a clearer view of the playing field. Or I could abandon the industry altogether and try something new. Toughing it out at TWA, it had become increasingly apparent, would not be one of my alternatives.

While I was trying to make up my mind, I attended a cocktail party and ran into a woman I knew who told me that her new boss was Eastern Airlines president Floyd Hall. I of course remembered Hall, whose loud leave-taking from TWA I had overheard from my front-row seat nearly two years before. She said that Hall wanted to hire some young, capable finance guys to help evaluate the changing marketplace. After a number of conversations and one or two interviews, I received a job offer from John Carty, Eastern's treasurer.

The offer was not overwhelming—$11,000 a year to serve as manager of financial analysis in the company's New York office—and I didn't jump to accept it. It was tempting, but part of me thought I'd simply be trading one bureaucracy for another. Eastern, at the time, was smaller than TWA, and it was troubled. But the mid-1960s was a burgeoning period for air transportation in this country. It was clear that Eastern's situation would soon change. All the domestic trunk carriers—carriers that operate between major population centers—were getting very big very fast, primarily thanks to the advent of jet aircraft, which attracted more passengers and offered speedier trips than older aircraft did. I knew that as these organizations expanded, it would be possible for some people in the middle ranks to ride with them right to the top. But there was also a chance that those who didn't advance would be left in bureaucratic purgatory.

When I thought about abandoning the industry altogether, one of the possibilities I considered was opening a banjo-and-beer hall with a Harvard friend, Wayne Fabian. Our idea was to start one of these joints in Cleveland, where Wayne lived, patterning it after the successful Red Garter bar in San Francisco. We had a name for the venture, the Pink Pantaloon, and attempted to get Joel Schiavone, an older HBS graduate who ran the Red Garter, to co-venture it with us. But this would have constituted a major fork in the road, requiring me to live in a city that I didn't know and leave an industry about which I had grown passionate.

Although I was undecided, I felt strongly that I had to make a move, so I forced myself to give notice at TWA. This turned out to be a good call for purely personal reasons. TWA had an uncommonly friendly policy that allowed departing employees thirty days of free-pass travel after leaving the company, so I took advantage of it to sort out my options. I spent a week visiting an old school pal in Germany, tooled around Europe in a Volkswagen that I bought there, and eventually made my way down to the French Riviera.

Behind this exhilarating freedom, of course, lurked my professional dilemma. I was still of two minds, but one was being made up more quickly than the other. I looked out over the majestic Mediterranean one day on a beach near Nice and realized that I didn't want to make my killing in a bar.

Yes, I was firmly convinced that we would clean up with the Pink Pantaloon. The time was right. Our location was right. The name was right. We had good people on board and a chance to build a real franchise. But money alone was not the most important thing to me, it seemed. This came as something of a surprise—and even today it must be hard for some of my critics (and some of my supporters) to swallow—but I realized that I could never be happy over the long term selling beer to college kids. It would be fun until we got up and running, but then I'd be out the door. It was still a great deal, but in the end, it just wasn't the deal for me. I decided there on the beach that day to continue my airline career.

Eastern had some of the same negatives as TWA, but it at least offered a change of scenery and entry at perhaps an earlier stage in the company's development. Plus, in his two years on board, Floyd Hall was really starting to jazz up the company, or at least that's how it appeared to me from the outside. And indeed, from my first days in the company's offices in June 1965, I was taken by the differences between it and TWA. Eastern was a much sleeper place, but my new colleagues took their jobs very seriously. Also, there were no young people at my level in the New York offices, whereas at TWA there were plenty. Eastern's 10 Rockefeller Plaza outpost mainly housed the executive and treasury divisions, but its operational base, in Miami, was the true spiritual home of the company.

In New York, we were such a small, disparate group that there was no real feeling of community or common purpose. I missed the sense of being part of a team, but I was quick to see that there were some benefits to this pared-down environment. Across the board, Eastern had a much smaller staff than top-heavy TWA, which meant that I quickly assumed a lot of responsibility and had greater access to senior management. Often, I would venture upstairs with analyses of proposed leasing transactions or aircraft purchases for discussion with the company's high-ranking officers.

Like TWA, Eastern was struggling through some financial difficulties when I arrived. The company had lost more than $55 million ($540 million, or so, in 2024 dollars) over the previous four years, and Floyd Hall seemed to be spending money faster than he could borrow it. Hall was by now entrenched at Eastern's helm, looking to leave his mark everywhere. A former pilot, with a carefully trimmed mustache and a penchant for hand-tailored suits—with a handkerchief carefully folded in his breast pocket—Hall had inherited the daunting legacy of Captain Eddie Rickenbacker, who spearheaded the buyout of Eastern from General Motors in 1938 and had guided the company for more than a quarter century. Captain Eddie, on the few occasions he visited the Eastern headquarters, cut a larger-than-life figure.

One day, I asked my boss if I could meet Captain Eddie, who kept an office after his retirement from Eastern at nearby 630 Fifth Avenue, then known as the International Building. His modest office, maintained by Eastern, looked down at the Rockefeller Center skating rink, across from which was Eastern's own office. He seemed a subdued man in his later years, particularly to a twenty-five-year-old who had heard so much about the successes of this World War I flying ace.

Hall also inherited the lone innovation of Rickenbacker's

successor, Malcolm MacIntyre: the air shuttle. This hourly commuter service between New York and Boston and New York and Washington featured no advance ticketing and guaranteed seating. The shuttle was a huge and immediate success. MacIntyre had made an unprecedented pledge that was a stroke of marketing genius: Eastern would guarantee a seat on its hourly no-reservation flights and send out an extra plane even if only a single passenger couldn't get a seat on the first flight.

By the time I joined Eastern, the shuttle had flown nearly ten million passengers over the course of just four years and was on its way to becoming the company's most profitable service. During those first four years, Eastern needed to roll out an extra plane to accommodate a single over-the-limit passenger on only sixteen occasions, and each time the company reaped the combined benefits of free publicity and the everlasting goodwill of regular shuttle commuters.

For the most part, though, Eastern offered its passengers a shoddy product in 1965. The planes were dirty and in need of cosmetic repair. Even the shuttle's prop-jet Electra fleet was worn down, although business travelers were so pleased with the low fares and guaranteed seating that they were willing to look past the fraying seats and pinched carpeting. Hall made some honest attempts to change the company's shabby image, but he tried to do too much too soon. He hired the consulting firm of Lippincott & Margulies to put a new face on things before he made any substantive changes. He modernized Eastern's famous falcon insignia, called for new colors for the planes, and ordered new uniforms for the flight and ground crews. He even approved the company's new tagline: "The wings of man."

But the net effect, as I saw it, was that passengers thought they were being duped by the surface makeover. The lesson I learned from Hall's mistake is that you can't change a corporate image overnight or at will. Years later, in the 1980s, I would say at Continental that we couldn't reposition our airline's advertising or change our aircraft color scheme until we had a product change to back up our claims. Floyd Hall wanted the world to think everything was wonderful at Eastern before his product was ready. I'll never forget flying one of Eastern's particularly ragged-looking DC-8s and noting the new company logo on a decal on the seat back in front of me. On closer inspection, I could still see the old emblem peeking out from underneath, and I remember feeling sheepish, and even a little ashamed, that I worked for an airline that would make such a transparent attempt to fool the public.

Some of Hall's finishing touches were simply not cost-efficient, either. In a misguided attempt to promote the airline's first-class service, for example, he started using elegant Rosenthal porcelain china, which was not the sort of china that made practical sense for commercial flights. Rosenthal was expensive and certainly classy but had a tendency to chip—and disappear. On average, regular glassware lasted around twenty airline flights before it had to be replaced. Our expensive Rosenthals were out of commission in less than three trips—if they even made it to their first wash cycle. The china was so beautiful that our biggest problem became theft.

---

The highlight of my brief tenure at Eastern, however, had nothing to do with my job. Since returning from six months at Fort Dix, I had resumed a friendship with Bob Carney, an HBS friend whom I had known casually at school and who was then working in investment banking. We met for lunch a couple of times when I was working at TWA, and after I landed at Eastern, whose office was just across from his at 1 Rockefeller Plaza, our lunches became more frequent and our friendship blossomed. He had gone to work at S. G. Warburg & Co. just before I joined Eastern. Previously, he had been at Dillon, Read & Co., where he started right out of business school.

Bob and I were an odd match. He was quiet, while I was relatively outgoing. He was conservative; I was more of a risk-taker. But our differences were healthy—he had a strong finance background, while I was stronger in marketing—and after many lunches at Charley O's, a midtown burger joint, we found some real common ground. We were both around the same age, both bachelors, and both stifled by our corporate constraints.

Our discussions kept coming back to the changing face of airlines. It wasn't hard to see, even from my lowly vantage point at Eastern, that the industry was undergoing a transformation. The seeds of what would later be airline deregulation were clearly blossoming. Supplemental airlines—the charter carriers of the time—were being given increased authority, and Bob and I both recognized an early opportunity there.

The charter business was, and remains, attractive because within it, you can control costs and load factors (the percentage of seats occupied), thus keeping ticket prices down. You might set up a charter once a week, from New York to Cancún, let's say, and sell all the seats on the departing flight to one tour operator and all the seats on the return flight to another. Then you'd have a New York–Cancún "track," which could be profitable even with only one round trip each week. Today, the charter business is wide open, but in the 1960s, the Civil Aeronautics Board (CAB) kept an iron fist around its precious supplemental charter certificates.

Gradually, we formulated a plan to sell ourselves as airline industry advisers, which was a brassy thing to do considering that between us Bob and I each had less than three years of experience. Still, we put together a business plan (including the idea of building a new supplemental airline), which we circulated to potential investors. We didn't quit our day jobs right away—after all, the only thing we had was a fairly thin idea—but we began devoting most of our spare time to the venture.

We had some trouble getting financing, which we anticipated. Bob arranged for a pitch to his boss, Siegmund Warburg, before which I had to submit to a bizarre handwriting analysis conducted by a Swiss woman the financier kept on his payroll and after which I reminded myself that even the most successful businessmen were sometimes held together with loose screws.

There were similar (although less amusing) frustrations at every turn, and it began to look as if we might never get off the ground.

Finally, after the traditional sources of capital kept turning up dry, Bob and I thought about gearing up without any outside funds. Neither of us had families or extravagant lifestyles to support. If we had to, we could work out of our apartments for a while on the cheap.

Fortunately, Bob's zeal matched my own, and we resolved to leave our jobs at the first opportunity. I was not at all disappointed to be leaving Eastern. I was tired of having to do things a certain fixed way just because that was the way things were always done. I had no stomach for having to back up my bosses when I knew that what they were doing wasn't necessarily good for the company. I didn't enjoy the way my superiors sometimes took credit for ideas or grunt work that originated with me or my colleagues or the way some bosses were quick to dismiss a fresh approach simply because it came from someone too low in the corporate hierarchy to be taken seriously. The entrepreneur in me was aching for change.

In resigning from Eastern, I went to see Todd Cole, Eastern's senior vice president of finance, a man I respected and with whom I had worked closely on a number of projects. I told him of my plans, and he responded with a standard speech about my leaving a promising career. He let on that he could see me as Eastern's treasurer in short order. I was flattered at the suggestion but reasoned that "short order" probably translated to five years, which to me seemed an eternity. I'd be thirty-one—middle-aged, as I saw it then.

It was the first week of August 1966, and as I walked out of 10 Rock for what I thought would be the final time, I stopped (appropriately) by the revolving doors to chat with Bob Arnold, one of the company's senior treasury executives. He wanted to offer his good wishes; I wanted to talk about our new venture and the challenges ahead. I was bubbling with excitement and wound up comparing a company like Eastern to a huge building. Lorenzo, Carney & Co., I suggested, would be more like a sort of helicopter, able to alight on any floor of the skyscraper without having to worry about stairwells or elevator banks or, most important, organizational structure.

Arnold clearly didn't expect to hear my enthusiasm couched in such philosophical terms, but he got the point, and I've never forgotten the analogy. In fact, I share it with young people whenever I get the chance, because I firmly believe that the best way to get ahead, in any field, is to be unencumbered by the constraints of a big corporation. The ability to fail or succeed comes only with the freedom to fail or succeed.

Lorenzo, Carney & Co. was incorporated on August 6, 1966. Bob and I each put up $3,000 (about $29,000 in 2024 dollars)—in both our cases, around 50 percent of our net worth—and opened an account for the new firm with J.P. Morgan & Co., which we viewed as a prestigious old-line bank. The Donnell branch of the New York Public Library, off Fifth Avenue on West 53rd Street, became our first office out of necessity. Bob and I both lived on the Upper East Side at the time, and we began most of our days at a neighborhood coffee shop, later moving on to the library to go over the morning papers and plan our agenda for the day. Perhaps outrageously, we commandeered a library phone booth and used it to set up appointments. We also used library materials to research various companies we thought might be in need of our advisory talents. Nowadays, with the proliferation of databases and other inexpensive research tools, we could have gotten the same start with Wi-Fi and a computer, but back then we had to do things the old-fashioned way. Sometimes I wonder how many great business enterprises of the past might have been hatched in public libraries.

Even before we left our jobs, Bob and I had already researched the dozen or so existing supplemental airlines to see if we might isolate one for acquisition. Our thinking was that a carrier with an underutilized certificate could be had at an attractive price. Then, with aggressive new management and a more relaxed regulatory environment, a modest investment could turn into a potential gold mine.

One of the most attractive targets turned out to be Zantop Air Transport, which operated a ragtag fleet of DC-6s and DC-8s and was based in Ypsilanti, Michigan. Most of its charter business consisted of delivering Ford auto parts to production plants around the country. But the airline's most important asset, as we saw it, was not its fleet or its long-standing contract with Ford but rather its supplemental airline certificate.

We solicited an introduction through one of Bob's contacts, Arthur Norden, after learning that the Zantop family might consider a sale on the "right" terms. But we soon discovered that the key to the mergers-and-acquisitions business, which we were trying to master quickly, lay in optimism: Bob and I had to be a little more positive about our chances of producing a ready buyer than we truly were. Not only did we not have a buyer lined up, we also didn't have an office, stationery, or a return telephone number. But somehow, we never got around to discussing this with Howard, Lloyd, and Duane Zantop, who owned the company along with a fourth brother, Elroy Zantop. Bob and I flew to Detroit to get to know the brothers and their business and let them get to know us. Eventually, we structured a kind of phantom deal that made sense to the Zantops and to the hypothetical buyer, because even then we knew enough to realize that deals were rarely done unless there was a good fit on both sides.

Meanwhile, we had to find our ready buyers, and for this we turned to a boyhood friend of mine named Ken Wieck, who used to sit in on regular card games at my parents' house in Rego Park and was now working at the small Wall Street brokerage firm of Tobey & Kirk. Ken put us on the trail of another set of brothers, Dick and Don Matthews, who were looking to expand their stevedoring business into an airfreight operation. We walked them through a potential deal for Zantop, and they were intrigued by our proposal. The Zantops were still not actively looking to sell their airline, but Bob and I were convinced that they would be open to it if the right deal came along. It simply fell to us to turn the Matthews brothers into the right deal.

Over the course of the following several weeks, working mostly out of the public library, we arranged for the Matthews brothers to acquire Zantop. As compensation, we received a five-year consulting contract plus an up-front payment of $100,000. The contract brought in around $15,000 a month over the course of five years, although it didn't require much of our time. Bob and I would have preferred that the contract cover a longer period of time and had been hoping to play an active role in repositioning the airline, but the Matthews brothers decided they no longer needed the vast experience and resources of Lorenzo, Carney & Co. despite their continued payments to us.

Dick and Don Matthews changed the name of their new airline to Universal and proceeded over time to run it into the ground. They ignored their core business with Ford while fumbling for ways to get their passenger charter business going. The only way to do this, we thought, was to spruce up the fleet with some modern jets and compete head-to-head in the growing passenger and military charter business, which was ultimately what made supplemental airlines such as World Airways and Overseas National Airways so successful.

Sadly, by the time Universal Airlines went out of business, the Matthews brothers were financially ruined because they had personally cosigned loans on a fleet of Electra airplanes, which the company acquired. This reinforced for me one of the basic tenets of business: always keep your personal assets and commitments separate from your business assets and commitments. No investment is without some degree of risk, and I've been mindful of the Matthews brothers' experience ever since.

The Zantop deal answered any lingering doubts we might have had about our new career and the opportunities we might be able to find. It also gave us the important

## Lorenzo, Carney Open Offices

F. A. Lorenzo     R. J. Carney

Lorenzo, Carney & Co., Inc., a newly established financial advisory firm, has announced the opening of its offices in the Pan American Building at 200 Park Avenue, New York.

The firm's two principals are Francisco A. Lorenzo and Robert J. Carney. Mr. Lorenzo has been employed by two airlines, Trans World Airlines, Inc. as a senior analyst and more recently by Eastern Air Lines, Inc. as manager of financial analysis. Mr. Carney has an investment banking background, first as an associate with Dillon, Read & Co. Inc. and more recently as assistant to the managing director of S. G. Warburg & Co. Inc.

The firm specializes primarily in the air transportation industry, advising domestic and foreign air carriers on a wide variety of financial matters and assisting them in obtaining new capital through private transactions. The firm also plans to work closely with institutions and individuals interested in investing in public and privately-owned airlines.

Recently, Lorenzo, Carney & Co. was involved in the sale of Zantop Air Transport, Inc. to Universal Airlines Inc., a newly created company. Zantop, one of the supplemental air carriers recently awarded the "inclusive-tour" authority, is engaged primarily in freight operations and in terms of revenue is the nation's largest privately-owned airline.

Article announcing opening our first office atop the Pan Am Building (1967).

start-up capital we lacked. With our stake from the Zantop deal, we rented office space we still couldn't really afford—a small suite on the fifty-sixth floor of the Pan Am Building at 200 Park Avenue, which we subleased from the Italian oil company Agip. Our small office was right next to the Sky Club, which we thought was a prime location for a couple of would-be airline entrepreneur-executives.

---

One of Bob's old army buddies, an attorney named Don Urgo, pointed us to our next big deal, which involved an airline in the eastern Caribbean known as British West Indian Airways—BWIA, or Bee-Wee, as it was commonly known—then owned by the government of Trinidad and Tobago. Urgo's introduction followed a circuitous route that started with a meeting between Trinidad's prime minister, Eric Williams, and President Lyndon Johnson in which Williams appealed to the United States for help with his money-losing airline. Johnson's staff, in turn, contacted the TWA president, Charlie Tillinghast, to see if TWA would be interested in pursuing an involvement with BWIA, and the airline responded in the affirmative. (Coincidentally, Tillinghast had been a managing partner at Hughes Hubbard & Reed, Don Urgo's former employer.)

TWA saw this potential tie with BWIA as a way into the Caribbean market, which made good political and business sense. One of the biggest draws for Tillinghast, in addition to the prospect of winning friends in the Johnson White House and at the Civil Aeronautics Board, was that experience operating in the Caribbean was often a factor in new route awards. There was also potential synergy between BWIA and TWA's Hilton International subsidiary. At the time, Hilton was considering the development of a first-class two-hundred-room hotel and resort complex on a pristine twenty-eight-acre parcel of beachfront property in Tobago known as Rocky Point.

Bob and I were brought in during the summer of 1967 to advise R. W. Pressprich & Co., where Urgo worked and which TWA brought in for investment banking assistance with the hotel project and BWIA. The more we looked at BWIA, however, the more we realized how difficult it would be to rescue the company from the financial mess it was in, despite its obvious potential. The airline was operating a handful of Boeing 727s, largely from New York and Miami to Antigua, Barbados, and Trinidad. But the 727 was not the ideal plane for these routes. The safety equipment required for long hauls over water added considerable weight, and the obligatory extra fuel reserves—in the unlikely (but not unheard-of) event that one of the island airports was shut down because of bad weather and the plane needed to divert to another island—compounded the problem.

Even more troubling than the operational issues were the political ones. Politics and business don't always get along, and in this case the airline's ties to the Trinidadian government, which controlled it, were very unsettling. The BWIA chairman, Sir Ellis Clarke, who was also Trinidad's ambassador to the United States, tried to run a fairly tight ship, but his government position made it impossible. Sir Ellis, his management team, and prior management teams awarded so many jobs, many of them nonessential, to various friends of government that the ratio of employees to passengers was nearly twice the industry average.

Almost immediately, we began structuring a multimillion-dollar refinancing package with an eye toward an equity investment for ourselves and our Pressprich partners. However, we were never able to put together the major equity deal we had hoped for, so we focused our attention on the airline. We recommended across-the-board cuts in personnel, advised on aircraft acquisitions, and arranged for an extension of the $18 million debt the airline held with Barclays Bank.

Eventually, Bob and I—without Pressprich's involvement—were hired as advisers to the airline at a retainer fee of $4,000 per month. We were able to attract to Trinidad an old friend of mine from TWA, Bob Gallaway, as BWIA's general manager. (I would also involve Bob in our airlines years later.) Bob worked at professionalizing BWIA while we worked on putting together an investment plan. By September

1967, Prime Minister Williams had accepted in principle our proposal to reorganize, refinance, and expand the company. We persuaded two investors—Herb Allen Jr., of Allen & Company, and Dick Pistell, of Goldfield Corporation—to put up $1.5 million, which allowed us to buy a 49 percent stake in BWIA through a new company we formed called Caribbean International.

On Boeing demo flight with Bill Allen Boeing president and Sir Ellis Clarke, BWIA Chairman and Ambassador to US (1968).

As president and director of Caribbean International and as a director of BWIA, I commuted to Trinidad on a regular basis—every other week or so, usually for two days at a stretch. One of our first moves was to reposition the airline. To accomplish this, we upgraded the name slightly to BWIA International, introduced a new logo—a steel drum surrounding the BWIA insignia—and hired the advertising agency of McCaffrey & McCall to help spread the word. Because we were operating just one flight a day to New York and Miami, we had a limited advertising and promotion budget—only $150,000, which even in those days wouldn't have been enough for a full-scale campaign in those cities were it not for a windfall of free publicity.

To get the widest reach with our limited dollars, we decided to go with a signboard campaign on the New York City bus and subway system and on commuter railroad platforms. The agency came up with a particularly clever piece of advertising: a picture of a glorious stretch of white sand underneath an inviting blue sky, a landscape enhanced by a shapely young woman, shot at a distance, her back to the camera, with visible tan lines where her bikini was supposed to be. The tagline: "The unheard-of airline, to unheard-of islands."

I'll admit that the ad was mildly suggestive, but there was certainly nothing lascivious or objectionable about it, certainly not by today's standards. Had it run as planned, the campaign might have made a small splash and brought us the slow trickle of warm-weather seekers we so desperately needed to turn things around. But New York's Metropolitan Transportation Authority, in its prurience-phobic wisdom, rejected the ad, which they claimed did not meet its standards of community decency, and once we were banned from the subways, buses, and commuter railroad platforms, we were all over the news. We couldn't have planned it better. Suddenly, our unheard-of airline was much talked about, and we didn't even make a dent in our advertising budget. It turned out to be the smartest $150,000 we never spent. It also turned out to be a valuable lesson for me about publicity instead of just advertising, which I would put to use many times in later years.

Like the Zantop deal, the continuing advisory fees from BWIA helped stake our company at an important time: very early on. Regrettably, the equity position we took in Caribbean International turned out to be nearly worthless by the time we got out of the airline, in 1971. But in many ways, it offered an invaluable lesson. Where else would a couple of kids, still shy of thirty, have gotten the opportunity to virtually run an international airline? It was an incredibly rich learning experience even if it wasn't very profitable. I learned what it was like to head a big company, deal with foreign governments and our own State Department, implement a seat-of-the-pants marketing strategy, negotiate aircraft purchases, and bring competing and sometimes conflicting interests to the bargaining table.

Most importantly, I learned how to manage. As a mid-level analyst, and later as an adviser, I never really had an opportunity to direct a team of employees, authoritatively assess a colleague's strengths and weaknesses, hire and fire, motivate, and generally ensure that the whole was greater than the sum of its parts. Here, to my surprise and pleasure, I found that I enjoyed bearing direct responsibility for the full range of decisions facing any business leader and that I thrived on delegating authority to good people. At each new vantage point—from TWA and Eastern to Zantop and BWIA—I was discovering things about my inner entrepreneur to go along with everything I was learning about business. With three key deals to our credit, I was confident that Bob and I would do great things before too long.

---

Midway through our protracted BWIA association, our ranks at Lorenzo, Carney & Co. swelled to include Rob Snedeker, who had been a young star at Time Inc., and Andy Feuerstein, a freshly minted Harvard Law School graduate. The two hires gave us sorely needed depth, but they also put some pressure on us to produce income. Despite our relative success, Bob and I didn't take any real money out of the business for the first year or so. We didn't need to. Our lives *were* the business. We had no major personal expenses. Most of our lunches or dinners during the week were with prospective clients; we were as likely to be out of town as at home; and we never took conventional vacations, even if we did enjoy an occasional free day in Trinidad. The only time I had to dip into my own pocket was to pay rent on my apartment or pick up the tab on a date.

But suddenly we had two guys on the payroll, and the pressure was on. Right away, even when it was just the four of us sniffing out deals, Bob and I thought it was important to institute some formal structure for our growing company. I became chairman, and Bob was president and chief operating officer. He was the guy who handled day-to-day problems, and I was the big-picture, more external guy. Bob and I would scout the deals and, with Rob and Andy, develop the strategy and see them through.

We looked everywhere for potential deals. No aviation company was too small or too remote for our consideration. We even found an opportunity in Canada. We were retained in 1968 by Transair, a Canadian regional carrier based in Winnipeg whose business was built on milk runs (regularly scheduled flights with several stops) up to the Arctic—places such as Yellowknife, Flin Flon, Whale Cove, and Repulse Bay—and cargo work for military outposts throughout the Northwest Territories. We wound up advising Transair on aircraft purchases, financing alternatives, and plans for general expansion. We even advised its board with management strategies and selection.

Back in New York, one of the areas Bob and I wanted to move into was aircraft leasing. Computer leasing companies were doing enormously well at the time, and unless your head was buried in the sand, you could see that the concept of leasing had exciting applications in other areas—such as aviation. Leasing companies essentially relied on the residual value of assets for most of their return. The only trouble with computer leasing, as we saw it, was that the equipment was often obsolete long before the lease term had ended. With aircraft, we believed, the residual asset values would be more predictable, more substantial, and spread over a far longer term. This was particularly the case with the new short-haul aircraft that Boeing (with its 737) and McDonnell Douglas (with its DC-9) had developed, aircraft that we thought would have a long life.

In February 1969, we watched with keen interest as a small insurance company later called Integrated Resources held a public offering before logging even a minute of operating history. It was plain from the prospectus that there was no business behind the company, and yet there they were, going public, with nothing to offer investors beyond a potentially sound idea and the modest track record of its principals in related ventures. Bob and I decided that if it was good enough for Integrated Resources, it was good enough for us, and we immediately hatched a plan for a public offering of our own.

In May 1969, we filed an S-1 form and an eight-page prospectus with the Securities and Exchange Commission for an aircraft leasing company called Jet Capital Corporation. The offering was handled by my old friend Ken Wieck, who was still with Tobey & Kirk. Because we had no operating history behind us, major underwriting houses such as Goldman Sachs and Merrill Lynch would not have given us an appointment, but for Ken and his partners, who had never done an underwriting prior to our association, we were a risk worth taking. Besides, there was tremendous upside in it for the underwriter: public offerings could be very profitable, and we had a sound business concept.

Over the years, I have frequently done business with old friends, people with whom I've enjoyed a certain history and trust. All things being equal, it can make sense to go with someone you know, and in this instance it was important to give our speculative offering every advantage. With Ken and the modest resources of Tobey & Kirk, I thought we could have a successful offering without the backing of one of the big underwriting firms. For our purposes, Ken's firm was plenty big.

Bob and I provided Jet's original risk money of around $100,000, which we had slowly accumulated at the firm, and we also cut Rob and Andy in on the stock. Just prior to our filing, we sold another $250,000 worth of stock to a small number of friends at around 25 percent of the anticipated offering price. In our public offering, we expected to sell around 400,000 shares and warrants at $10 per unit, but the market had worked against us during the long delay between our filing and our offering, in January 1970. Airline stocks were particularly weak during that period.

Ultimately, we sold 150,000 shares and warrants, raising about $1.5 million, and we knew we were lucky to get the deal done at all. Within weeks, the Dow Jones Industrial Average dropped nearly 5 percent, and our Jet shares tumbled sharply. The constant fluctuation in the stock price gave me something new to worry about, and it took a tip from my Harvard classmate Jim Clark, an architect and investor and one of our outside directors at Jet, to settle me down. Jim persuaded me to quit fretting about the day-to-day movements in our stock price and instead concentrate on building the company. That advice helped me weather many difficult trading periods in the years to come.

Almost immediately, we looked to put our new investment capital to work. Our $1.5 million was a tremendous amount of money for a couple of young airline advisers, but it just wasn't going to provide equity in a whole lot of airplanes, even in 1970 dollars. We tried to leverage the initial capital with the Enterprise Fund in Boston, a 10 percent holder in our company from the public offering. The fund had preliminarily agreed to put up another $5 million in subordinated debt, but that deal fell through as financial markets continued to weaken.

In the end, we looked for another few months before giving up on finding another investor, and we were left worrying that Jet would become a company with a couple of leases instead of a full-fledged leasing company. Even if we could pull it off, we couldn't justify tying up all our borrowing power in just a couple of airplanes.

The only way out of this dilemma, as we saw it, was to shift gears. The world had changed in the months we spent trying to leverage our $1.5 million stake. In May 1970, the Dow had sunk to its lowest level in more than seven years. In June, the Penn Central railroad filed for bankruptcy. Regional airlines were entering the normally busy summer travel season not knowing if they'd survive until the fall. The transportation industry, and the country at large, braced for economic recession, and it no longer made sense for us to concentrate on leasing alone. In this fragile economy, there appeared to be other, better opportunities for an aggressive aviation company with $1.5 million to spend.

But we couldn't go out and use the money as we pleased, not with the way the "use of proceeds" clause was written in the Jet prospectus, so we decided to try something fairly unusual. We went back to our new shareholders with a perquisite vote—a nonbinding ratification that we hoped would allow us to consider purchasing an interest in an airline in addition to pursuing leasing opportunities. We prepared a new business plan and asked our hundred or so shareholders to reconsider their investment. They did—and more than 95 percent approved.

---

With the new flexibility effectively granted by our shareholders, in August 1970 we set about evaluating several troubled airline properties. We focused on four regional carriers: Mohawk Airlines, Ozark Airlines, Southern Airways, and Texas International Airlines, in descending order of our interest. Each of these companies was in weak financial shape, but all had great potential and were small enough for us to consider, given our modest capital base.

Mohawk Airlines, our prime target, was based in Utica, New York. With a fleet of around twenty-five BAC 111 aircraft, it had a corner on the upstate New York market, with regular service to Syracuse, Rochester, Buffalo, and Boston. As regional carriers went, Mohawk was one of the biggest—bigger, even, than the Pittsburgh-based Allegheny Airlines, which would later become USAir—but it still had trouble making money. The company had lost more than $8 million in 1968 and 1969 and was facing a potential pilots' strike near the end of 1970. The airline needed an infusion of cash and was open to the idea of a merger or buyout.

Despite its troubles, we liked the way the company looked. After an introduction by Rob Garrett, a Smith Barney investment banker, and with the support of Mohawk's Chase Manhattan bankers, we sat down with the airline's president, Russ Stephenson, and hammered out a financing agreement. The highly leveraged deal, which called for Jet to put up most of its capital, was contingent on the swift resolution of a pilots' strike, which had in fact come to pass during our negotiations. We just didn't like the cash-flow dips that could be expected after a long labor dispute, and a deal that looked good in November 1970 would have been far less attractive to us after a long pilots' strike.

As we turned the corner into 1971, however, the strike dragged on, and by then the numbers no longer made sense. The deal started to look risky to the people at Chase Manhattan as well. Jim Mitchell, Chase's senior aerospace banker, eventually persuaded us to drop our pursuit of Mohawk and let him introduce us to one of the other regionals on our list of troubled airlines. Mitchell, who held the debt of a number of airlines—nearly all of the small regional airlines, many in trouble— dangled the promise of a better deal if we could help coax Mohawk into considering a merger with its fiercest rival, Allegheny.

The Allegheny–Mohawk merger was done by early spring, but there was a sad footnote. As the deal neared a close, I began hearing reports about Bob Peach, Mohawk's founder and principal shareholder, and his distress over losing control of his company. One of the most likely reasons for his depression, I suspected, was that he blamed himself for allowing Mohawk's fortunes to unravel. He was a sound, aggressive, and in some ways trailblazing businessman who had built his airline into a regional force only to see his power eroded and ultimately swallowed up by a smaller carrier—his nemesis, at that.

Apparently, Peach began to behave in odd, unsettling ways. His closest associates could no longer figure him out. I will never forget a February 1971 lunch meeting I had with him in a Clinton, New York, restaurant at which he displayed a very unnerving paranoia. During our lunch, he kept insisting that the people at the next table were talking about Allegheny. At Bob's pleading (and as closely as discretion would allow), I actually listened to their conversation and heard only personal small talk. They were not connected to the industry in any way, it seemed, but Bob was adamant and continued to shift about nervously during our meal.

I wish I had attached more significance to his behavior at the time or knew how to get him help. A few weeks after the merger, Bob Peach committed suicide.

# CHAPTER THREE

# Milestones

## The Growth of Texas International
## 1971–1975

WITH MOHAWK out of the picture, my partners and I at Jet Capital needed to look elsewhere for an airline to take over. We refocused on the other three on our original list: Ozark Airlines, Southern Airways, and Texas International Airlines.

Ozark and Southern were fine carriers, and we would have been interested in a deal. But we also had to be practical. Texas International Airlines (TIA) was the most available. It was the highest on Chase's list of most troubled carriers and in the toughest position as far as its debt structure was concerned. It was the airline with which we had the most leverage, although I must admit that it was running a distant third in terms of our initial desires. We were genuinely concerned about its overdue debt. In TIA's favor, on the other hand, was that the state of Texas seemed like a promising business environment and that, most importantly, the banks were encouraging us to take it on.

Naturally, it wasn't just what we wanted but also what was doable. TIA management was very willing to work with us and willing to cede control, since they didn't control the airline from an equity perspective anyway. They viewed the Minneapolis group that did control it as erratic and difficult to pin down on decisions: they normally flew in and went back in short order, often the same day. TIA executives called them absentee managers. The banks didn't like that aspect of the Minneapolis group's control, either.

True to his word, Chase's Jim Mitchell, shortly after the Mohawk deal fell through, arranged a meeting for us with the management team at TIA. As we expected, it turned out to be a sleepy, underperforming regional with more debt than it could service. The company was headquartered at the maintenance end of Houston's William P. Hobby Airport, which was where we had our initial visit.

TIA had a colorful history dating to the early 1900s, when an entrepreneur named Earl McKaughan established the Houston Transportation Company, which hauled timbers by mule team to the Humble oil fields. McKaughan eventually added airplanes to his cargo business, and Trans-Texas Airways (TTA) was incorporated in October 1947. By 1966, the McKaughan family had sold its stake in the airline for $12 million to an investment company headed by Minneapolis financier Carl Pohlad, who promptly saw his airline run into trouble.

Pohlad grew up dirt poor but eventually became a billionaire. He made his fortune in banking and later in his career went on to buy the Minnesota Twins baseball team and develop an outstanding business record. But when it came to his airline, he was saddled with the company's spotty safety and service reputation and loss-making operations. At the time we came along, it had only recently been renamed Texas International Airlines. The "international" part of the name came from a single route, a money-losing milk run from the Texas border town of Harlingen to Tampico and Veracruz, on the Gulf side of Mexico. Local people weren't impressed. They continued to derisively call the airline TTA, for Tree Top Airways, ever since one of its Convair CV-240 planes flew too low over a wooded area in the Rio Grande Valley and landed with a mess of bramble clinging to the fuselage.

From 1967 through 1971, TIA had consolidated losses of more than $21 million. This was an astonishing figure when set against only $257 million in total revenues (including $25 million in federal subsidies). But the main reason for our interest in such a financial basket case was its attractive potential. The oil business was booming. Texas was a rapidly growing state, and the fact that the Civil Aeronautics Board had awarded potentially lucrative new routes to the company might well pay off. We also could see that the airline had a lot of unnecessary and redundant expenses that could be trimmed by a more hands-on management. For all its faults, TIA held promise as one of the nation's eighteen certificated airlines, albeit in the position of number 18—the smallest. Moreover, the federal government wasn't issuing any more scheduled-airlines licenses—not at that time, anyway.

Despite its potential, TIA's poor operating results and tenuous financial position made it available at an attractive price. The management was actively looking to refinance the airline, and one possible option was to seek outside investment in exchange for an equity position.

In April 1971, we signed on as advisers at a retainer fee of approximately $15,000 a month ($115,000 in 2024 dollars). Our stated purpose was to restructure some of the airline's long-term and short-term debt, advise on the acquisition of new aircraft and the retiring of some of its existing fleet, and examine route and scheduling changes that might improve results. Underneath that mandate, though, we had marching orders from TIA management to finance a substantial investment in the airline's equity, which could give us a shot at control of the board.

This last objective was not expressly stated, because TIA management was working somewhat at cross-purposes with the board of directors. Pohlad and his Minnesota Enterprises group didn't want to see their control of the airline diluted in any way. They were out looking for capital at the same time we were, and the financial community was small enough for us to occasionally find ourselves trying to shake money from the same trees they were shaking.

Pohlad was an enigmatic fellow—cold and calculating one moment, shy and kindly the next. He had a fondness for airline investments but was well known for his inability to attract and retain competent management—at the airline, at least. For example, Bob Sherer, TIA's first president after Pohlad took over the airline, found himself out of a job after taking a hard line in labor negotiations. Pohlad apparently didn't want a labor confrontation and caved in to the demands of the pilots' union, which had threatened a slowdown unless Sherer was removed from his position. To my mind, such a move is almost always disastrous for a company. There is simply no way to keep strong managers if they need to live in fear of labor unions or anybody else.

Three months after our first meeting, Jet Capital presented a refinancing deal to TIA's management. It called for the deferral of more than $20 million in debt, the conversion of $13 million in subordinated debt into equity, and an infusion of $1.5 million in new capital. A portion of the new capital ($250,000) would be committed by National Aviation Corporation, an investment firm in New York with many substantial airline holdings. Jet Capital pledged to put up the rest. National Aviation was run by my old friend Don Burr, who was eager to see our deal get done and about whom you will read more in subsequent chapters.

TIA's management team enthusiastically endorsed our proposal and presented it to the board, which approved it. On May 26, 1971, we signed a letter of intent, giving us the exclusive right to structure a deal to take over the company. The airline's tenuous position with its banks, and the active involvement of Jim Mitchell and his staff at Chase, who supported our plan, naturally served as a strong incentive to TIA's board to go along. While our plan didn't provide a lot of new equity, Mitchell and Chase were happy to see that we would bring hands-on management to the airline.

Pohlad and his team, meanwhile, were still out trying to arrange their own refinancing, despite Jet's "exclusive" arrangement with TIA. Then a third party joined the hunt—of all people, Howard Hughes! Air West, operating on the West Coast and by then controlled by Hughes, who had renamed the company Hughes Airwest, was looking to absorb TIA and then go after Southern Airways in an attempt to create a new transcontinental airline. Ever since Hughes had lost control of TWA, he yearned to get back into the major airline business. In November 1971, Hughes's longtime confidant, Jack Real, met us in our New York office. He was hoping to persuade us to abandon our letter of intent with TIA and instead throw our resources behind his reclusive billionaire boss. But this time—the second time—I wasn't all that thrilled to be crossing professional paths with Hughes.

"Listen," Real said, "If you let us take over this deal, you'll all be millionaires." But we had no interest, even if what he was claiming was possible. We weren't out to make a quick buck just so someone else could get rich unlocking TIA's long-term potential. We wanted to turn TIA around, and there weren't too many other opportunities for a deal of this kind. We weren't about to back off just because Howard Hughes thought we could be bought.

On December 8, 1971, we reached an agreement with the board to acquire control of TIA, giving Jet Capital 24 percent of the company's equity and 58 percent of its voting shares. TIA's creditors, with approximately $25 million in bad debt (most significantly, Chase as lead bank), pressured the board to accept our proposal. Of the $1.5 million in new capital required to close the deal, only $1.25 million came from Jet, and of that amount, we needed to tender only $900,000 in cash. The balance, approximately $350,000, constituted our uncollected fees as advisers to the company and investment bankers on the deal.

So there we were, with control of a CAB-certificated airline—for only $900,000! "It may be the world's smallest airline," I joked to one of the reporters at the news conference announcing the sale, "but it's still an airline."

---

There was still the matter of winning approval from the Civil Aeronautics Board, a process that we knew could take a year or more. During that time, I spent my summer weekends in the Hamptons learning to fly, since the lawyers didn't want us to be around the company before CAB approval. Earning my pilot's license had long been a goal, and given that I was going to be co-owner and manager of our own certificated airline, it seemed advantageous to have a firsthand knowledge of the mechanics of flying.

I enrolled in flight school at the air force base in Westhampton Beach, New York, and dutifully completed the requisite coursework and training flights. I took my first solo flight on September 6, 1971, in a single-engine Cessna. It was, and remains, one of the most exhilarating experiences of my life: up there alone, free and untethered, soaring among the clouds.

I also noticed something else. When I was at the stick, my mind tended to wander—to the TIA deal or to any number of other pressing matters. That lack of focus is not a good trait in a pilot. Then I nearly flunked my flight test with an FAA examiner. I had to make three "touch-and-go" landings, in which the pilot touches down on the runway and then taxis along for an immediate takeoff. It's a relatively simple procedure, but on my first touch-and-go, I forgot to raise the wing flaps I had just lowered for landing. As I rolled down the runway with increasing speed, the plane was just too heavy to lift off. I finally made the correction and took off in time to save my license. But the instructor told me later that he was within seconds of taking over the controls. Once I secured my license, I didn't use it very often, although I enjoyed several solo weekend flights in later years in a chartered aircraft. But within four years or so, I gave up flying altogether. I had decided that the worst kind of pilot is a part-time pilot, and running an airline didn't allow for a lot of weekends away.

I ceased flying solo in other ways during the final flight school hops and hurdles of the TIA deal. In early May 1971, I'd met a stunning woman, Sharon, at a New York Yacht Club party, but we fell out of contact. In the fall, while at a Yale Club mixer, a voice called out to me from across the reception hall. I spun around and wonderfully, unexpectedly, found Sharon. I remember thinking there was no one else in the entire room; everything else just fell away. Many years later, my heart still jumps when she walks into a room.

We had our first date a few days after the Yale Club mixer at Gino's, a favorite Upper East Side haunt. I reserved the last table in the rear, on the left side, because it was one of the quietest corners of the otherwise noisy restaurant. I had almost let her get away, and I wanted to be sure there were no distractions on this second pass. Later, Sharon would tell me that what I had thought was a romantic first date actually seemed like a job interview to her—but I was out to learn all I could.

Sharon is the oldest of three children raised in Pelham, New York, an affluent suburb just north of Manhattan. She studied art and dance and spent a summer living in France when she was nineteen. At the age of twenty, she worked as an intern for Senator Charles Percy, an Illinois Republican, during the turmoil of the race riots in our nation's capital. She served on President Nixon's task force on youth affairs. Most interesting—to me, anyway—was Sharon's love of sports and the outdoors. As an undergraduate at Mount Holyoke, she taught herself to ski at nearby Mount Tom. She was already an avid sailor and loved walking and biking.

I was happy to learn about her father's career in business, because I took it to mean that Sharon would not only be open to the demands of my own but also familiar with the language and trappings that went along with it. A World War II Marine veteran, her father spent roughly a quarter century at Union Carbide before retiring as a senior vice president there. Then he began a second career as president of Mundo Gas, a gas importer located in Bermuda.

At the time, Sharon had just begun a career of her own, as a paralegal at the New York law firm of Sage Gray Todd & Simms. Her background and interests left her well qualified in the area of art appraisals, and she did a great deal of probate work, evaluating the art collections of various estates (Sage Gray had a major trusts and estates practice). One of her best finds was an original Toulouse-Lautrec. It had been consigned to a thrift-shop heap during an estate appraisal in a large apartment on the Upper East Side before Sharon recognized it for what it was.

We had some wonderful times together from the very beginning. We'd go out to the Hamptons, and Sharon would keep me company while I logged the necessary flying hours for my pilot's license. We'd go to dinners and concerts. Gradually, our talks shifted to family and children. I was reluctant to press her on these matters so soon in our relationship, but I didn't want to get too involved with a woman whose career was a bigger priority than marriage and family. Sharon said she wanted lots of kids, which I loved to hear.

Things were going so well between Sharon and me that I took her home to meet my parents for Thanksgiving dinner that first fall. I imagine Sharon regarded surviving a classic Spanish meal of chorizo, paella, and other traditional fare from my parents' kitchen as a key "test." What I remember most fondly about that first visit is that no one seemed particularly anxious. My parents were always terrific in potentially tense situations like this; they were gentle, caring, polite, and open to meeting new people. Sharon, too, had an ease and facility with people that I had already come to admire.

My mother took to Sharon right away, but then Sharon was always easy to take to. And she was a good sport, rolling up her sleeves and helping my mother in the kitchen. She even posed for a picture with the first sausage she'd ever stuffed. My mother served a Spanish dish called empanada that day, bread stuffed with various meats and tomatoes. Sharon later confided that she was practiced enough in the fine art of stirring her plate to make things look eaten when they hadn't been.

Our courtship was put on pause for a family tragedy. It was January 6, 1972, and I was having dinner with some friends—Larry Twill and his wife—at a seafood restaurant at Third Avenue and 72nd Street, a couple of blocks from Bob Carney's apartment, when I received an urgent phone call from Bob on the restaurant phone.

"Frank," Bob said rather ominously, "you need to come up here right away. I need to talk to you."

"I can be done with dinner here in a half hour or so," I said.

"It's important," Bob insisted. "Make it as soon as you can."

It was pretty unusual to get a call like that from Bob. He wouldn't tell me what it was about, but it was clear from his voice that something was terribly amiss. My first thought was that things had come unraveled on the TIA deal—why else would he want to pull me out of a dinner? But then I started to think something else was wrong. If it was the deal, he would have said so.

I excused myself and raced the couple of blocks to Bob's apartment. My head was filled with a dozen worst-case scenarios. "What is it?" I said breathlessly as soon as he opened the door.

"Your mother called," he said, trying to sound calm. "You need to call her back."

I grabbed Bob's phone and dialed. "It's your brother Larry," she said when she picked up. "He's very sick." I could hear the anguish in her voice as she told me that my big brother had suffered a heart attack. She told me what hospital he'd been taken to, where his wife was, where I could meet up with the rest of the family, and on and on. I took it all in, and I knew she wasn't telling me everything. Maybe she didn't want to tell me what she had to tell me over the phone, or maybe she couldn't find the words.

She called back a few minutes later to tell me what I had by then figured out: my big brother Larry was dead. The news hit me like a kick to the stomach. I was stunned and heartsick. It didn't seem real at first, and then, as it sank in, the weight of it was overwhelming. During my youth there had not been a lot of death in our family, at least among relatives with whom we were close, and I was not at all prepared for it. Clearly, none of us was prepared to lose Larry at the age of forty-two.

Larry and I had not been especially close for a number of years, but he was my brother, and I loved him. Our ten-year age difference meant that we were raised in almost separate family environments—with my other brother, Val, straddling the middle—so there was a lot we never knew about each other. We were different people from the same place. He got married right after college, quite suddenly, to a woman we hardly knew, and from that moment on he was somewhat removed from the rest of us. He had two children—a boy, Larry, and a girl, Laura—before I was even out of college. As adults, we didn't often get together when it was just the two of us, although we did meet for a sandwich near his Wall Street office just a few weeks before he died.

Larry worked as an options trader at Bache & Co., a large brokerage house. On the afternoon of his death, he had gone out to lunch with some guys from work for a birthday celebration. They drank a little and ate a lot. Then Larry went back to work and shortly thereafter slumped over his desk. He was rushed to Beekman Downtown Hospital, where he was placed in intensive care long enough to regain consciousness and visit with his wife, but then he suffered a second massive heart attack three hours after the first. The second attack killed him, and what troubled us years later was that if his heart attack had occurred today, his death might have been prevented, given all the advances that have since been made in the treatment of heart attack victims.

I had to go down to the city morgue with Larry's wife, Lynn, to identify the body. It was one of the saddest, most difficult things I have ever had to do. The medical examiner pulled back the white sheet that had been covering Larry's face, then set it down again a moment later, and in that instant, it finally hit me, full, deep, and hard. I looked down at my big brother, at the pale, blank expression on his face, and I wept. I'll never forget that moment. But as painful as it is to remember, it's not something I ever *want* to forget. It's the last image I have of him, but it is not the most abiding. When I think of Larry now, I flash back and forth between images of the times when I knew him best—as a gangly teenager, taking care of his baby brothers after school, waiting for our mother to come home from the beauty shop to give us dinner—and when I knew him least, in that final glimpse of him, there on that last day at the morgue.

My mother took Larry's death hardest of all, which was to be expected. He was her first child. She gave birth to him at the age of seventeen, when she was still nearly a child herself, and there was always a special bond between them. My father may have been her husband and her lover, but Larry was like her best friend. Now that I have children of my own, I realize how difficult it must have been for her to accept his death.

---

I had begun to think about moving down to Houston full-time and wondered how that move would affect my relationship with Sharon over the long term. There was only one way to find out.

I stopped at Gordon's Jewelers in Houston's Galleria mall and picked out a ring—a gold Tiffany setting with a modest diamond, my dream ring for a dream girl. Then I booked a table for lunch at the restaurant in Rockefeller Center in New York, which during the summer months moved its tables outside, over the skating rink. The lunch was set for Tuesday, July 25, 1972, and when it came around on the calendar it was a beautiful, sunny day—a picture-perfect setting for what I hoped would be a moment to remember.

Sharon's face lit up in genuine surprise when I leaned over the table and asked her to marry me. It was like she had no idea this was coming. We'd talked around it a number of times, enough to know that our plans and views were compatible, but we'd never let the conversation take that specific turn—I wanted to save it for the real thing. Sharon would say that I played my cards close to the vest in this area. She said she was wary of bachelors like me who wouldn't make their intentions known, and she truly had no idea that I was thinking of proposing, but I'm not so sure I believed her. After all, she'd already thought of Houston: she was open to the idea of living there and was prepared to offer the right answer without hesitation.

Sharon remembers this proposal the same way she recalls our first date—as if I were closing a business deal. I had hoped to present myself in more romantic terms, but if my proposal is to be remembered in business terms, I'm happy to report that it was the best deal I ever made.

---

As Sharon made plans for our fall wedding, I turned my attention to the CAB approval process, then in its final stages. The board took eight months to make its decision, and although the hearings lasted only a few weeks, the deliberations stretched on and on. The reason was the opposition by Jack Real and the Howard Hughes gang. They argued against CAB approval, maintaining that Hughes Airwest was better financed and better qualified to run the company. I was cross-examined by Hughes's attorneys in front of an administrative law judge in Washington, where Hughes Airwest presented hours of opposing testimony, getting their experts to corroborate Hughes's assertion that Jet was too small and inexperienced and TIA too damaged to be suitable for anything other than absorption by a larger carrier.

Ultimately, the CAB rejected the Hughes bid and approved our deal. Why did they choose us over an airline legend such as Howard Hughes? We had a signed contract, our financing was reasonable, and the CAB had always favored supporting an independent airline over a merger. It was August 24, 1972, and we immediately set the closing of our refinancing plan in motion. Then we flew to Houston later that same day for our first board meeting, during which I was appointed president and chief executive officer of Texas International Airlines, Inc. Bob Carney was named executive vice president for planning and development. Rob Snedeker, our financial analyst, became senior vice president for finance and administration.

We were finally in business, and our first task was to stanch the bleeding. The refinancing had bought us just about a year to turn things around. If we couldn't meet our short-term objective, to stop the flow of red ink, we wouldn't be around long enough to implement any long-term plans.

Our trouble spots were apparent. TIA had too many unprofitable routes. Our developing routes in larger markets were years away from being profitable. The pilots flying our nineteen-seat Beechcraft planes, for example, were drawing the same salaries and benefits as the pilots on our fifty-six-seat Convairs. Even with competitive pricing and government subsidies, and even if we could fill every seat, we couldn't turn a profit on the Beechcrafts.

Our initial strategy was to shrink the airline down to a sound break-even structure. Like a gardener who prunes back a plant to help it thrive, we grounded the Beechcraft fleet, cut back schedules in some unprofitable markets, and reduced our available seat miles by 12 percent for the second half of the year. We also strengthened maintenance procedures and tightened maintenance costs system-wide, cutting our operating expenses by 7 percent in the remaining months of 1972. In December, we inaugurated our Houston–Mexico City service. Despite fierce competition from Pan Am and Air France, it quickly became one of our most profitable runs. We also invested heavily in the airline's future, ordering two McDonnell Douglas DC-9-30 aircraft, valued at $11 million each, a big deal for us then, for delivery in the summer of 1974.

The number of TIA employees was reduced to its lowest level in four years, mostly through early retirement and attrition but also through a series of distressing layoffs. These layoffs offered my first unpleasant learning experience in hard-line management. It was a lesson I would have happily deferred but that could not have been justifiably avoided.

For the most part, however, and despite the cuts, morale among our two thousand or so employees was surprisingly high. There was change in the air, and it was exciting. Our owner-management team promised long-term stability and growth, and the message to labor was clear: you do your jobs, we'll do ours, and we'll all be in business together for a long time to come.

It helped that we also kept executive salaries at an industry low, in part to demonstrate to our people and the unions that we were not motivated by greed. In 1972, I drew an annual salary of $56,000 ($416,000 in 2024 dollars). Bob Carney earned $45,000 ($334,000), and Rob Snedeker was at $35,000 ($260,000). While we were all able to live quite comfortably, our paychecks were far smaller than those of our counterparts at comparably sized regional carriers.

The only wrinkles in our otherwise smooth relationship with our employees were my continuing ties to New York. As outside, out-of-town investors, we had to weather some initial skepticism about our dedication to the company and the community of interests we now served. Some people believed that we'd sell our stake after six months, which back then was the length of time a property had to be held in order to qualify for favorable capital gains tax treatment. The fact that I returned to New York frequently during this period while Sharon stayed on at her New York firm simply fueled speculation that we were out to make a fast buck on a quick breeze through town. Of course, that wasn't our plan, but it was difficult to sell our intentions to some of our employees and to members of the business press until our personal lives had a chance to catch up to our careers. A month after we were married, Sharon and I rented our first Houston apartment—at 10010 Memorial Drive, on the ground floor—but we continued to take turns visiting each other on weekends.

---

Gradually we entrenched ourselves in the ways of Texas, and concerns about our selling abated. We quickly expanded beyond our core group at Jet, recruiting some of the best and brightest young minds in the industry, although our efforts had actually started during the months we were awaiting CAB approval. Bob Gallaway, our old associate on the BWIA deal and at TWA, joined us from Frontier Airlines, where he had grown tired of his responsibilities and prospects as executive vice president. He signed on as our executive vice president and head of operations, proving to be a key early hire. In all my years in the business, I never met a more engaging, people-oriented manager than Bob, and he helped set the tone for our new company.

Jim Arpey came on board, also from Frontier, where he courageously gave notice before we formally closed on the deal for TIA. He became vice president of technical services and eventually succeeded Bob Gallaway as head of operations. Jim knew his way around an airplane hangar better than anyone I have known, and he worked tirelessly to control maintenance costs while improving reliability. He was a tremendous asset.

We also made good use of the several strong managers already in place at the airline, including Sam Ashmore, Don Breeding, Dan Thompson, Jim Cassady, and Bob Lemon. Bob had made such a strong impression on us as head of TIA's Air Line Pilots Association (ALPA) local that I promoted him to vice president of flying operations, something many people would find hard to believe. These men and a handful of others provided much-needed continuity between the old regime and the new.

Jim O'Donnell, whom I'd first met during our abandoned negotiations for Mohawk Airlines, joined us a few months into the effort as director of public affairs. As always, I was careful not to create dissension among incumbent management when I brought in senior guys from outside the company. O'Donnell reported to Jim Cassady initially, though I pledged to move him through the ranks as opportunities arose. Indeed, Jim ultimately took over our advertising and marketing efforts and showed himself to be one of the most creative, uninhibited thinkers in the field, a key resource for the company during my entire tenure. Jim was something of a free spirit, and his public relations and positioning sensibilities were unmatched. He had the best "nose" for the consumer I've ever encountered and taught me a lot about catering to our customers and the public.

Another important addition to the team was Don Burr. Don and I had become good friends in the few years since our meeting at an industry conference in 1970. In fact, Sharon and I shared a summerhouse in Point O'Woods, Fire Island, with Don and his then wife, Brigit, in the summer of 1972 while we were waiting on the CAB approval. He would also stand as best man at our wedding that fall. He was president of National Aviation, the aviation-oriented investment firm, but had become discouraged by the dreary work of managing other people's money. He used to call it a career "dealing with paper."

Don's eyes used to light up whenever our conversation turned to TIA, so in early 1973, I asked him to come down to Houston to be part of our effort. I was already stretched thin in a number of areas, and I wanted to bring in a competent executive to plug some of the gaps in my schedule and cover a number of external areas. However, some people criticized my hiring of Don because he didn't have any direct airline experience. Then again, none of us from Jet Capital, all under the age of thirty-two, had any great amount of airline experience, either.

We spent a great deal of time trying to reposition the airline in those first few months. Recall that one of the reasons we were able to buy the company at such an attractive price was that it had a poor record of on-time performance, an undeserved reputation for questionable safety (fueled by the "treetops" incident), and generally higher fares than rival Southwest Airlines in its intrastate markets. We needed to convince the flying public of our improved product, so we redesigned the company logo and adopted the tagline "We're on our way," which we thought conveyed a certain sense of excitement, movement, and change, all with the help of the new advertising agency we selected, Ogilvy & Mather.

The redesign signaled a new era for the company and, we hoped, communicated the same enthusiasm to passengers as our tagline. I was particularly enthusiastic about our new logo and aircraft markings, not only because they were attractive and effective but also because the change was so inexpensive. Our planes, I thought, were in serious need of a design makeover, which we just couldn't afford. But by using the lines and markings already painted onto our old planes, and by changing our corporate colors from gray, white, and purple to red, white, and blue, our team was able to repaint our fleet at only a fraction of the cost of a full paint job. At the time, a full paint job cost between $40,000 and $50,000 per plane; ours, making use of the existing striping, checked in at between $10,000 and $15,000 per plane, so the savings were substantial.

---

Sharon and I were married less than two months into my run at Texas International, on October 14, 1972, but the wedding didn't exactly signal an end to our hectic schedules. We both wanted to be married in Manhattan, even as our life was shifting slowly to Texas, since our family and friends were all in the Northeast.

The ceremony was at Saint Bartholomew's, an Episcopal church on Park Avenue near the Waldorf Astoria. Sharon was raised Episcopalian, and I was raised Catholic, but we were both flexible on the issue of

Inspection of the newly repainted TXI airplane (1973).

religion, although I had an inclination that Sharon's religion might make more sense for our children down the road because she was more religious than I was. Saint Bart's also provided such a stately and majestic setting that I couldn't imagine being married anyplace else. My parents, although they were practicing Catholics, were also very relaxed about where we were married.

The reception was held at the Junior League clubhouse, on 80th Street between Park and Lexington Avenues, and what I remember most fondly about the gathering was how radiant Sharon looked and the tremendous good feeling permeating the room. It was, without exaggeration, the single happiest day of my life, to be rivaled in later years only by the births of our children.

We spent our wedding night at the Plaza Hotel before departing for a ten-day honeymoon in Mexico City, Puerto Vallarta, and Los Angeles, followed by stops along TIA's route system through Texas and Louisiana. Eastern Airlines had just abandoned several Gulf Coast markets, and I needed to do some politicking there because these routes were being put up for grabs by the CAB.

Sharon returned to New York after the honeymoon to resume her paralegal work, and I returned to Houston. The plan was for her to eventually join me in Houston full-time, but she was enjoying her job so much and I was so engrossed in the TIA challenge that we didn't rush to give up her very attractive position. We continued to see each other every weekend, in Houston or New York.

We kept this long-distance arrangement up for more than a year, until the birth of our daughter Nicole Patricia, in New York. Sharon worked until December 21, 1973. The following evening, she went into labor, and baby Nicole made her appearance by morning. We picked her name because it had been on our short list of girls' names and because it echoed Saint Nicholas, appropriate for Christmas. Nicole was born on December 23, the same birthday as my deceased brother, Larry. I wept with joy when the doctor handed her to me, and I thought that this was what life was all about. I still can vividly remember singing Charlie Rich's "The Most Beautiful Girl" as I drove our small red

Fiat back uptown on Third Avenue to our apartment, on East 73rd Street.

After Christmas, Sharon and Nicole joined me in Houston on a permanent basis, and I started to feel, for the first time, that we had our life fully together. Sharon has never lost the image of one of our daily rituals in our rented apartment: me struggling to turn the pages of the *Wall Street Journal* while Nicole enjoyed her morning bottle in my lap. Regrettably, there were too many times when that was the last I would see of Sharon and Nicole for days at a time. I did a lot of traveling along the TIA system in those early months, trying to forge a relationship with our far-flung employees and the leaders in the various communities we served.

Sharon joined me on as many of these trips as possible, even after Nicole was born. In those days, before airline deregulation, when local officials were important in determining new route awards, Sharon was usually on hand to help christen a new plane, open a new route, or charm local officials at chamber of commerce visits. In time, though, she found she missed her career, and she enrolled in law school at the University of Houston when Nicole was only a few months old.

Meanwhile, we continued to streamline operations at TIA, finding new ways to save on costs and maximize performance. In 1973, we returned the airline to profitability for the first time in seven years, posting a modest net profit of $319,000. Revenues were up 5.7 percent from 1972, to $77.2 million; operating expenses rose only 4.8 percent, to $74.7 million; nonoperating expenses were down 24 percent, reflecting a reduction in interest payments and an improved cash position, to $2.2 million. Also, significantly, by cutting back on the subsidy-eligible portion of our route system, we reduced our reliance on federal subsidies over this period by almost 10 percent.

Next we adopted a program called Operation Speed Up, which helped bring the airline to an 82.7 percent on-time performance level by year's end, higher than any of the trunk airlines. We also completed approximately 98.4 percent of all scheduled plane miles, and improvements in both areas brought us to very competitive industry levels.

In addition, we improved our service with a number of user-friendly promotions, such as a new "quick ticket" for speedy passenger ticketing, in-flight snack and sandwich service on our short-haul routes, and the Texas Double—double-shot drinks for the price of a single, even though this brought us a much-publicized boycott by the local Baptists.

We were on our way.

With my partner Bob Carney in front of a new livery TXI airplane (1973).

Or at least we thought we were. Early on, we realized that we had to deal with the unique competition Southwest Airlines presented—unique because although we were subject to federal regulation, Southwest operated in an environment in which there was virtually no economic regulation whatsoever.

Southwest had been started by three ambitious airline entrepreneurs, the most famous of whom was the soon-to-be-legendary Herb Kelleher, and had opened for business with a clever plan. It would avoid government economic regulations by operating entirely within the state of Texas. A boast by one of the three partners, Rollin King, that Southwest was going to put TIA out of business had such impact that it scared away many potential buyers of TIA, in addition to scaring the airline's owners and creditors. In 1971, when Southwest started up, the company's then CEO, Lamar Muse, also threatened to put little Texas International out of business—not a difficult-to-believe proposition then—with its lower cost structure and lack of regulatory economic supervision. This taught us, long before 1978, when other carriers faced airline deregulation, what open entry and unregulated pricing would be like.

Another competitive advantage Southwest had related to the fact that the enormous and somewhat remote Dallas–Fort Worth Regional Airport (DFW) would soon be opening. Federal regulations required us to move our operations there, while Texas regulations imposed no such requirement on Southwest, and they were not bound by historical airport use arrangements.

While the new airport would better showcase our product and provide us with more gates for connecting flights, its disadvantages for TIA were significant. For one thing, it meant roughly $2 million in additional operating costs, not to mention the considerable costs associated with the move. Even the time required to land, unload passengers, refuel, and take off again—so-called turnaround time—was considerably faster at Love Field because it was a smaller, simpler airport. But most troubling of all was the negative impact on our Dallas passengers, who clearly preferred the proximity of Love Field, close to town, over the more remote and inconvenient DFW complex, located between Dallas and Fort Worth.

By remaining at Love Field, and by being able to charge lower fares because of its much lower costs (which I will elaborate on below), Southwest was able to offer a much more competitive product. We had in effect been ordered by federal regulators to fight with one hand tied behind our backs. This was one of my earliest experiences with the way government regulation, however well-intentioned, can act as a trip wire to a thriving enterprise.

Explaining TXI route map with new Mexican destinations (1976).

On top of everything else, our turnaround that first full year was marred by a terrible, and avoidable, in-flight tragedy. On September 27, 1973, TIA flight 655 departed El Dorado, Arkansas, for Texarkana, Arkansas, at around 8:15 p.m. in the middle of a violent rainstorm. The scheduled flight time was around seventy-five minutes. The Convair 600 was carrying eight passengers and three crew members. Investigations later revealed that, despite the weather, the captain declined instrument guidance and opted for visual flight rules, thinking he knew the terrain well enough to maneuver through the storm.

To avoid the worst of the weather, he took a northerly flight path, requiring average minimum altitudes of around 4,500 feet. Still, he sometimes dropped to less than 3,000 feet. The first officer, according to the tape recovered later from the black box, was so concerned that the bad weather had taken them off course that he took out a map to verify their location. By the time he found their position, it was too late. The last voice on the tape was the first officer's, informing the captain that the "minimum on route altitude here is forty-four hund—"

He never finished his sentence. The recording was cut short by static and the sound of impact as the plane crashed into the woods on Black Fork Mountain (elevation around 2,500 feet), in the Ouachita Mountain Range near Mena, Arkansas.

Jim Cassady tracked me down in San Antonio to tell me that one of our planes was missing, and I immediately left for the area. At that point, all we knew was that the plane was missing, but we were braced for bad news. A dozen worst-case scenarios raced through my mind on my way to the scene. When I arrived, the plane still hadn't been found, and the terrain was so rough and densely forested that we knew we'd never find it until after the weather cleared.

We hired surplus army helicopters to help with the search, and I joined them on a couple of the missions. Finally, three days into our search, a student pilot up on a training flight spotted the fuselage. Actually, what he spotted was a burned trail in the woods that led us to what was left of our plane. The Convair was crushed like a beer can. There were no survivors.

I was prepared for this moment. Or at least I had planned to be, and I thought I was. I can't speak for my counterparts at other airlines, but I know that I lived in constant fear of a tragedy like this. I can't see how you can run an airline and not worry about it all the time. From the moment we closed on TIA, I knew the odds were that someday, despite our best efforts, we would suffer a crash. During my entire time at TIA and Continental, I was like an overanxious parent with a kid out late. Usually, every time I took a middle-of-the-night call from the system control department—which often was about something relatively benign, such as a passenger who tripped while deplaning—I'd get the report, catch my breath, and fall back to sleep. Sometimes, though, if it was a serious incident, I'd be up the rest of the night with worry or make my way downtown to the office.

But close calls are part of the business, and, regrettably, so are accidents—at least they were in those days. Here, though, just over a year into my run in airline management, I was not as fully prepared for this part of the business as I had hoped. I realized as I dealt with the aftermath of this awful tragedy that the only way to be fully prepared, or better prepared, is to struggle through it and learn from it. What I learned is that you must shoulder all the blame, even when airline management is not at fault, and that you must be there to offer emotional and financial support to the families of your fallen crew members and passengers as well as to your employees, who sometimes take the news very hard.

———————————

Our efforts to keep flying nearly stalled the following month with the October imposition of the Arab oil embargo. Virtually overnight, the price of jet fuel jumped from twenty-five to forty-five cents a gallon. Texaco, which supplied most of the airline industry in those days, informed us that airline customer allocations had been cut to 80 percent of previous levels and that they had no choice but to reduce our order by a corresponding amount. The price rise in fuel, we knew, could be largely absorbed by the compensating fare increases routinely granted by the CAB in such circumstances. But the drop in available supply was potentially disastrous: without sufficient fuel, we would have to cut back on flights, plugging up the revenue streams we needed to stay in business.

The first week of the embargo was like a bad dream played on fast-forward. We huddled that first weekend in the Blue Barn, our windowless offices, making frantic phone calls to members of our congressional delegation and other influential contacts we had in Austin and on Capitol Hill. On Monday morning, along with just about every other airline, we filed an emergency application with the Department of Energy to increase our allocated amount of fuel.

In our filing, and later in person, we argued that there were many small cities in need of our service, that we didn't have the financial reserves to counter the loss in revenue, and that big carriers such as Eastern probably spilled more fuel around their airplanes in an hour than all our aircraft burned in a day. This last argument, coupled with our service to remote communities, seemed to do the trick, because we ultimately found our allocation largely restored and our prospects not quite as grim as they had seemed going in.

At TIA, we turned the corner into 1974 with great expectations. Our front-burner project, in January, was the heralded opening of the Dallas–Fort Worth Regional Airport, which was seen as something of an industry marvel at the time of its ribbon-cutting ceremony and a great big deal for the community. But at TIA, we didn't see it that way, and we were very reluctant tenants in the beginning.

---

We took another hit later that year that was far more devastating than any of the other snags we'd encountered up to that point: a crippling strike initiated by the Air Line Employees Association (ALEA), which represented TIA's 1,100 or so station agents, reservation clerks, and clerical workers. In contract negotiations, ALEA leaders held firm on their demands for a 50 percent wage increase spread over three years. We instructed our labor negotiators to hold firm to a still-generous 21 percent pay hike over the same period. The impasse resulted in a four-month strike.

Airlines were rarely affected by strikes in those days, because at most carriers, employees had no reason to strike. Back then, negotiations between airlines and labor unions followed fairly standard lines of pattern bargaining. Wage increases were typically absorbed by imposing higher fares on passengers, which in turn were routinely approved by the CAB. The squeeze, for small airlines such as TIA, was that our pay scales were always compared by the unions to those at big trunk carriers such as American and United, while our revenue structures were nothing like those of the big carriers. We didn't have any large, protected hubs with high average fares, as the big guys did.

Here, too, Southwest Airlines had an advantage over us, yet we had to match their much lower fare structure. They were a new company and did not have to live under old union contracts, which allowed them to enjoy much lower labor costs. It paid its people less, and their productivity was much higher, largely because they didn't have work restrictions from union contracts to live with. They also had fewer people with the amount of seniority our people had—they enjoyed a younger workforce.

Southwest was the key issue in these ALEA negotiations, because no amount of expense cutting would restore TIA to health if our labor costs continued to make us uncompetitive with our intrastate rival. We also hadn't come to terms with the union representatives on our need to use more part-time employees at terminals and seek volunteers to work split shifts at some of the small airports along our fifty-city route system, as Southwest was able to do.

We didn't want to take the blow of a shutdown, but we felt very strongly that caving to union demands built around erroneous and outdated business assumptions would be disastrous for the company, even over the short term. On December 1, ALEA membership went out on strike, but our planes kept flying. I and around four hundred or so management employees gathered in Houston and spread out along our system, working around the clock—selling tickets, hauling bags, cleaning planes. This helped us keep most of our daily flights on or close to schedule, with service at or near normal levels.

Then, just four days later, our pilots joined the ALEA workers in sympathy, and the airline was effectively grounded.

With flight operations stalled, however, we could collect payments as a member of an airline mutual aid pact. The mutual aid monies covered our overhead costs while we were grounded and until we reached a settlement. Of course, these payments were intended only to subsidize member carriers during a work stoppage and would end the moment we resumed operations. But we were worried. The longer the strike dragged on, the more difficult it would be to win back our passengers and return to normal.

There were two developments of note during the work stoppage, both of which strengthened my resolve to see TIA flying again—on reasonable terms. The first was a buyout overture. Al Feldman, president of Frontier, called two months into the strike and drew me into a discussion of how tough things were with our unions, how lousy our cash position probably was, and how hard it was going to be to resume operations once the strike was settled.

"Looks like you boys are going through a difficult period," he said, underselling our operation at every turn.

"Yes, we are," I allowed.

"Have you given any thought to selling?" he wondered.

"No, Al, we haven't," I said. "We wouldn't have taken the strike if we wanted to sell in the short term." Then I told him that if he had a proposal in mind that reflected the long-term value of TIA, I would be happy to review it with our board.

Al was interested only in picking up the airline at a distress price, but I was flattered by his interest just the same and proud that our carrier held strategic value for a company like Frontier. I thanked him for his interest and told him we weren't for sale.

The second interesting development during the strike had a more lasting impact. On February 6, 1975, the Texas Aeronautics Commission, over our strenuous objections, granted Southwest authority to serve the lower Rio Grande Valley. The fact that we were grounded when the routes were awarded and unable to battle back competitively made the commission's action doubly hard to take. The lower Rio Grande region had accounted for approximately 10 percent of our revenues. It was a core part of our business and potential profitability. Our position, which was obviously not helped by the work stoppage, was that additional service to the area was not needed and that competition in these markets would have an adverse effect on TIA's ability to serve other Texas markets. This was true. However, it was also true that our ability to serve other Texas markets was not a matter of great concern to members of the commission, who tended to regard Southwest as a sort of favorite son and allowed its management to largely do as it pleased.

The commission's decision was pivotal. It sent a warning throughout our ranks that the days of cozy regulation were all but over for us. Southwest was the commission's pet, and for TIA to survive we would have to slug it out in the marketplace with no help from any regulatory authority, whether in Washington or Austin.

We settled the ALEA strike and resumed operations on April 4, 1975. In the end, we granted wage hikes of around 23 percent, and we won much-needed productivity gains and the right to split shifts and hire part-time workers.

But the four-month shutdown changed our economic picture in a major way. We restarted operations during a period of unusually depressed traffic levels. Fuel prices were continuing to increase significantly, and Southwest had taken advantage of our absence by undercutting our service with sharply lower fares and adding new routes and frequencies, in effect cornering the intrastate market.

Still, our willingness to endure such a potentially devastating strike sent an important message to our other unions. Negotiations for new contracts with our three other major labor groups—pilots, machinists, and flight attendants—were already underway when we resumed operations. Our straightforward and committed position in the ground workers' strike gave management critical credibility. As a result, we were able to reach an agreement with all our labor unions resulting in substantially improved economics for the company, in addition to substantial improvement in our workers' compensation, extending through 1977.

We closed the book on 1974 with modest net earnings of $401,000—our second profitable year in a row. For the year, revenues were up 19 percent to $92 million, despite the work stoppage in the last month of the year. Shareholders' equity rose to $7.8 million from $7.3 million at the end of 1973. And in our eleven months of operation, TIA had the highest rate of traffic growth in the domestic airline industry. If we hadn't lost December to the strike, it would have been a remarkable year for our young company. But this was a temporary recovery.

The 1975 results were another story. We suffered a net loss of $4.4

million, most of it concentrated in the first half of the year as we struggled to return to normal traffic levels after the strike. We expected it would take time to rebuild our business, and it did. Revenues dropped to $78.6 million, down 14.4 percent from the previous year. Fuel prices rose beyond our worst-case projections. To survive, we wound up cutting our prestrike flight schedule by roughly 20 percent and trimming our workforce yet again, this time mostly through attrition and early retirements. We also instituted several fuel efficiency measures, including the then uncommon practice of taxiing our aircraft on the ground with only a single engine in operation.

With the exception of the increased competition from Southwest, we were back to where we were at year's end, operating with 57 percent load factors in December (a record TIA level for that month, although an exceptionally poor load factor these days), and poised to continue the upward momentum that had been interrupted by the strike. But our euphoria about our poststrike recovery was abruptly interrupted in December, when our finance people checked in with a dire forecast. At current revenue and expense levels, we would run out of cash during February, leaving us unable to make some major lease payments coming due that month. For the first time in three years, we were facing a very real cash crisis.

I gathered our senior officers and asked them to reevaluate our budgets for the remaining weeks of 1975 and our preliminary budget forecasts for 1976. I'd put some figures onto a flip chart, and I remember making my presentation to our key executives with a lump in my throat. After I laid out the situation, we broke into a number of small groups and began a painstaking examination of virtually every aspect of our struggling company. The forecast was desperate, but not without hope, and we reconvened for a management conclave in Austin a few days later to hammer out a revised plan. The Austin weekend, as it became known, was the first in a series of regular management retreats and stood as a kind of dividing line between what our company was and what we all hoped it could be. As a consequence, the weekend was successful not only in helping us avert our coming cash crisis but also in redirecting some of our fundamental thinking to TIA's future, taking account of the major changes occurring in Texas air markets—changes that would move to the national level. Indeed, the persistent drumbeat for the feared deregulation of the entire domestic airline industry, already heard in Texas, had become too loud to ignore.

———————————

On a personal level, 1975 also had its highs and lows. At the low end, on June 24, I was suspected of being on an Eastern Airlines flight from New Orleans to New York's Kennedy Airport that crashed on landing, killing all aboard.

I was on my way from Houston to meetings in New York but made a change of plans in order to accommodate a confidential interview over dinner in Boston with a prospective marketing executive. I then planned a late shuttle flight back to New York that same evening. In those days, I normally flew Eastern on my trips to the Northeast, but at that point there was no nonstop flight from Houston to Boston. There was, however, a nonstop Eastern flight from New Orleans to Boston—much more convenient. I had been meaning to schedule a visit to our New Orleans personnel for a while, and this seemed as good a time as any.

I made the revised travel arrangements myself, setting the stage for the later confusion. After a brief session with our New Orleans team, I left to catch a noon flight to Boston, and in parting I mentioned to our station manager that I was headed for New York. This was true—New York was my ultimate destination—but it added to the later confusion; the ill-fated New York flight departed New Orleans around the same time as my flight to Boston.

Sharon, meanwhile, was back home in Houston, midway through her second pregnancy. We stayed in pretty close in touch about our schedules in those days, but not so close that I would trouble her with each stop on my daily itinerary. Sometimes, when I scheduled meetings in two or three cities before reaching my destination, I would simply tell her where I'd end up; on this trip, all Sharon knew was that I was spending the night in our New York apartment. My mother was also aware that I was coming to town but knew nothing more of my plans.

Therefore, when the horrible news of the JFK Airport crash flashed across the wires, the people loosely aware of my schedule thought I might be on board. In those first moments, everyone on the flight was presumed dead, and after a frantic call from my office, Eastern confirmed that there was indeed one nonrevenue passenger on board in the first-class section. With a corroborating call from our New Orleans station manager stating that I was indeed headed to New York, I was presumed to have been among the passengers. The airline wasn't releasing passenger names at that point, but everyone at TIA assumed I was the nonrevenue passenger in first class.

Bob Gallaway headed out to our house to break the news to Sharon while I was touching down at Logan Airport, very much alive and innocent of the drama that was being played out in New York and Houston.

"Sharon," Bob announced when he stepped in the front door, "we think Frank was on board an Eastern flight that crashed earlier this afternoon."

Sharon recalls that Bob was white with concern when he delivered this bulletin and that her first response was disbelief. Bob was careful to remind Sharon that my presence on board had not been confirmed, and everyone seemed to take some small comfort in this. Sharon was obviously shaken by the news, but she'd been with me long enough to know that with my schedule, I was as likely to have been on that plane as not.

At around the same time, still unaware of the accident, I stepped out of Logan and flagged a cab to Anthony's Pier 4 restaurant, an old favorite, for my dinner meeting. On my way, over the car radio, I heard the news about the Eastern accident and called home as soon as I reached the restaurant to clear up what I feared would be some very distressing suspicions. "My God," Sharon exclaimed as soon as she heard my voice. "Am I glad to hear from you!" Then she cried. It had only been around twenty minutes since Bob arrived with the news, but Sharon says they were the longest twenty minutes of her life. With this call from me, she finally spilled the bottled-up emotions of those tense moments.

Next I called my parents and found my mother distraught and in tears. She had heard about the crash on the news and called Sharon to ask about my whereabouts. When she learned I was indeed scheduled to be in New Orleans before traveling to New York, she broke down. She had just buried one son a few years earlier, and the thought of losing another was a great weight for her to bear. Thankfully, I reached her only a short while later. Even today, whenever I read about the occasional airline crash, I am reminded in a very personal way of the impact such tragedies have on the loved ones of the people aboard. There's nothing like an ounce of personal experience to add pounds of concern about the safety of the passengers and crew on any airline I've helped manage.

The high note of that year was the birth of our second daughter, Mercedes Ana (Mercedes being an old family name and Ana being my mother's name), but even this joyous occasion was laced with some disappointment. I was marooned at the A Bar A ranch in the middle of Wyoming.

This was no ordinary ranch outing. I was being initiated into Conquistadors del Cielo, an organization of two hundred or so senior aviation executives. Because Nicole's birth had been late, we figured this second pregnancy would likely follow a similar pattern. We also figured I could jet back to Houston on short notice, crossing our fingers that I wouldn't have to. Sharon and I had been taking a refresher course in natural childbirth and were both looking forward to being together in the delivery room. If I had thought there was a serious chance I would miss out on that special moment, I would have postponed my initiation to the following year for sure.

The initiation ceremony was a big deal, with members dressed up as real Spanish conquistadors, wearing ornate robes and makeup. Twenty minutes before the ceremony, I was listening to final instructions from Bob Six, the Continental chairman who would go on to play a major role in my career, when I received a harried phone call from Sharon.

"Frank," she said, near tears, "my water broke."

I tried to calm her down. Her contractions hadn't begun, so I told her there was no need to panic, even though that was just about all I was doing on my end of the line. I told her to make arrangements to meet her doctor at the hospital and ask Bob Carney for a ride there. I also suggested that she ask his wife, Nancy, to babysit Nicole.

Then I sought out Bob Six. "I've got to get out of here," I said. "My wife's going to have a baby!" I knew there were a number of private aircraft parked at the nearby airfield and thought one of them would be available for charter, but none was. So I resolved to load up on coffee and drive to Denver (a four-hour trip), leaving at 3:00 a.m. for the first flight to Houston.

I landed on the morning of September 6, a few hours after Mercedes was born. I was crushed when I learned I didn't make it but of course was overjoyed to learn that Sharon and the baby were doing fine. My regret at not being there melted away the moment I cradled our newest baby daughter in my arms. Nothing else mattered. Mercedes was miraculous and, just as her sister Nicole had done before her, she gave my life new meaning and a sense of wonder. Rebuilding an airline, however exciting, was nothing next to moments like this.

Nevertheless, a battle was coming that would pull some of my attention to other matters. It was gestating in Washington. And it would have a major impact on the future of passenger air travel in America.

# CHAPTER FOUR

# Changes in the Air

*Deregulation and the Launch of Peanut Fares*
*1975–1978*

A S TALK of airline deregulation grew louder through the 1970s, I had mixed feelings about the issue. Philosophically, deregulation appealed to me. If Washington bureaucrats were no longer dictating our prices and routes, airlines could operate more efficiently, try innovative ideas, and reduce fares. Deregulation would also help invigorate airline management ranks. My years of recruiting told me that talented business school graduates were reluctant to join an industry that moved so slowly and had many of its critical decisions dictated or second-guessed by government agencies.

From a practical standpoint, however, I knew that deregulation would likely spell disaster for TIA and its employees. The deregulation proposals that started hitting Capitol Hill around 1974 would have permitted large carriers to freely enter the small feeder routes (usually the short ones that bring passengers into large city hubs) that were so basic to us and use their economies of scale to kill small regional airlines such as ours. Southwest, on the other hand, would suddenly be free to fly anywhere outside Texas, undercutting us on the profitable interstate routes from Texas that we operated.

In addition, a deregulated Continental Airlines could open a Houston hub (as was rumored) and put us out of business overnight with its large aircraft fleet and much stronger marketing muscle. Without some protection against these larger players, TIA and other regional airlines probably would not last long enough to give the public the improved air travel choices that deregulation promised—at least not from us, given our modest balance sheet.

Massachusetts senator Ted Kennedy was the first and loudest proponent of airline deregulation, as was the counsel to Kennedy's Judiciary Committee Subcommittee on Administrative Practice and Procedure, Stephen Breyer, who would later become a distinguished Supreme Court justice. They convened hearings on the subject in late 1974 and 1975. During those hearings, airline analysts and other industry insiders painted a vivid picture of federal regulators collaborating closely with major airlines, usually at the expense of the fare-paying public. It was of concern to us to note that the liberal Senator Kennedy was working closely with the conservative Senator Howard Cannon from Nevada, chairman of the Senate's Commerce, Science, and Transportation Committee. Both shared strong support for the measure—the liberals because decreased regulation would mean lower fares and the conservatives because they were largely opposed to government regulation.

The CAB had been founded in 1938 to regulate the industry almost as if it were a public utility. It controlled fare structures, limited route authorities, upheld the rights of incumbent airlines over new entrants, and generally discouraged competition. Between 1951 and 1976, a total of seventy-six companies applied to the CAB for permission to run new airlines and compete for major national trunk routes, and every one of those applications was rejected. Thanks to a Depression-era law, the industry was run like an exclusive country club, with the CAB posted at the door to turn back prospective new members.

When Senator Cannon launched his own investigation into the CAB through the commerce committee's aviation subcommittee, I finally got a chance to speak my piece about deregulation. At the time, I was chairman of the Association of Local Transport Airlines, the trade organization for small regional carriers such as Aloha, Piedmont, Frontier, TIA, and others. I made our case to a congressional aide named Bob Ginther, a young attorney who was helping draft Cannon's deregulation legislation.

My basic argument was that we small carriers could be important tools of competition in a deregulated environment, but only if we could be protected from predatory price competition from the major carriers. I also pointed out that one of the most troubling ironies of the legislation was that it encouraged price competition, which would drive down fares but did nothing to help airlines reduce their costs of operation. Instead, deregulation would leave us with the same old established cost structures and fixed labor costs that were already running small carriers into the ground.

I told the same story to Ginther's counterparts on Senator Kennedy's staff, including a young attorney named Phil Bakes, who worked under Stephen Breyer. Bakes fully grasped my arguments and was both polite and sympathetic. (I liked Bakes enough to hire him years later.) He and Breyer agreed that deregulation might put some small carriers out of business, but they added that, from their perspective, those failures would be a small price to pay for the greater good. Like everyone on Capitol Hill at the time, they accepted the equation that lower fares for the public justified any adverse side effects caused by deregulation. Consumer price inflation in 1975 was running at more than 9 percent, and it had hit 11 percent the year before. In that kind of economic environment, the promise of cutting prices on *anything* was politically irresistible.

The subsequent Cannon aviation subcommittee public hearings in the spring of 1976 were quite a show. The Eastern Airlines CEO, Frank Borman, brought in an elaborate display consisting of two rows of airline seats. He claimed the seats were set at a greatly reduced twenty-nine-inch pitch (the distance between seats) and that this kind of crowding would be commonplace in a deregulated market. Then he gestured to his rows of seats and invited some of the senators down to the floor to try them out.

The sight of Howard Cannon, who would have had a hard time fitting comfortably into any airline seat, struggling into Borman's cramped rows was perhaps the most visually compelling argument against deregulation imaginable. Senator Barry Goldwater, who sat on the committee, also came down to sample Borman's deregulated comfort levels, and he had an equally tough time sitting down. It really was quite a funny scene, and there were photos of the clearly uncomfortable senators splashed across the front pages of newspapers nationwide the following morning.

What struck me about Borman's exhibit, however, was that the short distance between seats seemed to be a bit exaggerated. I'd been eyeballing seat pitches in airplanes for many years, and Borman's seats looked like they'd been set a lot closer than twenty-nine inches, which would have been just a few inches shy of the normal economy-seat pitch of thirty-one or thirty-two inches.

As it happened, a *Washington Post* reporter I knew was sitting next to me in the hearing room, and I couldn't help sharing my doubts with her. I also offered—with some mischief, I'll admit—to lend her a tape measure, which I always carried in my briefcase so I could size up the competition's seats while traveling. She took me up on my offer, and it turned out that the seats in Borman's exhibit were actually pitched at an impossible twenty-six or twenty-seven inches. I doubt that Borman ever knew his exhibit was a deception. But it made for terrific theater, and it sent a warning that passengers might have to pay for their cheaper fares with a sharp decrease in comfort, a situation that has certainly come to pass.

As the deregulation movement continued to gain momentum through 1976, we came to see the issue from a more realistic perspective. We were young guys with long careers ahead of us, and deregulation was clearly destined to shape those careers. So we decided to stop fretting about short-term disruptions and direct our energies toward deregulation's long-term opportunities. We knew that if we stopped fighting the inevitable and instead offered Congress our support, we stood a much better chance of influencing the few details in the deregulation bill that concerned us most.

In 1977, I also appeared for the second time in congressional hearings, this time in the House. The first time, during the Senate hearings the previous year, I had questioned the legislation and pointed out the damage it would do to small carriers. But by the time the House hearings rolled around and I was asked to testify as the head of the smallest carrier, we saw that deregulation was inevitable, and my testimony emphasized the fact that the consumer would enjoy lower fares and a wider variety of services. But before we took that position, we had extensive "negotiations."

Shepherding the bill through the House was a bipartisan effort, and Bob Ginther and Phil Bakes were working hard to assemble a consensus of support for it among airline presidents, senior executives, lobbyists, industry analysts, academics, and economists. United had been the first major carrier to come out in favor of the legislation, but as a condition of its endorsement, it had asked that the bill provide "free entry" (the ability to fly anywhere within the United States at any time, depending upon the availability of appropriate space) for airlines seeking new domestic routes. Even though staffers had already planned to include free entry in the proposed legislation, Dick Ferris, who was running United at the time, wanted an explicit commitment in exchange for his support. There were others in the process, carriers and legislators alike, still opposing free entry, and Ferris wanted to make sure the provision stuck, over their objections. United had reasoned that without free entry, because of its large size, it would receive a relatively small number of future route awards under a regulated entry structure—as indeed it had. Frontier Airlines was the only local service carrier to initially support deregulation. It had become increasingly clear to us that with the support of United, virtually assuring passage of the legislation, regional carriers would end up merging or being merged into several surviving very large carriers.

As a result, when I sat down again with Bob Ginther to discuss the pending legislation and our support for it, I was ready to tell him exactly what we wanted on the bill in exchange for our approval. Our conditions were simple, fair, and, above all, they took the long view. First, we wanted time limits imposed on the CAB, so that applications for new routes and other privileges would be acted on in a timely fashion. (The CAB was famous for taking years to make decisions.) We also wanted time limits imposed on the government's consideration of airline mergers and acquisitions. We had vivid memories of deals that died simply because of bureaucratic inertia, and if airlines were ever going to run efficiently, mergers and acquisitions needed to be transacted the way they were in other industries.

I told Ginther that the most important item on TIA's agenda was a provision that in the long term would totally remove the CAB's and Department of Transportation's authority to review the acquisition of one airline by another. We argued that all anticompetition and antitrust questions should be left to the Justice Department, as they were in other industries. Ginther responded as I expected. He told me that Senator Cannon would never relinquish DOT authority to approve airline mergers, but I had my fallback position ready.

I pressed for the deregulation bill to allow investors from outside the airline industry to purchase an airline without government approval. I told him of the agonizing delays CAB put us through during Jet Capital's acquisition of TIA in 1972. Such an amendment had no direct impact on our ability to acquire another airline in the future, because TIA was an "inside investor" within existing regulations. But government review of airline purchases by industry outsiders had the effect of depressing airline stock prices. As we saw it, deregulation would work better for us if it freed up capital markets, increasing TIA's value in the process. (Unfortunately, our proposed change would hurt us in a deal for TWA some years later.) Ginther told me he thought he could sell our request to Senator Cannon and that we had a deal. The provision was added to the draft legislation, and I did not think much more about it until almost a year later, but I'll get to that.

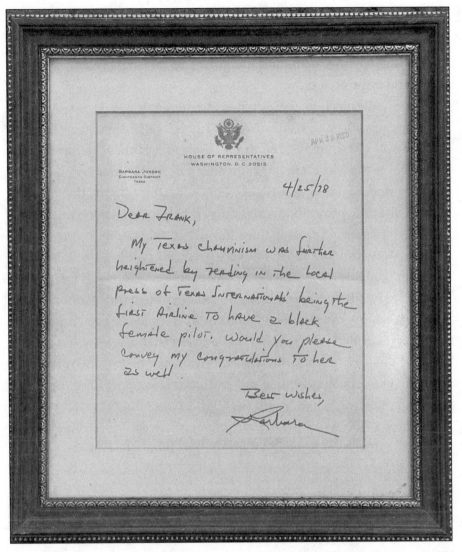

HOUSE OF REPRESENTATIVES
WASHINGTON, D. C. 20515

BARBARA JORDAN
EIGHTEENTH DISTRICT
TEXAS

4/25/78

Dear Frank,

My Texas chauvinism was further heightened by reading in the local press of Texas Internationals' being the first Airline to have a black female pilot. Would you please convey my congratulations to her as well.

Best wishes,
Barbara

TXI recognized as being first airline to hire a black female pilot (1978).

While the deregulation legislation was taking shape, something else was taking shape in the Lorenzo family. On February 13, 1978, Carolina Grace Lorenzo was born—our almost–Valentine's Day surprise. Our third daughter was named for our two grandmothers: Carolina, the mother of my dad, and Grace Murray, the mother of Sharon's father, Glenn. Sharon remembers vividly that when Carolina was born, our physician, whose wife had gone to Sharon's alma mater, announced at her birth, "One more for Mount Holyoke." Carolina emerged as a breath of fresh air with her singing and dancing, which gave rise to her career as a yoga instructor and therapist specializing in wellness counseling and mindfulness.

Meanwhile, in June 1978, when the deregulation legislation was getting ready to be passed into law, I got a call from Ed Smart, the chairman of TWA, telling me that his lawyers had suddenly noticed language in the bill allowing outsiders to buy airlines without government review. The big airlines were not happy about this change, because the new provision would make it easier for someone to swoop in and grab control of companies like TWA, whose stock was widely owned. We wondered if the lawyers involved had been asleep, since they were only now waking up to this proposed change in the regulations, although it was a tiny change involving the removal of only four words ("and any other person") and could easily have gone unnoticed.

Smart had been advised by his lawyers that we were the proponents of this change, and he was calling to ask us to back down. He wanted me to contact Ginther and rescind our support for that part of the bill. Following Smart's call, we all discussed the potential benefits of agreeing to TWA's request, particularly since we were trying to buy some DC-9-10 aircraft from TWA at the time, but in the end, we decided against it. I mentioned to Smart that the DC-9-10 purchase was important to us, but that didn't help get him to agree to the sale. In addition, however, we were committed to the change because we believed it would increase TIA's access to capital as well as its value to shareholders, and we believed it was the right thing to do for the markets.

---

The Airline Deregulation Act would finally be signed into law by President Jimmy Carter on October 24, 1978. It called for a gradual six-year phaseout of CAB controls over fares and routes and for the ultimate dissolution of the CAB after that. But the CAB had begun loosening its grip on fares long before the law was formally passed. Back in

1975, in the heat of the Kennedy hearings, President Gerald Ford, upon assuming office, replaced CAB's then chairman with a committed deregulationist named John Robson. It was thanks to Robson's indirect encouragement that we produced one of our most valuable and lasting airfare innovations, even before deregulation formally passed.

During the summer of 1976, the airline business hit a slump largely thanks to the CAB's sudden boost in regulated airfares for family travelers. Under pressure from the major airlines, which wanted more revenue, the CAB had rolled back a set of previously authorized family discount fares—just in time for the summer vacation season. Because I had recently booked my brother's family's vacation trip to Houston that May, I had firsthand insight into the impact of the fare increase. The five round-trip tickets that had cost Val's family $750 that May were selling for $950 just a few weeks later. For the average family, that was a substantial hike. By merely responding to the pressure to raise fares, the CAB had neglected to anticipate the resulting sharp reduction in traffic levels. Americans took their travel dollars elsewhere that summer, and the airline industry suffered.

Not long afterward, I vented my frustration over the summer slump during a meeting with Robson and some of his staff. I complained that we had to do something to boost the personal travel and leisure market, but the CAB and most airline executives were insensitive to the effect of fares on the average consumer. "Deregulation is coming," I told him, "but we still can't provide more competitive fares because the CAB won't allow it."

Robson proved to be the perfect sounding board. He said that contrary to my assumptions, the CAB just might allow reduced fares before the actual passage of the deregulation law if they were perhaps on an "experimental" basis. His position came as a pleasant surprise to me that day but made perfect sense. As deregulation loomed, he was prepared to send a message that the CAB was already open to a more enterprising spirit of competition.

I left the meeting thrilled. I was determined to use a reduced-fare experiment as a tool to help us promote our name and boost traffic in markets where we remained relatively unknown. Strange as it sounds, no other airline had ever gained approval to cut fares across the board as a purely competitive move, at least not on the sustained basis that I envisioned. Continental had an "economy fare" program in the early 1970s, and National had used a "no-frills fare" to help restore traffic levels after a long labor strike. Discounting had been successful over a brief period of time, and in a poststrike situation, but no one had really tried it as part of an ongoing competitive strategy.

As a federal agency, CAB did not press its authority over our intra-state Texas routes, and we had had some previous success with an introductory discount fare on a new route between Houston's Hobby Airport and Dallas–Fort Worth. We had launched the service with a "calendar fare," cooked up by our marketing genius, Jim O'Donnell, and his team. The idea behind the fare was alluring and simple: "The date you fly is the price you pay." For example, on the first day of our promotion, passengers could fly standby for one dollar in either direction; on October 2, we charged two dollars, and so on up to our regular weekend fare of $15. (The regular weekday fare was also a bargain at $25.) On opening day, our gates were jammed with standby passengers eager to snap up the first one-dollar fares in airline history. The crowds kept coming all through those first two weeks of the service, along with TV news crews to record the commotion.

The calendar fares provided us with proof that discount fare promotions could gain us media attention and increase passenger loads, even on high-priced flights. And yet even within our own shop there was a lingering reluctance to cut ticket prices. I recalled that when the CAB raised ticket prices for families during the summer of 1976, our vice president of planning proudly proclaimed that the move would surely drive up our revenue yields in the coming vacation travel months. Like many of my industry colleagues, he took continued business from the little guy, with his limited pocketbook, for granted. Most airline executives, I had found, tended to see the world through the eyes of expense-account travelers who aren't price-sensitive and don't generally stop traveling when prices climb. During the slump in passenger traffic that summer, nobody in the airline industry pointed to increased family fares as the cause. To do so would have been anathema, like blaming ourselves.

One natural fear aroused by fare cutting was that if competitors responded in kind, a price war might break out, and all the airlines would lose in a race to the bottom. But I was convinced that if a fare promotion played to an airline's unique market position, discounted fares could build meaningful market share and leave competitors flat-footed. So for our fare-reduction experiment, we targeted half a dozen routes where the TIA name was fairly unknown at one end or the other. We flew from Houston to New Orleans, for example, but our round-trip originations were overwhelmingly from Houston. A New Orleans resident, planning a round trip to Houston, would likely look for another carrier with a more prominent presence in his hometown. Similarly, on our Dallas–Albuquerque–Los Angeles flights, our business was dominated by Dallas-based customers, and we were far less known in the more western markets.

The plan was to offer one such unrestricted discount flight each day in target markets such as New Orleans, Albuquerque, and Los Angeles. We selected each day's least profitable flight (usually in midafternoon or late evening), assuming that any additional traffic would be a windfall, even at drastically reduced prices, and that the full-fare spillover would help our other flights throughout the day.

The "come-on" strategy was to advertise the lowest possible fares (Houston–New Orleans for $24, for example) and get people excited enough to book the cheap flights. If they could be flexible in their flight plans, they could save money; if they couldn't, it was likely that many of them would book with us anyway at the full fare, then maybe take the cheaper flight for the return trip. Either way, we came out ahead, and even if travelers wound up not flying with us on a particular trip, there was a good chance they'd remember us the next time around.

The toughest part of the program launch turned out to be the question of what to name it. After Jim O'Donnell and his marketing team kicked around ideas for a couple of weeks, they put together a presentation using the name "Value Fares," which struck me instantly as a real bore. As he and his people walked me through the proposed campaign, with storyboards and charts, I had a feeling that they wanted to hide our exciting and truly innovative program in a plain brown wrapper.

I held my tongue, though, because I wanted to be fair to Jim and take some time to think it through. I also trusted Jim's instincts and wanted to give mine enough time to catch up to his. I was always careful, in these situations, not to give away my emotions too readily. Everyone always looked to the president for his reaction, and nine times out of ten my gut feelings would change, so I always smiled politely and held back. If I jumped on a group of enthusiastic managers for something I didn't like, then clearly it would be that much harder to get a strong, enthusiastic effort from that group the next time out. No one likes to work for a boss who's impossible to please.

I thanked everybody on Jim's team and said we should all go off and think about it. I planned to do the same and left that afternoon for a series of meetings in Florida. But on the plane out from Houston, I couldn't shake Jim's presentation. It was all I could think about. "Value Fares" just didn't cut it for me, and I couldn't sit on my feelings any longer. I called Jim during a stopover in New Orleans and sent him back to the drawing board.

Some days later, the team returned with the theme of "Peanuts Fares." The moment I heard it, I thought this was the way to go. *Peanuts Fares. Fly for Peanuts. Say Nuts to the High Cost of Flying.* It was memorable and different. It was even a little controversial, as a subtle nod to president-elect Jimmy Carter, whose peanut-farming roots were very much in the news in November 1976.

I listened to Jim's presentation with the same noncommittal response I displayed on the first pass, only this time I was trying to contain my initial enthusiasm. In fact, the only thing I didn't like about the name was that I liked it so much. My experience with these kinds of presentations was that I rarely recognized a good idea at first sight. In fact, most good ideas seemed truly lousy until I had a chance to try them on and get used to them. Conversely, most of the concepts I liked right away turned out to be losers, so I was a little leery about my enthusiasm for the Peanuts campaign. I wanted to give it a chance to resonate, and I wanted to canvass our senior staff people for their reactions.

Many of our managers didn't like the Peanuts idea at all. They worried it was too frivolous and undignified and that it might cheapen the airline's image. One of our senior executives was aghast that we would even consider such a name, calling it "the stupidest thing I've ever heard." So many of our operations people were strongly opposed to it that I began to have second thoughts. Maybe it did cheapen the product. Maybe there was another way to go. Ultimately, though, I decided to trust my gut and Jim's judgment. We rolled out the Peanuts Fares campaign with great expectations and only a few reservations.

We made our formal application to the CAB in December 1976 for our discount fare "experiment" and used the occasion to hold a press conference in Washington, DC. The timing was perfect. Jimmy Carter was just about to take office, and Jim O'Donnell commissioned a large-scale caricature of the president-elect dressed as a peanut and wearing a huge toothy grin. We used the picture as a backdrop to our press conference, which wound up getting us wide media play in the nation's capital as well as back home.

We still had to wait thirty days for CAB approval, so we used the interval to drum up consumer awareness and prepare for what we all hoped would be markedly increased loads in our selected markets. Our new advertising agency, Scali, McCabe, Sloves, came up with a clever series of ads featuring a Captain Peanut character to represent Texas International. In one spot, there was a fleet of low-flying planes tethered to the ground in a tangle of strings; above them was a fleet of flying peanuts, smiling and wearing captains' hats and sunglasses—with no strings attached. Up to that point, any low fares that the public had seen had restrictions such as a required "Saturday-night stay."

Our Peanuts Fares went into effect on February 1, 1977, with 50 percent fare cuts on low-load-factor flights in five major markets. Almost immediately, we tripled the number of tickets sold. Load factors approached 80 percent on flights that used to run no more than 30 percent full. And traffic held at these new levels even after our competitors scrambled to respond.

TXI's Mr Peanut at the airport greeting Nicole, age 5 (1978).

Profits for all flights in these markets surged to $1.8 million for the first nine months of 1977, up from just $141,000 during the comparable period a year earlier. We were ecstatic, and the spillover to our other flights was beyond our best-case projections. That was the true test, after all, since Peanuts Fares would not have been a success unless it helped us sell more full-fare tickets. Fears that discounting some flights would "cheapen" our product turned out to be unfounded.

The other airlines quickly countered with "super saver," "chicken feed," and "small potatoes" fares (and we were worried about *our* name!). But we'd gotten the head start and remained two steps ahead. Even Southwest Airlines, whose regular fares were competitive with our reduced fares, was deluged with callers seeking Peanuts Fares. The Southwest chairman, Herb Kelleher, told me once that for years after our promotion, his reservationists kept getting calls from customers requesting Peanuts. It became a generic name for low airline fares, and this didn't make the Southwest chairman happy, given that his airline had a history of low fares in Texas.

Peanuts Fares did so well during the initial months that we extended the campaign throughout our intrastate markets, where we saw dramatic boarding increases despite aggressive competition from Southwest. We applied the same concept to interstate routes as well. When the CAB granted TIA authority to fly from Dallas to Baltimore later that year, we inaugurated the service with $79 one-way fares. The following year, we kicked off our new Las Vegas service with $78 round trips from Houston and $98 round trips from Dallas–Fort Worth, all under the Peanuts Fares banner.

Convinced now of the powerful effect of discount promotional fares, Jim O'Donnell hatched all sorts of crazy stunts that nicely fit in with our hustling, aggressive marketing approach. Our inaugural service to Guadalajara, Mexico, for example, offered seats for as little as forty-nine pesos (around two dollars) to the first fifty passengers who showed up in our terminal wearing the most unusual swimsuits and another fifty passengers who offered the most unique rendition of the song "Guadalajara," to the accompaniment of our mariachi band. Another promotion, when we started service to Kansas City, was a Peanuts parade with elephants, which was really a great attention-getter.

# Kansas City doesn't need Texas International's low fare service.

Braniff Airways
-Kansas City Star, May 23, 1978

# Nuts to that.

Texas International Airlines
-June 12, 1978

We're not saying nuts off the tops of our heads. We've given Braniff's attitude a great deal of thought.

And indeed, there may be people who, even in this day and age, don't need Texas International and our low Peanuts Fares.

But who are they?

Who doesn't need 50% savings on non-stop flights to Dallas/Fort Worth?

Who doesn't need 35% savings on flights to Houston, San Antonio, and other cities?

Who doesn't need assurance that every seat on every Kansas City flight is a low fare seat?

Who doesn't need convenient low fare access to Guadalajara, Mexico's Yucatan peninsula, and Las Vegas, which we'll offer by the end of this year?

Who doesn't need the new Peanuts Fare non-stops to Houston, Milwaukee, Minneapolis/St. Paul, and Oklahoma City for which we've applied?

In all of Kansas City, there's only one party we can think of who doesn't need Texas International and our Peanuts Fares.

Braniff.

## Texas International

For low fares to Texas call your travel agent or Texas International at (816) 474-3377.

Edgy advertising intro for Peanut Fares in Kansas City (1979).

Another program with long-term implications from Jim O'Donnell's department was the first-ever loyalty program for airline customers. His program paved the way for today's frequent-flier plans in many ways. The TIA plan was the trailblazing Payola Passes campaign, which offered passengers $10 coupons on flights between DFW and Tulsa or Oklahoma City and $20 coupons between DFW and St. Louis. The coupons could be accumulated and redeemed for full-fare seats on TIA flights or applied toward a full-fare ticket with the balance to be paid in cash.

The impact of all these promotions on our bottom line was extraordinary. For 1977, as Peanuts pricing extended its reach throughout the TIA system, we surpassed three million annual passengers boarded for the first time in our history, a 25 percent increase over the previous year. Total revenue reached $145 million ($742 million in 2024 dollars), a 20 percent increase from the previous record year and double our income in 1972, the year we took over the company. Load factors rose to 57.7 percent, up from 53.6 percent in 1976, which had been our previous best; during December and several summer months, our planes exceeded 60 percent average loads for the first time. That was a very high load factor in those days.

Also extraordinary was the way TIA's fortunes had shifted relative to the airline industry as a whole. Year-end earnings for 1977 showed a 5.5 percent return on revenues, exceeding the industry average. Profits more than doubled, to nearly $8 million.

The Peanuts experiment was such a resounding success that we continued to use the name long after the one-year CAB "experiment" had officially ended and long after airfare discounting became the order of the day. The Peanuts name was a symbol of one of our greatest successes. We were known for it, even beyond the reach of the TIA system. With Peanuts Fares, we had turned markets that were traditional losers into winners, proving that airlines could increase their earnings by decreasing fares. TIA enjoyed the highest traffic growth rate in the industry in 1977, prompting no less an authority than *Forbes* magazine to call us "one of the airline industry's most innovative and exciting companies." Texas International was openly acknowledged as the pioneer in system-wide low-fare pricing—by our rivals at competing carriers, by our colleagues throughout the airline industry, by the press, by the financial community, and, most importantly, by the public.

Presenting new TXI flights to Baltimore with Karl Sattler Maryland Aviation Administrator (1979).

But our innovations weren't confined to our fares, although that is what we were best known for. One time, around mid-1977, I was flying from Houston to New York on Eastern Airlines when I noticed a man in first class light a cigar and saw the whole cabin fill with smoke for a few minutes. It seemed to me that this was crazy. At the same time, we were looking for ways to distinguish ourselves from other airlines and show an interest in better service to our passengers. After some discussion among our senior staff, we decided to file with the CAB and become the first airline to ban cigar and pipe smoking on our aircraft. However, American Airlines stole our thunder by filing the next day to do the same, and it was American's filing that really got press attention. But in fact, we were the first.

Peanuts Fares were a step in the right direction, but they were only a step. Real, substantive change would require a total makeover of the company to deal with deregulation, and we hadn't yet figured out what that would be. At the start of 1978, we redoubled our efforts to keep costs down, reducing our workforce yet again. We again shed some of our least profitable routes at that point. We looked everywhere for ways to make the company more efficient. We even removed the hot oven installations on some planes so that we could add a few more paying seats.

However, these measures would not be enough for us to survive as a small regional airline. The wide attention heaped on our low-fare promotion stepped up our image and broadened our horizons. The landscape was changing fast, with deregulation on the way, and no matter how highly we thought of ourselves at the Blue Barn, the reach of Texas International's system and identity extended only sparsely beyond the Gulf and the Southwest. We needed to grow fast.

CHAPTER FIVE

# The Pursuit of National Airlines

*Seizing Opportunities*
*1978–1979*

A S WE were about to enter the post-deregulation period, our most immediate need was for the strengthening of our balance sheet, and in April 1978, we raised more than $27 million through the sale of units of subordinated debt and common stock in what was then a very large public financing for a regional airline. This gave TIA substantially greater liquidity and flexibility to pursue various strategies for dealing with deregulation. It certainly gave us more downside protection.

We also raised our visibility in the capital markets by listing our stock on the American Stock Exchange. At the ceremony for our formal induction into AMEX, a limousine was sent to our New York offices to take a group of us downtown. On the way, it occurred to me that my father, my very first financial adviser, would get a big kick out of this moment, so I had the driver stop by the beauty shop to see if my dad was free to join us. It didn't take much persuasion. Dad was beaming all through the ceremony. All my life, he had drummed into me the message that anything was possible in his adopted homeland, and there I was, running a company listed on the American Stock Exchange. It was truly a proud day for both of us.

With this new infusion of capital, it didn't take us long to come up with a rather unplanned use for it. On Memorial Day weekend, both Bob Carney and I took home some other airlines' annual and quarterly reports, and both of us noticed that National Airlines presented an opportunity: its shares seemed unusually depressed. While we had looked at some potential merger targets among the ranks of undervalued and underperforming airlines, Florida-based National stood out to both of us, independently, that weekend. It was essentially the same distress-sale thinking we had used to identify our very first deals at Lorenzo, Carney earlier in the decade.

At the time, National was one of the smallest of the country's trunk carriers. Its routes essentially ran from Florida up the East Coast. It also had a southern extension from Florida to the West Coast, with a stop in Houston. The company had some routes to Europe, too. With its sleepy, conservative management, National seemed like a natural target for purchase. Never mind that its revenues were more than three times the size of ours or that it flew five times more revenue passenger miles (the number of miles traveled by paying passengers) than we did. The coming of deregulation called for a bold move, and this qualified as one.

As we saw it, National had great investment value. In addition, it complemented TIA. National had Florida; we had Texas; between us, we had two of the nation's fastest-growing Sunbelt states. They had the brand name and financial resources; we had the management and energy. Even our fleets complemented each other. National had big 727s for medium- to long-haul flights, and we had the small planes, DC-9s, for feeder markets, which would be so important after deregulation. Our Houston hub could serve National's route structure well, and indeed we had good connecting links already established in Houston. The two companies were a very good fit. In fact, I had attended a press briefing given by National in Houston at which its salesperson showed the company's route map stretching across the country and up the East Coast, with Texas International connections in Houston shown clearly in dotted lines.

But best of all, National's stock price, at around $18 per share, was extremely low compared to the net value of its equipment and holdings, which we figured could be as high as $75 per share. However, the $18 price at which the stock was trading was at a high for the previous twelve-month period—the low had been $9. In terms of financial strength, we saw National as though it were a little bank; it had a strong and clean balance sheet. Bob and I were very enthusiastic about the value and potential of the company.

Later that week, after Memorial Day, Sharon and I went up to Cambridge, Massachusetts, with Bob and his wife, Nancy, for our fifteenth Harvard Business School reunion. Bob and I had been in different sections at the school, so there were a lot of times when we were off at separate functions, but we were staying at the same hotel and had breakfast together in the mornings. Without fail, whenever we met, our conversation turned to National Airlines. We were both preoccupied by the opportunity. We attended one reception together, at a Boston art museum, and Bob and I kept scheming about National as we took in the collection. It was there, in that museum, that we decided to start buying National stock. Maybe there was a friendly deal to be done, but even without one, the stock seemed too great a bargain to pass up. And down the road, we wouldn't rule out a hostile bid for the company.

So when we returned from Harvard, we called Smith Barney & Co., our broker, and quietly began buying the stock. Smith Barney arranged for the purchases to be made through its arbitrage department for maximum confidentiality. To disguise the trades, many were made through accounts at other brokerages. We wanted to make sure that the specialist who handled the stock at the stock exchange wouldn't see the same name repeatedly buying the stock. The specialist was in reality a speculator focused on his own profitability in addition to being a market maker. If he sensed his stock was being accumulated, he would hold it in his own account, which would tend to lift the price, all things being equal. Bob and I were so conscious of leaks and disturbing the stock price that we didn't even discuss our initial purchases with our directors.

We also commissioned Smith Barney to undertake a thorough study of the company so we could see what type of bid might make the most sense. In addition, I made a call to National's chairman, L. B. "Bud" Maytag Jr. (a scion of the appliance family), whom I'd met several times at various industry functions, to see if a friendly meeting could be possible. After a few minutes of small talk about the latest deregulation news, we agreed to a lunch date in Miami for the following week. Two days later, though, Maytag's secretary called to cancel. Over the following few weeks, I called Maytag several times to reschedule, but I never heard back from him. I've always suspected that his lawyers warned him that my call was probably about doing a deal and that if he wasn't interested, he should keep his distance. That's not the way I would have played it had I been in Maytag's position, but I could certainly see their point of view.

Maytag's brush-off didn't bode well for our hopes for a friendly deal. But Bob and I decided to continue buying National stock anyway during June, by that point with our board members' approval. Everyone agreed: even absent a deal, National stock was still too great a bargain to pass up. Down the road, we thought, if we accumulated enough stock, we could consider a hostile takeover of the company.

---

Back in 1978, leveraged buyouts and hostile takeovers of companies in general were still extremely rare, and none had ever been attempted in the staid, highly regulated airline industry. But we knew that deregulation was bound to disrupt the chummy fraternity of airline executives sooner or later. Perhaps, we thought, it might make sense for us to take the initiative and set a new course. The odds of gaining control of National were probably no better than one in five, but since our evaluation told us that the stock could be a winner, we saw limited downside risk in trying, or so we reasoned.

Arni Amster, the head of Smith Barney's arbitrage unit, kept chipping away at the stock, buying up blocks in the tens of thousands, or just a few hundred shares at a time—whatever was available at a reasonable price. At the beginning of 1978, TIA had a net worth of $14 million, and the financing in April added $10 million. By the end of 1978, we would have nearly $60 million tied up in National, so it really was a huge gamble. Nevertheless, we proceeded with more optimism than caution, but probably just enough of each.

Around two weeks into our buying spree, I took a peculiar call from a Stanford University professor who claimed to be doing merger evaluation work for the Pan Am chairman, Brigadier General Bill Seawell, and said he was interested in pursuing discussions with TIA. So I called Seawell myself to see about his interest. I had gotten to know him at industry gatherings, and he probably viewed me as a kid running one of the ants of the business.

"What's this I hear about your interest in TIA?" I asked.

"We have some interest, Frank, that's true," he said. "Maybe we should get together."

We set up a drinks date for a few days later at the 21 Club in New York, in one of the quiet corners of the restaurant. It was the third week in June, and Bob and I were continuing to buy National stock, still without anyone noticing. Of course, there was no reason to inform Seawell of our expanding portfolio, certainly not until I heard what he had to say.

What he had to say was pretty much what I expected. Pan Am was indeed looking at several domestic carriers. Seawell seemed convinced that the way to ensure Pan Am's survival in a deregulated marketplace was to acquire a stake in a domestic airline and use that national carrier to help feed Pan Am's international routes. He and his people had done a preliminary evaluation of TIA and liked what they saw. His exact words were that TIA "looked decent," which I took as high praise. "We'd like to look at it further, Frank," he said, "but only if you have any interest."

"Sure, we're interested," I allowed, even though in fact I was not. I didn't really think Pan Am was such a logical suitor or that Seawell was all that serious in his pursuit, but I wasn't about to close the door before I heard his offer. It made sense to keep talking and continue our National stock purchases.

On Thursday, June 29, just as Sharon and I were looking forward to a trip to London and a short vacation beginning the following Saturday, Amster called me, barely able to contain his enthusiasm. "There's National stock all over the place this morning, Frank. We could do a cloudburst today." This is an arbitrageur's term for what happens when you buy such a large block of stock that you start to draw out anxious potential sellers. By that point, with our steady buying, we were about 100,000 shares short of the 4.9 percent ownership threshold that would require us to file a schedule 13D with the Securities and Exchange Commission, publicly declaring our holdings and our intentions.

We all expected that this day would probably come, but to be honest, I was caught unprepared. It was barely a month since Bob and I had hatched our National-buying plan at Harvard. Actually, to call it a plan was generous. All we were really doing was buying up some stock and buying time to figure out our next move. I wasn't ready to go public with our efforts, although the regulations gave us a ten-day window in which to file our disclosure. Most buyers used the ten days to snap up even more stock before the disclosure would send the stock higher.

The common tactic, as Arni laid it out for us, was to fall just short of the 4.9 percent mark, then go over it in a big way. The large blocks at issue that Thursday would certainly put us over the 4.9 percent mark, but I wasn't sure we wanted to buy through at that level just yet. From a strategic standpoint, I didn't think we were ready to announce to the financial community, or to our employees, that we had taken such a large stake in National. And we weren't ready for the public relations frenzy that would surely follow. Also, on a strictly personal level, it was important to me that word of our position wouldn't hit the Street while Sharon and I were out of the country.

"Look, Arni," I said when he called to tell me of the large block that had become available, "I just don't think we should do this today. I want more time to think about it."

"You're making a big mistake, Frank," he cautioned. "The market waits for no man."

"I'm uncomfortable being out of the country when we have to file with the SEC," I said.

"So change your plans," Arni quite practically countered. "Today's the day. You might not get another chance like this."

I still wasn't ready to take that last leap, but Arni felt so strongly about the opening that he came to our New York office later that morning to make a final pitch. In the end, he won me over. I quickly canvassed our executive committee for affirmation and gave Arni the go-ahead in time to make his big buy. And buy he did. By the time the market closed, we'd nearly doubled our holdings, buying close to 275,000 shares, most of it in two big blocks, at $17.375 per share. We learned later that our buying spree was fed by a stroke of luck: earlier that morning, Shearson, Hammill had downgraded its evaluation of National to "sell" based on an expected deterioration in earnings. (Without Bloomberg terminals and the technology we have today, we didn't learn of the Shearson sell alert until the next day.) After the sell call, the institutional investors holding large blocks of National stock were suddenly eager to unload their shares, and we were there to take them off their hands. National was one of the most active stocks on the New York Stock Exchange that day as a direct result of our cloudburst, and the *Wall Street Journal* reported the next morning that National did not know of any reason for its stock's level of activity.

By coincidence, earlier in the spring, Sharon and I, along with a number of Houston dignitaries, had been invited on the maiden flight of Pan Am's Houston–London route. We didn't normally travel in such rarefied circles, but Pan Am was counting on TIA to provide feed traffic for the new service by virtue of our modest (at the time) Houston hub, so we were invited on the flight and to the inaugural celebration in London over the July Fourth weekend. This was the origin of our vacation plans.

While in London, the Pan Am guests were feted in a grand manner. We were all put up at the plush InterContinental Hotel, which the airline owned at the time, and there were several receptions held to commemorate the occasion. On Tuesday, July 4, there was a formal dinner to cap off the festivities, and before the meal I sought out Seawell and asked if he could carve out some time the following morning. As a courtesy, I thought I'd let him know about our National shares, given his expressed interest in pursuing a deal and given that we would be on the short vacation we had planned in Switzerland over the coming weekend, which would also coincide with our public disclosure the following Monday.

We arranged to meet the next morning after breakfast, although we were more tired than expected. At four o'clock that morning, there was a fire in the hotel kitchen, and the building was evacuated. Imagine the scene outside the hotel: all Seawell's guests, including the mayor of Houston and other dignitaries, piling into the street—half asleep, half dressed—some of them carrying books or briefcases or handbags, whatever was important to them. General Seawell paced in front of the building in his robe and pajamas, huffing about the indignity of the fire, making frantic apologies. He seemed embarrassed to the point of tears that a freak kitchen fire should upset his distinguished guests on the last night of such an important occasion.

But we were all back in our rooms a short time later with our valuables in tow and a story to tell for years afterward. I went up to meet Seawell in his suite later that morning as planned and dropped my bombshell: "General," I said, "I know you're going to be out of the country for a while, and I wanted to let you know that we're going to announce on Monday that we bought some National Airlines shares."

There was no immediate response, and when I looked up, I saw a blank gaze on Seawell's face. He seemed thrown for just a moment, but then he collected himself. "Really?" he said, perking up. "That's great. I've been thinking about doing the same thing, but I could never get our board to approve it." I felt it was important that Seawell hear this piece of news from me, on a confidential basis, not only in consideration of his interest in our company but also out of respect for a man who had been very gentlemanly to me. I also used the opportunity to discuss the opening of the new Terminal C at the Houston airport and how Pan Am and TIA would fit into the plans for it. But this subject, however important, seemed decidedly minor to Seawell in comparison to the news about National.

---

With my personal obligations to Seawell out of the way, Sharon and I took off for Geneva later that afternoon to begin our relaxing drive across Switzerland. We took a few days getting from Geneva to Zurich, arriving as scheduled the following Monday and checking into the beautiful Dolder Grand hotel, located in the hills just outside the city. This hotel had been a favorite of mine since my first stay there, with my parents back in 1955. We dropped our bags in our room and immediately went to the local Smith Barney office. It was nearly three o'clock in the afternoon in Zurich, nine o'clock in the morning in New York, and I wanted to see how the market would respond to our announcement—planned, coincidentally, for that time.

I couldn't have timed it better if I had been a choreographer. Sharon and I walked into the brokerage office almost the moment the news came across the Dow Jones broad tape: "Texas International announces 9.2 percent ownership of National Airlines." The account reported that we had paid a total of $14.35 million for our shares and said that TIA was "considering the possibility" of seeking control of the Miami-based company.

I was, frankly, a little nervous now that the veil of secrecy had been lifted. We were out in the open and still not entirely sure of our next move. I knew we would make news, but I didn't fully realize what an explosive piece of news it was. The brokers in the Zurich office, who didn't know who we were, buzzed with the story. We later learned that the market had the same general reaction: "Texas who?"

The reports that came across the tape throughout the day all noted our size. One analyst likened our move to "a rabbit trying to buy an elephant for a pet." Another called us "a sardine chasing a shark." A UPI wire story referred to the filing as "a frog-that-swallowed-a-whale merger attempt." And *Barron's* columnist Alan Abelson, avoiding these animal kingdom metaphors entirely, simply gave us his "chutzpah of the year award." In newspaper accounts, we were painted as pesky little guys looking to topple one of the industry's big boys on the eve of deregulation.

The market responded in kind: National shares jumped 25 percent, to $22, by the closing bell, while our own stock climbed sixty-two cents to close at $12. Almost immediately, there was wide speculation that other suitors were readying their own bids for the company; Braniff's name was among those bandied about, and Pan Am's surfaced as well. By the end of the month, National stock was trading at more than $26 per share, while TIA had climbed to more than $14.50 per share, up more than 25 percent from its price before the announcement. (It was, and remains, unusual for shares in an acquiring company to rise in a takeover bid, and the fact that ours did most likely reflected the Street's view that we were making an attractive move—and, of course, that we were already registering a substantial paper profit on our stock holding.)

Meanwhile, with the price of National shares soaring, we were no longer sure which way we wanted to go. On its face, our investment was paying off, but the full-scale acquisition that looked extremely attractive at the $20 level was suddenly looking a lot more expensive with the stock nearing $30. With commitments to spend another $70 million on eight new DC-9s by the end of 1979, I wasn't exactly confident that we could raise enough money to finance a takeover.

A provision of the Federal Aviation Act of 1958 stipulated that owners of 10 percent or more of an airline's stock were "presumed to be in control" of that airline. Consequently, because we wanted to be able to continue buying, we had to act quickly. On Friday, July 28, with the dust still unsettled and our course unclear, we made a formal application to

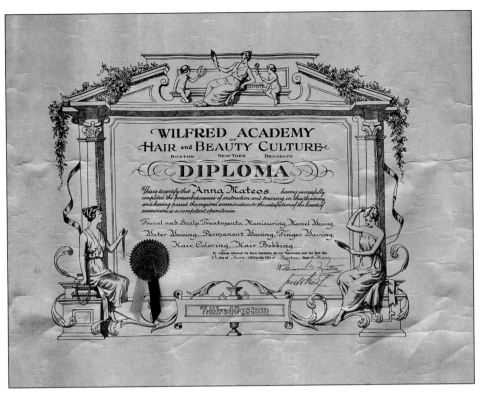

Mother's graduation at age sixteen from beauty school (1928).

My parents at the opening of their own business, Larian Beauty Salon (1937).

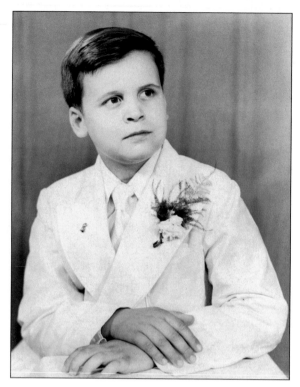

My first Holy Communion when I was nine (1949).

TWA 749 Constellation at LaGuardia, the plane we flew to Europe (1955).

My father, brother Val stationed in Germany, and myself at the Frankfurter Hof hotel (1955).

My brother Val, myself, father, and brother Larry, who passed away at forty-two (1964).

Our new BWIA livery showing stylized steel drum on tail (1968).

This is to certify that

FRANCISCO A. LORENZO

has graduated from the Federal Aviation
Administration approved **Primary Flying
School-Airplanes** curriculum given by

SUFFOLK AVIATION, INC. under the terms of

Air Agency Certificate Number 11-EA-57

Final Grade 85

I certify the above statements are true

*R. A. Reuthard*

chief instructor

APRIL 29, 1972

Date

Cessna
PILOT CENTER

Getting my flying license at thirty-two (1972).

With Sharon, cutting our wedding cake (1972).

## Cease and Desist, Please, Howard Hughes

**Lorenzo and Carney of Texas International**

Early in 1970, **Francisco A. Lorenzo** and **Robert J. Carney** raised $1.4 million in the stock market to go into the aircraft-leasing business. But the bottom soon fell out of the airline business and the young entrepreneurs—they were all thirty at the time—worked as financial consultants while they searched for another place to put their money. One of their clients was Texas International Airlines, a troubled regional carrier serving the Southwest.

Although Texas International's revenues climbed 22 percent a year from 1967 through 1971, to reach $61,716,-000, its losses mounted phenomenally, growing at an average rate of 128 percent a year. Any of fifty creditors, from the Chase Manhattan Bank to local caterers, could have thrown the company into bankruptcy. But Lorenzo and Carney convinced them all to go along with a major restructuring of the company's debt—and, a year ago, the two men wound up in control. Last July, after some rescheduling, cost cutting, price changes, and aggressive marketing, President Lorenzo and Executive Vice President Carney announced Texas

International's first loss-free twelve months in six years.

Before it is again a solid profit maker, Lorenzo says, the airline must still clear some hurdles, most notably paying for the operation of a terminal at the new Dallas–Fort Worth Regional Airport that will be bigger than the *main terminal* at New York's LaGuardia Airport. It must also fend off continuing take-over attempts by Hughes Airwest, which tried to obstruct Civil Aeronautics Board approval of the refinancing last year. At that time, Lorenzo told the CAB that a representative of Howard Hughes had told him Airwest wanted to acquire Texas International and Southern Airways, to create a new transcontinental airline. Lorenzo says Airwest made another pass at his company this summer but he turned them down. "Our plan," he says, "has not been to get refinancing only to get a quick return on our money." Although Airwest general manager Irving T. Tague concedes his company does want to take over Texas International, he denies that Howard Hughes plans a nationwide airline.

*Fortune* piece after victory over Howard Hughes (1973).

Being introduced at local airline convention with Bob Carney (1973).

Sharon sees a newly repainted TXI airplane in Austin (1973).

Sharon and I with Nicole at her baptism at St. Bart's Church in New York City (1974).

My father in the yard of Rego Park house with Nicole (1974).

Surrounded by flight attendant managers at the graduation ceremony before we started hiring male flight attendants (1975).

Newly repainted TXI airplanes at Houston terminal A (1976).

Discussing airplane part with TXI mechanic Bob Bonventura (1976).

Chatting with fellow employee at our company picnic at Forest Club (1978).

Chatting it up with employees at another company picnic (1978).

On the TXI ramp at Houston (1978).

During overhaul on airplane talking with mechanics (1978).

TXI listing ceremony at the American Stock Exchange. From left: AMEX specialist, US Securities and Exchange Commission Chairman Arthur Levitt, Bob Carney, flight attendant, myself, my father, and Don Burr (1978).

Cartoon depicting the fight for National Airlines (1979).

Fred Smith, founder of FedEx, presenting the Wings Club speakers' award (1979).

the CAB to acquire control of National Airlines, prompting National's board to convene an emergency meeting that weekend to review the matter. Even after nearly three weeks, the National board had given no formal response to our filing and from all appearances seemed to be either still reeling from our initial announcement or just feeling like a fly had landed on an aircraft and needn't be dealt with.

In our CAB application, we pledged to place our current and future National holdings in a voting trust, voting proportionally with other shareholders in any action, enabling us to expand our stake in the company beyond the 10 percent level used by the board to determine controlling interest. Our intention, we stated, was to avoid any controversy on the issue of control while continuing to acquire shares up to the 25 percent ownership level established by the CAB on pending mergers. At that point, we would suspend our buying program until we had a final ruling and until we had completed a merger agreement with the National board. The 25 percent level, we figured, would be more than enough to give us working control of the company, if approved. To seek any more, we feared, would jeopardize our chances with the CAB. Of course, as we explained, we were also taking the risk that if the board turned us down, we'd have to sell our shares, probably taking a big loss.

Our filing defended our acquisition of National shares and our desire to buy more: "[Texas International] saw an investment opportunity and made what it considers to be a prudent and lawful commitment of its capital. There must be room in this industry, as there is in unregulated industries, for free management choices of this type. Such a free climate in the capital markets goes hand in hand with the board's encouragement of a more competitive operating environment."

It continued, "Undoubtedly, opponents of the acquisition will contend that Texas International has acquired control of National without prior board approval. They will insist that Texas International dispose of the stock acquired so far before the board considers the transaction on its merits. But acceptance of that approach would represent a return to the old, protective approach toward the industry."

With the market price of National continuing to climb and trading levels shooting higher amid rumors of interest from other airlines, particularly Braniff and Pan Am, we were eager to continue to purchase the stock. We really thought the CAB would understand the marketplace consideration and the consequences of denying us the ability to buy more of National. We were taking the risk essentially without any voting rights.

On the very afternoon of the filing, the CAB responded with a formal warning that our plans might have constituted a "knowing and willful violation of FAA regulations," which made it unlawful for one airline to enter an "interlocking relationship" with another without first obtaining CAB approval. John Golden, deputy director of the CAB's bureau of compliance and consumer protection, further cautioned that if we continued to purchase National shares before the board made its ruling on the matter, we would be subject to civil penalties or other disciplinary action.

We were treading on new ground with the CAB in creating a type of trust that had never been done before. But I thought it was critical to have this ability to go to 25 percent, thus pushing the envelope. The trust arrangement to buy stock was a good gambit—our only one, it seemed. I knew that if we waited to buy more stock until the final CAB ruling, likely many months later, we would risk losing the deal entirely. The stock was now in play, and bigger airlines could push the price out of our reach if we had no opportunity to add to our position. In our filing creating the trust, at least we wouldn't lose any ground waiting for the final CAB action. If the board ultimately rejected our proposal, then we would be forced to sell the stock out of the trust; but if it approved our bid, as we fully expected , then we would have kept our advantage over the other suitors.

As National shares headed still higher, it was clear that we would have to replenish our war chest if we hoped to secure a toehold. We had sunk most of our new working capital into National, and there was still a long way to go, so we looked to the European financial community for some quick financing—a Eurodollar deal, as they were called. In those days, it was much easier to raise money overseas than it was at home: you could simply prepare a prospectus, visit investors, offer the securities, and close the deal within a few days without the volumes of paperwork or the long waiting periods required by the SEC on transactions in the United States. At the time, however, no American airline had ever arranged European financing, so this, too, was new territory.

Our investment bankers arranged a five-day "road show" to London, Paris, Geneva, Zurich, and Frankfurt, and I pitched our offering of convertible subordinated debentures at fancy lunch and dinner gatherings at each stop. At the time, oil was a very hot commodity, and the image of the Texas oilman had become a global symbol of wealth and largesse. All our potential investors wanted to hear about was Texas, Texas, Texas, so I gamely played up that image wherever possible. I did everything short of donning a ten-gallon hat and telling these European moneymen that there was oil underneath our runways.

The overseas offering was a quick sellout, raising $25 million in 7.5 percent convertible subordinated debentures, and we returned home rearmed for our run at National. But while we were off raising money, Bud Maytag finally mounted his counterattack. On Tuesday, August 8, National urged federal officials to block our takeover bid on the grounds that we had violated the Federal Aviation Act of 1958 and various antitrust laws.

National also complained to the SEC, alleging that our April financing failed to disclose an intent to acquire National in the "use-of-proceeds" section. This allegation prompted the SEC to investigate us for months, but these charges were eventually deemed without merit, as was National's subsequent effort to prove that our European financing left us in potential violation of a federal law restricting foreign ownership of domestic carriers. National also aimed its legal guns at Jet Capital, the holding company that controlled TIA, arguing to the SEC that Jet was an investment company and required to register, which for an operating company is a very bad turn, imposing extensive regulation, operating limitations, and added cost. This charge was also dismissed by the SEC. Maytag and company had a bagful of harassment tactics, and when one failed, they reached in for another. They succeeded in spinning our wheels, spending our money, and redirecting our attention, but we pressed on.

Finally, at an August 17 CAB "sunshine" hearing to consider our bid—so called because formal CAB meetings were required to be conducted in open forums—the board voted to issue an order allowing us to proceed with our purchase plans while continuing its full investigation of the matter. In an unprecedented ruling, the CAB chairman, Alfred E. Kahn, held that our buying did not violate the Federal Aviation Act and that we could continue acquiring shares of National stock subject to formal approval, which could come as late as March 1979. If the board ruled the arrangement unacceptable at that time, we would be forced to divest ourselves of the newly acquired stock—which was understood.

With Kahn's ruling, we moved on to buying more stock right away—sooner, in fact, than we should have. Arni Amster had been champing at the bit, watching National shares climb to the $30 level in the weeks following our disclosure, and the stock was particularly active on the afternoon of the CAB sunshine meeting, when it appeared that there was another large buyer in the market. After I walked out of the meeting, I phoned Arni and told him to resume buying, even though I wasn't all that comfortable at these high levels. At $30 per share, we were showing a $7 million paper profit—not bad for two months' work—and here we were sticking our necks out even further. But I knew we had to protect our position, particularly if we were headed for an auction. I also knew that the longer we waited, the more we'd have to pay to stay in the game.

We ran into some trouble at that point, but not a lot. Shortly after we disclosed these added purchases, in yet another effort to block our bid, National accused us of jumping the gun on our stock purchases immediately following the CAB meeting. Technically, they were right. We *were* jumping the gun by a few days. Although Kahn had verbally approved our application to place additional shares in a voting trust, it would be a week or so before we had the formal paper document officially sanctioning our continued buying. We were guilty according to the letter of the law, but the board held that our infraction was not malicious and assessed only a token fine—a small price to pay given the substantial amount of stock we accumulated in the intervening period and the subsequent jump in price.

---

On August 23, four trading days after the sunshine meeting, the other buyer surfaced: Pan Am announced that it had amassed a 4.8 percent stake and was offering $300 million to buy National—or $35 per share. The bid, which confirmed that Seawell had finally gotten his board to act, would have merged the two companies into one of the world's largest airlines. From TIA's perspective, it would have sent any competing offer for National into the stratosphere cost-wise.

The news set off a flurry of activity in the market and made us rethink our strategy. At $35 per share, our interest in acquiring the airline was lukewarm at best; it would be a tough price to justify to our shareholders. But we never had to make that decision, because the market pushed the stock right through the $35 level almost immediately. At $40, which was where the stock was quickly heading, the price was way beyond the point where a deal for us made sense. Believe it or not, Bob Carney and I tended to have a conservative streak, so we did an about-face on strategy and started thinking of ways to maximize our profit on the deal rather than how to acquire the company.

Within a week of Pan Am's offer, we backed off thinking of ourselves as buyers and focused even more on thinking of ourselves as sellers. But even though we were then looking at National as a pure stock play, we weren't about to let on that our goals had changed. It was in our interest to publicly pursue the deal and keep pushing the stock. In late August, Pan Am and National agreed on a merger at $39 per share, up from the $35 offer. Shortly thereafter, on August 29, to pressure National and Pan Am to up the price of their merger beyond

$39 since the stock was already trading over that price, we swallowed hard and bought 320,000 shares at $40—a $12.8 million purchase, easily eating up most of our recent financing in a couple of hours. I'll confess I didn't sleep too easily that night.

Two days later, Pan Am and National raised the merger price from $39 to $41 per share, and we were still in the picture. In fact, the news accounts from that period—and this was a big deal, so there were a whole lot of news accounts—all mentioned that TIA had yet to make a formal offer for National. This was true, and there was none forthcoming. In one interview, I allowed that we had no specific plan for a takeover. "We don't have one in writing," I said. "We don't even have one on the back burner."

Still, there was wide speculation about our next move, and even while Pan Am and National came to a final agreement on September 7, the market seemed to be waiting for the other shoe to drop.

Bud Maytag continued to dodge my calls. The only communication we had during the late summer and early fall was in a series of open letters from Maytag (really, of course, from his lawyers and investment bankers) to our board of directors. "At this point," Maytag wrote in one letter, dated September 25 and released to the press before it arrived in our offices, "we can only conclude that Texas International has embarked on a venture it can't finish—one that is not in the best interest of its fellow National shareholders. In effect, [TIA] wants to fly now so all the rest of National's shareholders can pay later."

The tone, like that of all Maytag's public missives, was challenging and hostile, although I couldn't read them without also hearing the uncertainties and misgivings of a man whose company had somehow gotten away from him. By mid-September, Pan Am's stake in National had grown to 18.1 percent, TIA held 20.1 percent, and both airlines had applications for control pending with the CAB, although unlike Pan Am, we had not filed for any merger approval. Maytag appeared in the torrent of press accounts as a stumbling corporate figurehead, clearly bound for the door; the only question that remained was which exit he'd be forced to take.

Bob Carney and I came off looking like a couple of feisty, visionary thirty-eight-year-old upstarts, an obvious exaggeration or possible untruth, but we weren't about to quibble. *Forbes* ran a piece in October 1978 titled "Lorenzo the Presumptuous," in which I was dubbed a "Goliath-baiter" and TIA was hailed as one of the industry's "most innovative companies." Considering the competition in those regulated days, the bar was not very high. In another account, I was quoted as saying that acquiring National would cost $32 million less than buying a "modest" fleet of ten Boeing 727-200 jets and spares (support equipment and services)—a rather brazen comparison, it seems to me now. And the *New York Times*, in an article titled "No Longer Tree-Top Airways,"[2] called our bid "a mouse-that-roared strategy that raised eyebrows both in the industry and on Wall Street."

*New York Times* cartoon showing TXI bid to acquire National Airlines (1978).

In October, we still had some buying room from the CAB order, but then we were looking at suddenly reduced prices in National stock. Just as the overall market entered a period of sharp contraction, and

---

[2]  *New York Times*, November 8, 1978.

with National's future and the CAB decision still up in the air, the price of its shares took a surprising nosedive, to the $25 level. Investors were doubting whether any deal would win CAB approval. But we held on to our game plan, and on October 17 snapped up another 174,200 shares at $25.875.

This last block brought our holdings to 1,892,500 shares, or 22.1 percent of the company, for a total cost of $52.3 million, which actually meant that we were showing an overall loss of just over $2 million. Nevertheless, we continued "buying the stock down" over the next several days, confident that the price would eventually return to its previous much higher levels.

Beginning in November, Pan Am began racking up a series of civic endorsements in support of its control-merger proposal. New York City officials testified on Pan Am's behalf before the CAB, the Miami-Dade board of county commissioners voted 4–2 in favor of Pan Am's application, and the Florida cabinet passed a resolution supporting a National–Pan Am merger. We countered with the unsolicited endorsement of Alfred Kahn, freshly retired from the CAB, who stated publicly that a National merger with TIA would be better for the industry and the flying public than a union with Pan Am. Even out of office, Dr. Kahn was a great champion of deregulation and competition, and he had some difficulty hiding his strong beliefs, whether or not his comments were appropriate.

---

Then in December, the playing field changed. Unaware of these next developments, I was in Washington on Thursday, December 7, 1978, for a meeting of the Air Transport Association. These gatherings were always a good place to canvass the industry on matters of mutual interest, and at this event, the pending National deal was a major topic of conversation. Strangely, I was even questioned about the deal by a colleague from my early days at Eastern, Charlie Simon, who was Eastern's chief financial officer. What struck me as peculiar about

Charlie's interest was where we were at the time: in the men's room, at adjacent urinals.

Now, Charlie was a very discreet guy, his choice of meeting places notwithstanding, and I'm confident he would not have asked me about our National deal if he'd known that his boss, the Eastern chairman, Frank Borman, was mounting a bid. Borman, who had publicly opposed Pan Am's bid and vowed to fight its merger with National on antitrust grounds, spent the following weekend huddled in Miami with his board and his lawyers, preparing yet another offer for National on his own. On December 6, the day before, the National president, E. F. Dolansky, had testified before the CAB that the airline was still open to offers that might exceed Pan Am's, which stood at $41 per share, and Borman must have seen this as his last chance to get in on the bidding.

On Monday morning, December 11, I took a courtesy call from Borman, who wanted to let me know that the announcement of an Eastern offer for National, at $50 per share, would be crossing the tape in a few minutes. I was ecstatic that there would be a third bidder for the airline, but of course I kept my reaction to myself. In Borman's mind, at least, we were still competing on the deal, and he had just upped the ante by $77 million. Bill Seawell, I later learned, wasn't quite so cool about keeping his emotions under wraps; when Borman made a similar courtesy call to him, the general apparently hit the roof.

"It's a new ball game," Borman later told reporters. Indeed, it was.

The move took us all by surprise. In a proposal to the CAB, filed concurrently with his bid to the National board, Borman asked that Eastern's offer be considered on the same timetable as TIA's and Pan Am's, claiming that an Eastern–National merger would "promote competition, especially across the Atlantic." This last claim played to the new pro-competition bias of regulators, although it struck me as somewhat unfounded. There was no masking the fact that there was a great deal of overlap between Eastern and National on some very major routes, and on antitrust grounds alone, it seemed doubtful that Borman's bid would pass muster.

Many airline and market analysts viewed the Eastern bid as a purely defensive move made in order to upset a planned January 15, 1979, meeting of National shareholders at which they would vote on the Pan Am deal, although some also recognized the value of National's newly granted London, Paris, Frankfurt, and Amsterdam routes to Eastern's plans for international expansion.

We could not have cared less about Borman's motives or his chances. What we liked about this latest development was the prospect of yet another run-up in the price of National stock. But unfortunately, Borman's offer didn't spur a whole lot of movement in the stock (Eastern wasn't buying until it had a favorable ruling from the CAB). National continued to trade in the $36–$40 range in the weeks following Eastern's bid, which we took to mean that the arbitrageurs, who by then owned most of the non–Pan Am and non-TIA stock (around 50 percent of the shares), didn't think Borman stood much of a chance.

On Monday, January 22, the Justice Department officially opposed the efforts of Pan Am and TIA, even though the CAB had not ruled on either merger. The assistant attorney general, John Shenefield, claimed that the proposed mergers were anticompetitive and would likely hurt consumers as a shrinking number of major airlines tightened their grip on pricing practices.

The Justice Department rejection was a setback and sent National shares swooning, but I don't think any of the parties looked on it as a major blow because the CAB had the final say. Still, the very public objection to our actions put us all back on the front pages, and even on some prominent editorial pages, the following morning.

The *Washington Post*, in an editorial, urged the CAB to ignore the Justice Department and allow the free market (and National's stockholders) to determine the outcome. "While such a decision could spur more merger proposals," the *Post* editorial read, "it would be in keeping with the spirit of deregulation. A decision blocking either or both of these takeover bids would suggest the government is not yet ready to let go of the regulatory reins it has kept on the airline industry much too long."[3]

Finally, after nine months in the game, we decided to make our first formal offer to acquire National Airlines. Up until this time, all we had done was amass a 24 percent ownership position in the company with no specific takeover plan. We'd taken a great deal of heat for our sit-back-and-wait strategy, but it made sense for us to conceal our hand. At that point, though, we wanted to put some additional substance behind Eastern's offer price (especially since the arbitrageurs were dubious of the Eastern offer), and the way to do this, it seemed, was by making a conventional bid of our own, as best we could.

On Tuesday, February 20, we matched Eastern's $50 bid, with a per-share offer of $8 in cash, one share of TIA stock (which was trading at around $12), and various debt securities. Ours was almost entirely a "paper" deal, and we never expected National to bite on it. At these high prices, we weren't really trying to buy the company so much as we were trying to push the Pan Am deal price up to Eastern's $50 level. Certainly there was always the chance that National would accept our offer, and we would have to "eat" the deal. In order to protect ourselves from this long shot, we had to make sure our proposal was structured in such a way that it was credible and we could live with it if it went through. This ($8 in cash and $42 in equity and debt securities) was a deal we could live with.

Predictably, National wanted no part of our proposal, so we nearly doubled the cash component of our offer in the ensuing days, but they turned us down again. In addition to sweetening the deal, we also inched closer to the 25 percent ceiling established by the CAB, grabbing another 121,000 shares of National stock on March 14 (at an average price of $40.41) and bringing our stake to 2.1 million shares, at a total cost of approximately $59.2 million. It was like a high-stakes poker game, and we were determined to stay in the bidding until the very end.

---

[3]  *Washington Post*, January 22, 1979.

We added to our treasury at this time by completing one of our most interesting financings. We still had seven new DC-9s on order from McDonnell Douglas and had completed a major deal with Swissair to buy twenty used DC-9s over the course of a couple of years, in addition to the possible National needs. As a consequence, on April 11, we closed on $35 million of guaranteed floating rate notes due in 1986 in the Eurodollar market. I should point out that the very somber "guaranteed" was that of TIA, not of some staid financial institution, as was often the case.

A funny background to this financing: in early March, I had a meeting with an investment banker in New York who mentioned that Citibank had just completed an offering of Eurodollar floating rate notes with interest at 1 percent over the so-called LIBOR—or London interbank offered rate. Given the quite high profile of TIA at the time, certainly in Europe, I inquired whether we could sell a similar security, adding a few points more in interest. The banker came back a few days later, after checking with his London office, and said that while that type of offering was normally only done by major institutions, they were willing to give it a try. Thus was born our floating rates deal, and we got our money in three weeks, thanks to the simplicity of the Eurodollar market in those days.

The administrative law judge in our and Pan Am's control case delivered his opinion on April 5, calling on the CAB to reject our bids. Naturally this news was unsettling, but we were prepared for it, because law judges were often centuries behind the real world and we were confident that the full CAB would see it differently. The CAB immediately announced that it would take up an expedited review and not let the law judge decision stand as the final word.

On April 25, the Justice Department and the Department of Transportation finally checked in with their rulings on Eastern's application to buy National, declaring in separate filings to the CAB that such an acquisition would violate both antitrust and aviation laws. Eastern was still in the game, pending the CAB decision on the matter, but that now appeared unlikely.

In April, Pan Am raised its bid yet again—to the $50 level previously offered by TIA and Eastern. Naturally, we were ecstatic.

---

On Tuesday, July 10, 1979, the CAB finally ruled on the National situation, unanimously approving our proposal along with Pan Am's and rejecting the law judge–recommended decision—ironically, a full year after our filing of schedule 13D, which disclosed our National stock purchases. Publicly, I expressed disappointment that Pan Am was deemed an acceptable partner and allowed to remain in the running alongside TIA. Privately, I was thrilled: with Pan Am being granted government clearance to complete its merger, I knew there'd be a ready buyer for our 2.1 million shares—maybe the only buyer.

National stock, which had been hovering around $40 prior to the CAB decision, shot to $46 when trading resumed Wednesday morning. It was clear to Bob Carney and me that the time had come to fold our hand. After a call from Bill Seawell in which he asked to buy our shares in order to strengthen his position against a higher Eastern bid, we agreed to sell.

We announced the final deal with Pan Am on July 28, and it provided for the immediate sale of our initial 790,700 shares at $50 per share and the later sale of our remaining 1,309,300 shares on the same terms by the end of the year. The staggered buyout was structured to allow TIA to realize the capital-gains tax advantages for the National shares we had held less than the required one year. In the interim, we pledged to withdraw our April 12 offer to merge with National and agreed not to purchase any additional shares or to sell out to any other party. In total, we received $105 million (about $449 million in 2024 dollars) from Pan Am—a $46 million profit (about $197 million in 2024 dollars).

Combined with our three financings over the course of the nearly twelve previous months, we'd be sitting with nearly $125 million in reserves ($534 million in 2024 dollars)—a fantastic amount, considering our small size and our $14 million net worth eighteen months earlier. The real beauty of the deal for us was that we kept all the cash, although we had to pay taxes on the gain. Had we bought the stock on margin, or secured by a bank loan, we would have had to repay the debt on sale. Therefore, since we borrowed on an unsecured basis, we were able to put the sale proceeds directly into our treasury.

Word on the Street had us immediately going after another airline, but that wasn't our plan, although we were diligently analyzing several prospects. We were flush with cash and ready to grow in the new challenging deregulated environment.

# CHAPTER SIX

# The Birth of New York Air

*Braving the Winds of Deregulation*
*1979–1981*

T HE NATIONAL deal left us a very cash-rich yet structurally challenged small airline eager to play a winning hand in the game of airline deregulation. Strategically, we continued to focus on a merger or acquisition that would make sense while at the same time continuing to build our airline operations.

As was widely reported at the time, Braniff, Western, and Continental were having problems adjusting to the newly competitive marketplace. These three airlines came into our sights, and we analyzed them extensively. Braniff's financial difficulties were well known, but I went through the motions with its president, Harding Lawrence, just the same. Harding was one of the truly colorful characters in the airline industry, and I had long been one of his admirers. At the time, though, he had been under fire for some of the moves he made in response to deregulation—including his crazy-quilt acquisition of unused route authorities, which he had initiated during the early months of 1979.

Harding had a spectacular office on the Braniff campus at the new Dallas–Fort Worth airport, connected to an equally spectacular apartment he kept there. In 1980, when I went to his office so that we could take each other's pulse on a potential deal, he pushed on the wall, and it rotated on its axis to reveal his living room, and I remember thinking it was like something in a James Bond movie. But the jet-set accommodations masked some real trouble spots at the company. I had grave concerns about Braniff's finances, concerns that were not necessarily incompatible with doing a deal provided that Harding would be forthcoming in his appraisal of his airline—which he turned out not to be. There were also potential antitrust complications in a Braniff–TIA merger. Curiously, Lawrence referred to the possibility of merging with Texas Air Corporation (see page 140) rather than with Texas International Airlines a number of times. It seemed to me that someone had told him that Texas Air Corporation was where the cash was, and that was the only interest he had.

Talks with Western progressed somewhat further, although the airline offered no real fit. It had a nascent hub operation in Salt Lake City and some strength in Denver but no presence in Houston. Moreover, its fleet was made up of DC-10s, 727s, and 737s, which didn't match our small-plane DC-9 fleet at all. But despite these negatives, we still spent a fair amount of time evaluating Western, principally because the Western president, Dominic Renda, was openly soliciting offers, and we wanted to explore every merger and investment opportunity.

Continental looked like it offered better possibilities than the other candidates. The airline was developing a Denver hub and had a substantial number of flights in Houston. It had a complementary fleet of wide-body aircraft and a positive national reputation for service and innovation. I had some doubts about the ability of the airline's management to adapt to the changing deregulated environment, but that would only be a short-term worry if we took over the company. The real problem with Continental was that it had already stated its interest in negotiating a merger with Western, whose offices were just down the street from Continental's and whose executives were very chummy and had already expressed a preference for a merger with Continental. Therefore, it was clear that the only transaction likely available to us would be an unfriendly one, and we weren't prepared for that—at least not yet.

Still, throughout that summer, there were all kinds of rumors that TIA would go after Continental. There was even an item in the business pages of the *New York Times* speculating that we were behind a recent surge in buying of Continental stock and preparing to tender for control of the company. In fact, we didn't even have a token investment position in the company at the time—reminding me yet again not to believe everything I read in the press.

The rumors persisted in August, while I was spending some time on Nantucket with my family and training for my second of four New York City Marathon runs. While there, I received a call from the Continental president, Bob Six, responding to some of these rumors. I assured him that we weren't the ones doing all the buying even though I thought his stock was a great value.

"Just checking," he said. "All my friends on Wall Street say you guys own a lot of our stock."

"I hear the same thing," I said, "but it's just not true." It wasn't at the time.

---

Bob called a few more times before the month was out—whenever the market traded a big block of Continental stock—but I had nothing different to report. After a while, the calls became kind of funny, especially considering that we were about to embark on a completely different and altogether modest buying program that no one would have suspected. Our aim: Trans World Airlines, part of a holding company called Trans World Corporation.

If some observers considered our quest for National to be Goliath baiting, going after TWA was like going after a whale. TWA's airline operations were around fourteen times the size of ours, depending on which measures we chose for comparison. TWA flew nine times as many planes as TIA, employed twelve times as many people, and yielded twenty times our revenue. No matter how we looked at it, TWA was a big fish, but it kept turning up in our sights as a perfect target. It offered a good fit and tremendous upside at an extremely attractive price. It was also a very well-known brand. In addition, its management did not appear to have developed a strategy to deal with deregulation and therefore might welcome an amalgamation that better prepared it for the newly competitive landscape. One could also sense from public comments that TWA management had a low regard for the airline compared to its hotel and other holdings.

Ironically, it was the very size of TWA that gave us a unique advantage over any other potential suitors. We knew that Braniff and Northwest simply didn't have the appetite for such a merger and that antitrust concerns would prompt the government to block bids by United or American. All the other major airlines, including Pan Am, National, Continental, and Western, were already too deeply entangled in other mergers to pursue TWA. If we wanted to get into the game, it appeared we'd have the playing field all to ourselves.

In September 1979, we began buying shares of Trans World Corporation, TWA's parent company, while we formulated a proposal that would separate a merged TWA–TIA from the rest of Trans World's holdings. TWA's parent was a diversified corporation whose most valuable assets were the Hilton International hotel chain and Canteen, a vending-machine company. Hilton and Canteen together had pretax profits of $240 million over the previous five years, while TWA airline operations had pretax losses of $102 million during the same period. It was apparent that TWA was a cash drain on Trans World and was regarded by Wall Street as a negative for the company. Trans World had also just announced plans to further diversify by acquiring the Spartan Food Systems restaurant chain and the Century 21 real estate firm. Presumably, these acquisitions were viewed in a more positive light than buying new aircraft for TWA.

Trans World stock at the time was trading so far below the value of the sum of its parts that the Hilton International hotel unit *alone* was probably worth Trans World's market valuation. The more we ran the numbers, the more obvious it became that spinning off TWA through a merger with TIA would unlock tremendous hidden value for Trans World's shareholders. We also knew from our National experience that it's often attractive to have a position in a target company so that if negotiations are unproductive, at least there is a possibility of a profit from that investment.

As we brought our Trans World holdings to just over 4 percent of the company (roughly 650,000 shares), we put together a formal proposal in which Trans World shareholders would enjoy the additional value of a second trading equity in the newly spun-off airline while Trans World's management would continue to control both companies. By absorbing TIA's people and resources, the merged TWA–TIA would invigorate its management ranks, gain a valuable Houston hub, and acquire an important position in Mexico. For TIA, we were willing to surrender control of our airline if it meant we could achieve a strategic solution to TIA's size problem while participating in the turnaround of TWA's sagging fortunes.

I thought the odds were high that this spin-off strategy would play directly to the personal strengths of Trans World's chairman, Ed Smart, whose background was primarily in the hotel industry. I arranged a breakfast with Smart at the Carlyle hotel in New York on September 13, 1979, and it was there I learned I had Smart figured completely wrong. He wasn't the least bit interested in what I had to say, and by the end of breakfast, he made it clear to me that he didn't want to do business with us, plain and simple. If he was going to do anything, he would do a big deal—or so it seemed.

Less than an hour after Smart's rebuff, I returned to our New York office to discover that rumors were already swirling about our interest in TWA. Perhaps someone had spotted Smart and me at the Carlyle and made the connection. More likely, someone in Smart's office had leaked it. Whoever decided to tip the market, it certainly worked to generate interest. Trans World shares and TIA shares were both going through the roof, and the betting line was that we were buying TWA.

I consulted with our lawyers and decided that the most prudent course, given Smart's rejection and the market action, was to issue a statement confirming our interest in TWA and announcing our 4 percent stake in the company. We also reported the unproductive breakfast meeting with Smart and said that no further discussions were planned. We weren't prepared to abandon the deal, but our lawyers believed that we should make our interests known. Then we could sit back and see what happened.

What happened was that Trans World stock continued to climb. We had done most of our buying at about the $18 level, and in the days following our announcement, the stock shot up to $26 as investors anticipated our next move. The business pages were filled with speculation about our strategy and TWA's response. A *Wall Street Journal* headline asked, "Who Says Little TIA Can't Buy Big TWA? Many Believe It Will."

But Smart's lack of interest had soured us on the realities of a TWA deal. No matter how attractive a streamlined TWA looked to TIA, it simply didn't make sense to enter another protracted and very public battle for control of another carrier. These deals are always difficult to win. For us, winning in this case was the ability to merge TIA and TWA, not just a stock market profit. So we pulled back in purchasing Trans World stock, and thirty days after our initial announcement, we began a sell-off of all our holdings. Instead of selling quickly and profiting from Trans World stock's inflated price, however, we allowed the stock to find its natural level in order to avoid accusations of market manipulation. This time, we actually wound up liquidating our position with a slight loss on the deal, which seemed a small price to pay for a credible shot at such a formidable and structurally attractive carrier.

In addition, we had been extensively focused on using our cash resources to build the company internally, taking advantage of the new operating freedoms brought about by deregulation and our strong balance sheet.

---

In the first week of January 1980, the heads of the New York and Boston airports came to visit us in Houston at my invitation with one thing on their minds—the need for more competition in the Northeast's air routes. Bob Weinberg, chairman of Massport (and a classmate of mine from Harvard Business School), which ran Logan Airport, and Peter Goldmark, executive director of the Port Authority of New York and New Jersey, which ran LaGuardia Airport, were both having problems with Eastern Airlines, whose shuttle service dominated air traffic in Boston and New York as well as at Washington National Airport.

At LaGuardia, where Eastern was one of the busiest tenants, Eastern's chairman, Frank Borman, was pressuring Goldmark's agency for concessions in leasing terms and other airport conditions. At Logan, he had threatened to pull out the shuttle service entirely in protest of new noise-abatement rules implemented by Weinberg's agency. Eastern flew more planes out of Logan than any other airline at the time, and the hourly shuttle flights to New York were a large part of Eastern's operations there. Borman complained that the tightened noise restrictions were causing delays in taxiing and takeoffs, especially burdensome for Eastern's short-haul commuter flights.

Weinberg and Goldmark basically pitched us on bringing TIA to their airports to give Eastern a run for its money. If TIA were willing to open a competing shuttle service at Logan and LaGuardia, the two pledged to do everything within their authority—in terms of passenger gates, maintenance space, favorable lease terms, whatever—to help us succeed and counter Eastern's outsize influence.

It happened that at TIA, we had already discussed and evaluated expanding into the Northeast, where the air travel markets were large and competition was scarce. Eastern's shuttle service dominated both the New York–Washington route (the nation's largest air passenger market) and the New York–Boston route (the third largest). I left the luncheon meeting thinking that starting up a New York–based airline, with Boston as a key market, was a very attractive idea.

Further study and follow-up meetings with Weinberg and Goldmark convinced me that a low-fare, high-frequency shuttle-type operation was the way to go. Geographically, the new airline would be far enough removed from TIA's Houston hub to avoid any danger of duplicating our efforts or stepping on our own toes. Strategically, the established shuttle markets, such as Eastern's Boston–New York route, were ripe for competition, while our New York hub would open new opportunities for low-fare service to other nearby cities, such as Cleveland, Buffalo, and Pittsburgh.

We were fortunate that two other significant developments at TIA would support our plans for expansion into the Northeast. We were already awaiting delivery of fifteen midsize jets from Swissair that would be perfect for commuter shuttle service. We were also contemplating a new corporate structure that would facilitate running the new Northeast service as a subsidiary operation. From a marketing point of view, having a separate subsidiary was a highly attractive feature, since I felt it essential that this new service have a distinct New York feel and not just be viewed as a branch of a Texas airline.

The way we came to buy those fifteen jets reveals a good deal about our entrepreneurial, fast-moving management style. I was reading *Aviation Daily*, the industry bible, over breakfast in my backyard early one morning in the spring of 1980 when I spotted an article about Swissair's plans to phase out its DC-9-30 fleet because of noise problems at Zurich's Kloten airport. My mouth watered at the thought of buying those planes at a perhaps distressed sale price. Most of Swissair's DC-9-30s were less than ten years old ("like new" in terms of airplane life spans), and everyone knew that Swissair maintained its planes extremely well.

I immediately got on the phone to Walter Fuchs, the Swissair executive quoted in the article, and introduced myself as a member of TIA's aircraft procurement office (which was not entirely untrue). Fuchs told me he would soon be authorized to seek offers for the aircraft, and I promised that someone would get back to him later that day. As soon as I got to the office, I relayed the situation to Jim Arpey, who also handled aircraft purchases. Jim jumped right on it.

In short order, before many in the industry even knew the aircraft were available, we were able to sign a deal for the fifteen planes at $6 million apiece with an option for five more and delivery spread over a period of two years. At the time, we still had no specific plans for expansion, but I had no doubt we'd put these planes to good use. With the advent of deregulation, I believed that new short-haul routes were bound to proliferate, and relatively small aircraft such as DC-9-30s would become increasingly valuable as a result. Smaller equaled lower risk, as I saw it—extremely important in the precarious deregulated world we had moved into.

---

In June 1980, we decided to implement a changed corporate structure. Under this structure, which would involve an umbrella holding company, TIA would operate as a separate company under a corporate parent. Given our bulging cash reserves of $125 million, one of the great advantages of such a structure was that the parent company's investments would no longer be subject to scrutiny by the DOT. We could finance a start-up airline on a completely separate basis, enabling us to build a family of individual airlines, each with a distinct identity, set of goals, and system of rewards for loyal passengers. And, crucially, any start-up airlines we launched would not be bound by existing union contracts at the now separate TIA.

Back in 1967, TWA had adopted this holding-company structure to diversify its holdings in other industries under the umbrella of Trans World Corporation. Our approach was different, though. We saw the umbrella company as a way to diversify our holdings within the airline industry itself. This was a radically new concept among airlines, but it wasn't long before most major carriers, including United, American, and USAir, would form similar holding companies, giving them the flexibility to establish new low-cost subsidiary airlines of their own. Ironically, today, major airlines such as Lufthansa and British Airways look upon their low-cost airline subsidiaries as the way of the future.

After we won shareholder approval of our restructuring, we transferred $100 million from Texas International Airways to the new holding company, which we called Texas Air Corporation. We chose the name Texas Air because we wanted to keep a close association with our flagship business and our base of operations. However, in an amusing twist—although it wasn't so amusing initially—in setting up the corporation, we were forced to buy the rights to the name Texas Air from a small Houston air-conditioning company of the same name.

In the holding company restructuring, TIA shares were swapped for TAC shares on a one-for-one basis, and the airline became a fully owned subsidiary of the holding company. We left around $25 million in the coffers at TIA—a tidy sum for working capital and expansion at such a small airline.

The new airline we planned would be based in Manhattan (the first new carrier to be headquartered in the city in thirty-four years), and we planned to start small by serving only the Washington, DC, market, with Boston to follow soon after. I had originally wanted to name the new airline Big Apple Air, but it didn't take us long to realize that native New Yorkers rarely referred to the city as the Big Apple (as a kid from Queens, I should have recognized this instantly). So we settled on the clean and simple New York Air.

To launch our new brand with a flourish, we asked our ad agency to develop a logo and color scheme for our planes—known in the industry as livery—using a stylized rendering of the New York apple on the tail of the aircraft and painting the planes a deep red. As far as we knew, no airline had ever used a "hot" color such as red for its planes, so it gave us a distinctive look, one that never got old.) (In the 1960s, Harding Lawrence's "jellybean" paint scheme for Braniff included red, but that red was a flat rather than vibrant shade.) Even our lettering was distinctive, although to some people, it was not quite distinctive enough. We displayed our name in a classic font reminiscent of *New York* magazine's title type, and the publisher was all over us about the similarity, but we smoothed things over by offering *New York* as our in-flight magazine.

I served as New York Air's chairman and chief executive, but only for our start-up period. The spirit behind New York Air was highly entrepreneurial, so we named Neal Meehan, former head of customer service at TIA, as the New York Air president, leading a team of young, hungry, innovative corporate officers. Jim O'Donnell would run the marketing efforts, and Andy Feuerstein, who had done well with us during our early days at Lorenzo, Carney, returned with us as New York Air's general counsel. Stephen Kolski left National Airlines to become head of flying operations. To sit on the board, we recruited no less an industry presence than Alfred Kahn, the former CAB chairman and principal architect of deregulation, who was then a professor of economics at Cornell University. He was a friend and mentor and was really enthusiastic about what we were doing.

---

Our plans hit their first obstacle with the ALPA, the Air Line Pilots Association. Our cost structure called for starting New York Air pilots at salaries of around $30,000 a year ($113,000 in 2024 dollars) for flying seventy to seventy-five hours a month—pretty normal compensation for trained pilots not working for legacy airlines in those days. However, TIA's unionized pilots were making $60,000–$70,000 a year ($226,000–$264,000 in 2024 dollars) for flying approximately sixty hours a month, and their ALPA representatives saw an immediate threat in the lower New York Air salaries. They claimed that our true long-term goal was to use the Texas Air holding company as a way to shut down TIA and transfer its aircraft and operations to lower-cost New York Air. But even if we wanted to, we could not use a shadow company to avoid a standing union contract, because there were "runaway shop" laws in place to prevent that. In any case, we had absolutely no intention of doing that to our pilots or any of our other employees, quite a few of whom had been with the airline for many years and whom we had gotten to know personally.

We countered by offering ALPA an explicit "fence agreement," which committed us to keeping TIA pilots flying at current levels and keeping all TIA aircraft at TIA, but the union refused to accept it. Instead, ALPA representatives insisted that New York Air planes should use TIA's unionized pilots. They also maintained that since New York Air's DC-9-30 fleet had been purchased from Swissair prior to our reorganization, those planes should be flown by unionized TIA pilots, even though we argued that these planes were not necessarily bought for TIA's direct use and that the court did not impose any such limitation on us.

The reality of the freshly deregulated marketplace was that there was no way to satisfy ALPA's demands without killing New York Air. We could not possibly use TIA pilots on New York Air flights without negatively affecting the costs of the new airline and bringing in TIA's machinists and flight attendants under their existing union contracts. To have done so would have doomed the strategy behind the low-cost airline concept, so basic in the new deregulated airline world.

It wasn't an anti-union strategy, as ALPA claimed. It was simply a competitive strategy that ultimately expanded job opportunities for airline pilots. It was good business. It was legal. It was ethical. It created jobs. It treated our people fairly—the ones in place, at TIA, and the ones we were hiring, at New York Air. And it financially strengthened TAC, the holding company, which could only have a positive impact on the health of all TAC units, including TIA. But none of this mattered to the union leaders at ALPA. They were fundamentally threatened by our pioneering strategy of opening a new airline unbound by existing union contracts within our holding company structure. And what was most dangerous to ALPA, as they saw it, was that we were setting a precedent that might pave the way for other airlines such as United and American to follow suit.

The average TIA pilot didn't see New York Air as a threat at all. Our pilots recognized the strategy as a practical move for management and saw no risk to their security or seniority. They realized what TIA was dealing with. They knew of the far lower compensation levels, for example, at Southwest and other competitors in the Texas area. They realized that deregulation would bring new competition. In fact, when ALPA leaders tried to mount a slowdown of TIA operations in protest, they failed to generate enough grassroots support among TIA pilots to pull it off. It had become very clear to everyone that ALPA was fighting us on behalf of the pilots of Eastern and other large airlines, not on behalf of the TIA pilots they represented, although that was the publicly professed reason.

So ALPA representatives began picketing TIA headquarters in Houston and the New York Air offices at LaGuardia Airport. They even picketed our bankers in midtown Manhattan, leaving me to personally apologize for the nuisance to the chairman of Manufacturers Hanover Trust, whose Park Avenue headquarters, among others, were harassed. ALPA leaders finally sought an injunction in federal court in Brooklyn, hoping to ground our new airline before we sold a single ticket. The injunction was denied in the early fall of 1980, but it succeeded in tying up our resources and attention for months on end. These labor struggles marked the first skirmish in what would become a years-long battle between the wealthy pilots' union and me.

Another obstacle in starting up was securing takeoff and landing slots at high-traffic airports such as LaGuardia and National. Traditionally, representatives of existing carriers managed the flow of takeoff and landing requests through "slot committees" composed of airline representatives, and these requests rarely involved anything more than minor changes in scheduling. The airlines added slots on a piecemeal basis, canceling one flight here, adding two there, and building their traffic to the desired levels in each market. In order to start a shuttle-type operation, however, we needed to open for business with a whole bunch of slots, then build from there.

Prior to New York Air, no new carrier had applied for such a full slate of flight clearances in a high-traffic "slotted" airport, and there was no established way to acquire these clearances. There was no secondary market for slots, as there is today, so we couldn't even buy the slot rights from another airline. We could, however, present a compelling argument that these two slotted airports were operating well below capacity and that the FAA should simply increase the number of slots to accommodate our request without having to reduce the number of flights of any other airline.

We petitioned the slot committees at LaGuardia and National to consider such a proposal. After all, we maintained, the slots had been established as a temporary measure in the late 1960s, in answer to increasing delays at our busiest airports, and were never intended to permanently restrict any new traffic from entering those markets.

Earlier that year, we had hired Phil Bakes, the Capitol Hill staff attorney who had helped draft the deregulation legislation under Stephen Breyer, as our senior vice president for legal and public affairs at TAC. He became the point man for our DOT application for expanded slotting. We argued that as the first new entrant into these slotted markets after deregulation, New York Air presented a litmus test for the government's commitment to competition in air travel. If a new airline couldn't get off the ground in the most heavily traveled corridor in the country, where the market was operating as an effective monopoly, then all the talk about opening America's skies to increased competition would be exposed for what it truly was—just talk.

As expected, our slot applications were opposed by every other airline with a vested interest in the decision—which was almost all of them. The slot committee summarily dismissed our request. Ultimately, though, the DOT approved our bid and awarded New York Air forty daily slots at LaGuardia and eighteen daily slots at National—just shy of our request, but enough to get us started.

Word of the DOT decision reached a group of us at our ad agency offices in Manhattan, where we were reviewing the latest designs for our flight attendants' uniforms. This was already a fun day for us, interrupting the mess of uncertainty surrounding our start-up, and the pretty models and stylish uniforms must have left us particularly receptive to good news. I was sitting with Phil Bakes, Neal Meehan, and Jim O'Donnell when I was handed a note about the slots and was positively ecstatic to learn that the department had awarded us most of the rights we requested in our application. We were all crazy with excitement—all of us, that is, except for Phil, ever the fighter and perfectionist, who couldn't get past the fact that we were denied two sets of slots, even though in every other respect it was a triumphant victory for our fledgling operation.

---

Certainly one of the bright spots amid all the difficulties in the months preceding the launch of New York Air was that it brought me back frequently to LaGuardia Airport. I was in New York often during that summer of 1980, and I tried to begin and end each trip with a visit to my parents' house in nearby Rego Park. On these visits, I remember, my father would pump me for information on our start-up venture. He was proud of the work I had done in Texas, 1,500 miles away, but New York Air gave him a front-row seat to something he could directly relate to. Hearing all about what we were up to in New York was a source of tremendous excitement and satisfaction for him.

My father had developed a serious case of skin cancer over the previous year, and by the summer months, after unsuccessful rounds of chemotherapy and radiation treatments, the growing melanomas on his body signaled only worse days ahead. Dad had been a healthy and active man, running the beauty shop until 1978 and regularly traveling to Houston with my mother to visit with their grandchildren. But as the summer of 1980 wore on, it became an effort for him just to get through the day and off to his outpatient treatments at Memorial Sloan Kettering Cancer Center, in Manhattan.

It was tough on my mother as well, not just because of the lengths she went to to take care of Dad but also because she had all that time to imagine what life was going to be like without him. My visits gave my mother a little relief from her endless caretaking, I think, and gave me a chance to spend some last precious hours with my father. I think it also acted as a kind of salve for him, easing him over his worst days, leaving him eager to see how it would all turn out, willing his son to finish on top. I will always be grateful for the chance to have given him that.

My father passed away on September 27, 1980, after being hospitalized with pneumonia. I was touched that so many TIA and New York

Air people made the trip to New York for the funeral. Only a few of them knew Dad at all, but they came because they knew what he had meant to me, and many understood the influence that his *gallego* spirit had had on me and, in turn, on our company. They came because he'd instilled in me a hunger to accomplish all that I could and a commitment to do so fairly and with integrity. My will to succeed was born in his.

It took Dad's obituary in the *New York Times* to remind me of just what he went through to build a good life in this country. My mother smiled when she read the piece, which listed Dad's age as seventy-five; she turned to Val and me and said, "Your father was no more seventy-five than the man in the moon!" When he left Spain, she explained, Dad was forced to shave a few years off his age to avoid the required military service for all young men seventeen and older.

One of the saddest consequences of my father's death, aside from his missing the beginnings of New York Air, was that he didn't get to watch my daughters grow up. He took such pleasure in them that it pained me, at first, to think of what he'd miss. Sadder still was that my children would never really know their grandfather. Nicole and Mercedes, at seven and five, were certainly old enough to always remember him, but Carolina, at two, was probably too young.

As it turned out, my sadness was a little misplaced, because my father lives on in the memories of my children. They have collected enough stories from me and from their grandmother to know what kind of man he was, what he meant to me, and what he did to make his mark on the world. We have many nice photographs of him from his healthy days. Mercedes keeps a special photograph of the two of them that I snapped several months before Dad died. What makes the picture special is that it won a local Father's Day photo contest and was printed in the *Houston Post*. (Sharon had entered the picture without telling any of us.) Dad happened to be visiting Houston when the contest results and the photo ran, and he was thumbing through the paper when he came across this sweet shot. It was a great surprise for him, and I can't look at the picture today without feeling glad for the way he chanced upon it. In the photo, his face is already ravaged by the cancer, but his eyes are smiling.

My father's legacy of honoring hard work made it easier for me to step back from my grief in the months following his funeral. I knew in my heart it would make him beam with pride if he could see me jumping back into the successful launch of our new airline. On December 19, 1980, with high expectations, we introduced New York Air to a ready marketplace. However, the start-up was anything but smooth.

Originally, we had wanted to begin service on December 14 and had been told by FAA staff that our FAA approval was essentially set. So we began advertising and announced the fourteenth as our launch date. However, as the day got closer, and with no word from the FAA, who claimed to have some paperwork problems, we had to cancel our launch and the many reservations we had. The delay and the cancellations were painful to us and to the passengers we disappointed. It made the evening news for a few days before the actual start-up, on the nineteenth. It was a big, unfortunate development.

About two weeks after the start-up, however, Sharon and I went to an out-of-the way restaurant in upper Manhattan to get a break when a gentleman with a strong New York accent came over to our table, having recognized me from the press photos. "Mr. Lorenzo," he said, "how were you able to arrange that government delay? What an amazing publicity stunt." I of course explained that it wasn't planned, nor was it what we wanted. But I did leave the restaurant realizing that I had learned an important lesson about the value of publicity.

———————

Our initial one-way fares were $49 peak and $29 off-peak, which compared very favorably to Eastern's $65 one-way fares. (At $29, traveling to Washington, DC, with us off-peak cost only fifty-five cents more than making the same trip on a Greyhound bus.) We scheduled ten round-trip flights each day—hourly for the early morning and late afternoon commuters and every two hours during the slower midday periods.

Unlike Eastern, we offered reserved seats and a wide variety of snacks and beverages. In fact, we extensively advertised the fact that we provided coffee and a bagel or muffin at no charge—unlike Eastern, which at that time provided nothing, since flight attendants were busy during the flight collecting fares.

We capitalized New York Air with $10 million from Texas Air Corporation in exchange for five million shares of New York Air common stock and 2.5 million shares of convertible preferred stock. In the days following our launch, we filed a registration with the SEC to take New York Air public, which had been one of our goals and one of the advantages of establishing it as a separate company. We went public on February 20, 1981, successfully offering 1,760,000 shares at $9.50 per share, raising $16.7 million before underwriting costs (about $57 million in 2024 dollars) and certifying our start-up strategy as an early success while adding to the airline's hefty capital cushion. For its era, the amount raised in the IPO was considerable—close to what other new-entrant airlines had raised. And of course New York Air had a substantial holding company behind it.

Less than two months later, in early 1981, we opened our New York–Boston service, with $39 peak and $29 off-peak fares, but not before staging another headline-grabbing promotion conjured up by our marketing folks. We offered twenty-nine-cent tickets to the first thousand passengers who showed up at Logan Airport and took a public oath to "never ever again" fly Eastern or drive to New York. The sight of a couple of thousand commuters crowded into our Boston terminal facility and pledging their allegiance to New York Air was enough to put us on the nightly news and on the front page from coast to coast, this time in a very positive way.

By all measures, New York Air was a runaway hit. In our first full month, we boarded more than 37,000 passengers and flew our planes at 58.1 percent of capacity. Load factors climbed to 64 percent by February, and we cleared the 100,000 mark in monthly passenger boardings by March. We cut significantly into Eastern's market share and, most importantly, succeeded in penetrating the public consciousness, mostly through a series of inspired promotions and a well-timed gesture of patriotism. That February, following the release of American embassy employees who'd been held hostage in Iran, we donated the New York Air plane on which the hostages and their families flew to New York for a homecoming parade. We were proud to be able to contribute to the celebration and receive a written commendation from Mayor Ed Koch, but I won't deny that there was an important PR component behind our goodwill.

---

Over time, we adopted several memorable promotional gambits, including our colorful "nosh bags," which included a fresh bagel, a roll and cheese, or some other snack, and complimentary newspapers; we even bought the airline rights for three years to the song "Theme from *New York, New York*," made popular by Frank Sinatra, which we retooled as "New York, New York Air" in our ads and as boarding music on our airplanes.

Throughout our system, we were known for the friendly, outgoing service of our crew and for our imaginative advertising. For one television commercial, we hired a contortionist to walk through the cabin of a plane outfitted in Eastern's colors (really just a studio set) and express doubts about Eastern's supposed cramped seating space. Then the contortionist sat down, folded both legs behind his head, sighed, and said he didn't have any problem getting comfortable on Eastern. Another commercial showed the Eastern president, former astronaut Frank Borman, crammed inside a spinning space capsule as the screen displayed the tagline "Just because Eastern's president flew inside a space capsule is no reason you have to feel the same flying to Washington." After I heard about this ad, I very quickly had it stopped because I felt it went over the top.

Even the bitter battle with the pilots' union played into our hands. Its efforts to shut us down had the effect of giving us more public attention. We would have all preferred labor peace, but the incessant picketing and leafleting made the development of New York Air a news story. It put us on the docket for public scrutiny, whereas without ALPA's very visible opposition, we might have had a difficult time getting noticed.

Meanwhile, once the courts rejected ALPA's appeal to have New York Air and TIA considered a single company, union leaders attempted to organize New York Air pilots directly, but our pilots weren't interested. They were reasonably paid; they maintained strong relations with management; they worked in a pleasant, enterprising environment; and they enjoyed the benefits of an extensive employee stock bonus plan that helped increase their stake in a thriving company. All told, New York Air pilots saw no reason to fork over 5 percent of their salaries for representation they didn't need or want. Airline unions pursued our other employee groups as well, but none succeeded in organizing any of them, for many of the same reasons the pilots opted against representation.

When a new airline called People Express launched from its Newark Airport hub in April 1981, we enjoyed a second round of publicity on the heels of that company's inaugural campaign. There was no direct competition between us (People Express initially served routes to Norfolk, Buffalo, and Columbus), but because New York Air was trafficking in such high-profile, media-dominated markets, we could hardly go unmentioned in any of the articles or news spots that trumpeted the birth of a new low-cost airline.

Also getting attention was the fact that People Express was the brainchild of Don Burr, who had been TIA's president for a year before quitting in January 1980. Don had been with TIA since 1973, and he left because he wanted to make his own mark in the industry by starting a new carrier, a move made possible by airline deregulation. When Don joined us, he had no airline operating experience, since he ran an investment company devoted to aviation. But he proved to be a quick study, learning the industry well at TIA. He had also participated in the planning meetings we held internally on starting a new airline. He had done yeoman work in directing operations, particularly when Bob and

I were up to our ears with the National deal, but Don was the kind of guy who needed to run his own show.

However, what bothered me a lot about Don's leaving was that it signaled the end of a good friendship. He had been best man at our wedding; we had vacationed together with our families; and just two months before he quit, Don and I both made our first try at the New York City Marathon after doing a good bit of our training together. We even crossed the finish line nearly simultaneously, in a little more than four hours.

When Don left TIA, he took our head of planning, Gerry Gitner, with him. He also took a few of our ideas, including a concept we had developed called "unbundling," a catchall term we used to describe the way we separated our various services and attached a price to each one, almost like the "options" tacked on to the manufacturer's suggested retail price of a new car. People Express took the concept to what was then an extreme by charging passengers extra for everything, even for coffee and tea. At the time, it seemed like an innovative way to pass on cost savings to the consumer, and it succeeded, at least at first, in whetting passenger appetites for absolute no-frills service and extremely low prices. Of course, the fees hated by today's fliers are an outgrowth of this unbundling strategy.

The initial popularity of New York Air and People Express struck fear into the hearts of airline executives around the country. At the time of our launch, Frank Borman claimed that New York Air wouldn't last six months, a prediction that became a kind of rallying point for our employees. When June rolled around, we celebrated our six-month "half anniversary" with a party at the New York Sheraton for the eight hundred or so workers who had been able to get the evening off. Neal Meehan hired a Frank Borman look-alike to appear at our party and say a few words of congratulations at the podium—where he was smacked in the face with a whipped-cream pie. The crowd went crazy. Later we found out that most of our people had been fooled and had thought our "special guest" was the real Frank Borman.

The press at the time foretold doom for the major airlines, and most of our competitors were hard at work developing their own low-cost subsidiaries so they could keep up with us. The airline unions, however, acted quickly to forestall those efforts by jumping into labor negotiations with demands for a new restriction: airlines could no longer set up "alter-ego" operations, as they were called, without hiring new employees in accordance with existing labor contracts and seniority rosters. Not surprisingly, no other airline set up an affiliated carrier under these conditions.

The major airlines were out to undermine our efforts in any way they could. Phil Bakes, who spent a lot of time flying in and out of New York and Washington during New York Air's start-up phase, noticed something unusual on those flights. Phil flew on the nonrevenue passes generally extended to senior executives of other airlines, and because Eastern Airlines had the only nonstop flights from Houston to New York and Washington at the time, he flew on Eastern. On a number of

New York Air cartoon depicting new flights (1982).

Sunday-evening flights, he saw the familiar faces of TIA's union organizers and members of ALPA's master executive council, composed of representatives from all major airlines. Sometimes there were as many as a dozen union leaders on his flights, and his continual sightings confirmed what we fully expected: Eastern was so nervous about our entry into the shuttle market that it was helping the unions by offering their representatives free travel passes.

---

By March 1981, we had introduced four new daily flights in the New York–Washington corridor and begun new nonstop service between Washington and Boston. In April, we extended service to Cleveland, with our sights set on Detroit, Pittsburgh, Columbus, and Buffalo in the months ahead. We even thought about establishing another start-up airline on the West Coast, where a San Francisco hub could offer commuter-type service to suburban areas of Los Angeles, San Diego, and Sacramento with growth potential for routes to Portland, Seattle, and Las Vegas. We evaluated the potential start-up San Francisco Air, and for a while it appeared that we might be able to get it off the ground—but it was not to be.

It was such an exciting time for us, but it came to an abrupt halt. On August 5, 1981, the 13,000 members of the Professional Air Traffic Controllers Organization (PATCO) walked off their jobs, in violation of laws prohibiting strikes by federal government employees. When all but 1,300 of the controllers ignored President Ronald Reagan's order to return to work within forty-eight hours, the striking controllers were fired and banned for life from federal employment. It had to be the most ill-advised labor action in the history of collective bargaining, and it was certainly the one with the most far-reaching consequences, but Reagan was that rare president who meant what he said.

Chaos ensued at airports all over the country as supervisors and military flight controllers tried gamely to fill in for the missing workers. Flight schedules were slashed at twenty-two of the country's most congested airports so that the fill-in controllers and freshly hired train-ees could acclimate themselves to the control towers. New York Air was affected profoundly because our business was based in two of the country's busiest airports, LaGuardia and National, where the FAA was forced to cancel a significant number of flights. We were compelled to give up our regular hourly schedules, and we even eliminated our Boston route for a short time just to shore up our Washington service. That was devastating, because we had already invested so much to penetrate the Boston market.

The resulting delays out of LaGuardia had a particular impact on short-haul traffic, driving many travelers to consider ground transpor-tation until conditions returned to normal. The delays were so long, in fact, that we had to apply for special permission to occasionally replen-ish our ice, beer, and soda stores *before takeoff* without losing our place in line. When there are twenty-six other planes in front of you await-ing clearance, it makes sense to commence your beverage service while you're still on the ground.

We watched helplessly as the larger carriers managed to turn the calamity to their advantage. Most of the FAA's scheduling cuts were made on the basis of an across-the-board percentage, and Eastern was big enough to absorb the canceled flights throughout its system while maintaining its regular shuttle schedule. It was even able to deploy its larger 260-seat A300 jets on its Boston–New York shuttle runs, pulling the neat trick of expanding capacity (and absorbing our former passen-gers) while trimming back its overall schedule to meet the emergency requirements as the FAA defined them.

Even some smaller upstart carriers, including Midway Airlines, based at Chicago's uncongested Midway Airport, were able to survive the controllers' strike relatively unscathed. United aggressively pro-moted its own low-cost Friendship Express service from LaGuardia to Cleveland, matching New York Air's fares and schedules once it was clear that our arrival in that market would be delayed indefinitely.

We were unlucky all around. As a new airline, we had geared ourselves for growth—with several new planes arriving shortly, new routes in development, several classes of new employees in training, and even a new West Coast operation in the planning phase—and all these efforts ground to a halt because of a slowdown in air traffic that lasted for the better part of a year. One moment, before the PATCO strike, we were flying high; the next, we were scrambling to stay in business.

On top of all this uncertainty, we were also distracted by events taking place on the other side of the Texas Air empire.

# CHAPTER SEVEN

# The Continental Acquisition

*An Epic Battle*
*1979–1983*

I N NOVEMBER 1979, Continental Airlines (CAL) held its annual board meeting at Houston's Warwick Hotel. I was invited to attend a reception at the local Hyatt Hotel on the evening of the meeting, because Texas International was an important feed partner in Houston for Continental. In each corner of the room was food from one of Continental's destinations, and somewhere between the Hawaiian luau and the Cajun cook-off, I bumped into Jay Pritzker, chairman of Hyatt Hotels Corporation and a Continental board member.

Jay and I had known each other for more than ten years at that point, ever since I tried to interest him in the BWIA deal in 1967, and our conversation quickly turned to Continental's sagging bottom line and questionable future. It was then that Jay quietly suggested to me that what Continental really needed was an energetic young group like ours. He added, "What this place needs is to be taken over by guys like you." I asked whether he thought small guys like us could ever pull off something like that, and he said there was plenty of financing available for deals of this type, provided that the acquiring company had good management.

Naturally, he made it clear that he wasn't speaking for anybody else at Continental. Nobody on the board was aware of his comment—certainly not Bob Six, who would not have been happy. But Continental's financial condition was bordering on precarious. I knew it was in Jay's nature to always be thinking in terms of deals, and of course we had already evaluated the possibility of a linkup with CAL. But it was really a strong confidence-building moment for me that a very successful guy such as Jay would think that this kind of deal was doable for guys like us.

To its employees and loyal passengers, CAL was known as "the proud bird with the golden tail." Its founder and chairman, Bob Six, was one of the last remaining pioneers of the prewar aviation industry. Six took over a small regional airmail carrier in 1936 and ambitiously renamed it for the Continental Divide, the north-south axis from El Paso to Denver along which he hoped to operate. Continental Airlines went on to build a fine reputation for service, but as airline deregulation took hold, its financial performance had been poor, and it seemingly lacked any direction.

Perhaps the biggest structural problem CAL faced was that it lacked a dominant market position in its principal cities. The emerging consensus under deregulation was that a viable airline in the new competitive environment needed a commanding market presence in at least one airport—a principal hub where its market position in terms of flights and numbers of passengers was so powerful that a competitor could not swoop in, add flights, and undercut its fares. The industry was beginning to refer to these as "fortress hubs." At the time, Delta had a strong one in Atlanta, and United had a large, profitable one in Chicago. But Continental's presence in Denver, where it did have a modest concentration of flights, was not particularly secure: it faced strong competition from the larger United and the smaller, more agile Frontier Airlines. Los Angeles, which Continental called home, also had a lot of competition, and CAL was a relatively minor player there. CAL was largely a hodgepodge group of routes scattered in the West, and it faced cutthroat price competition in just about every market it served. Its results showed it.

At the time of my chat with Jay Pritzker, Continental was also reeling from a series of unfortunate setbacks that had only exacerbated this problem. A bid it had made to merge with Western in 1978, which would at least have strengthened Continental's market share in Denver, had been rejected by the CAB over antitrust concerns. Then, in the summer of 1979, the FAA grounded almost half of Continental's fleet after an engine fell off an American Airlines DC-10. The plane crashed in Chicago shortly after takeoff, killing 273 people, and the FAA immediately stopped all DC-10 flights until July 13, when it determined that the engines were safe. (The probable cause of the accident was faulty maintenance.) It was Continental's misfortune that it was heavily invested in the DC-10 and was forced to cancel hundreds of flights during the summer travel season as a result.

Continental would close 1979 with a loss of more than $13 million ($56 million in 2024 dollars). Its stock had stagnated at around $10 per share, which gave the company a relatively meager market value, even for those days, of approximately $150 million. The equity in Continental's fleet was probably worth around three times that amount, so on those terms alone, a play for Continental looked very attractive.

A short while after the Continental board reception, we began buying some CAL shares. I still wasn't keen on making a hostile move for the company, but I wanted to enter into any negotiations with at least an investment position so that we might have the opportunity for a modest profit if a deal didn't materialize.

———————————

I made my first overture to Bob Six the following week, in a phone call to his Los Angeles office. "Bob," I said, "I think we should talk about where our two companies are going." This was pretty much my standard opening in a discussion of this type. It covered all the bases. After a few minutes of conversation, Bob invited me to his home in Beverly Hills for dinner during the first week in December. When the appointed day came around, I hopped on a TIA flight to Los Angeles, rented a car, and drove out to his address. Unfortunately, my navigating skills, in those non-GPS days, were no match for Beverly Hills, so I pulled into the Beverly Hills Hotel to call and ask for directions.

Bob's wife answered the phone. "What are you doing in town?" she said. "We're expecting you next week."

"Next week?" I said. "I'm in Beverly Hills and was headed to your place tonight. I was calling for directions."

"Oh, my," she said. "We have a house full of company. Let me put Bob on to sort things out."

Bob insisted that I had gotten the date screwed up and that he had no time to see me. I thought he might have at least tried to squeeze me in for breakfast or coffee the next morning, considering that I had made the long trip and would likely stay the night, but he said he didn't have the time. While I was put off by the mix-up and Bob's intractability, I didn't press the matter. When you're in the courting position on a deal, you're sometimes made to swallow certain etiquette lapses if you hope to achieve your goals, and there was no point in getting these discussions off on the wrong foot. I simply confirmed our appointment for the following week and caught the next flight home.

I retraced my steps one week later (this time with proper directions) and arrived at Bob's doorstep in Beverly Hills at the appointed hour. Bob's wife, actress Audrey Meadows, was best known for her role as Alice in Jackie Gleason's famous television series *The Honeymooners*. Sharon and I first met Audrey during the 1977 deregulation hearings in the Senate, and Sharon's favorite story from that time involves Audrey's taking her aside to offer some words of advice about being the wife of an airline executive. "Honey," she told Sharon, "keep your suitcase packed, and keep your eye on that man!"

The Sixes were delightful hosts. Audrey regaled me with tales of her Hollywood friends, and Bob held forth on his early days at Continental. He capped off the meal by offering me one of his fine Cuban cigars, and we retired to his study. There, I laid out a plan to merge our operations, which would create strong hubs with market power in Houston and

Denver. Our short-haul planes, which Continental lacked, would complement Continental's long-haul airliners, and our combined national marketing strength would help broaden our passenger base. The joint airline, I said, would fly under the Continental name. This last detail, I knew, would appeal to Six's pride, but it also made good business sense. Continental was clearly better known, while our Texas name was hardly appropriate for a national carrier.

However, I sensed that, much like Ed Smart at TWA, Bob thought we were too small-time to do business with. He listened to me patiently because his airline was in trouble, but he was clearly a status-oriented guy, with high-class friends, a world-class art collection, and a first-class airline humbled by hard times. It was clear during our meeting that he looked on TIA as a low-class operation, and after our public plays for National and TWA, he probably saw me as a sort of corporate raider as well.

Bob closed the evening by agreeing to look over our feed numbers and promising to get back to me. He also confirmed what I had suspected: he was about to hand off his president's job and remain with Continental as a nonexecutive board chairman. His handpicked successor, Al Feldman, the former head of Frontier Airlines, would later prove to be a relentless and tenacious opponent of a Continental–TIA merger—literally to his dying day.

———————

All through 1980, we continued to hold a considerable number of shares of Continental stock, never exceeding the 4.9 percent ownership threshold that would have required us to reveal our holdings or intentions. There was a great deal of activity in airline stocks during this period, and we moved in and out of our position according to market fluctuations. Under Feldman, Continental's stock price was particularly volatile, thanks to a strike threat by its flight attendants, persistent rumors that Continental was ripe for takeover, and a renewed merger agreement with Western Airlines, engineered and signed by Feldman.

The first merger attempt with Western had been rejected, but now, with deregulation, Continental thought a merger stood a good chance of getting government approval, so it went ahead with its second attempt.

A merger with Western would make Continental much less attractive to us, however. There was no logic to it, as we saw it, because combining the routes and resources of both carriers would only exacerbate the problems of each. Within our management group, we likened the merger to throwing a bowling ball to a drowning man to help him stay afloat. But if we were genuinely interested in pursuing Continental, it had become clear that we would have to move quickly. We would have to either attempt to block the Western merger or exit our position without losing money, since CAL stock was already weakening because of the prospect of a Western merger.

As of November 1980, just a month before we launched New York Air, we owned 4.24 percent of Continental—651,700 shares purchased at an average price of $9.19. Like our initial National purchases, the Continental stock was acquired in blocks small enough to avoid attention, and with a fairly modest investment of just under $6 million, we were well positioned to make a move—if we saw there was a move to be made.

Our opportunity came soon enough, but we nearly missed it. On Tuesday, February 3, 1981, an administrative law judge recommended that the CAB approve the Continental–Western merger, and time appeared to be running out on a bid from us. Normally, such a recommendation would have dissuaded us from any additional activity, but Feldman had left the door open by choosing to postpone the shareholder vote on the merger until *after* receiving formal CAB approval. In the previous merger attempt, Western and Continental each spent more than $500,000 on special shareholder meetings, but the votes had been rendered moot by the CAB's ultimate rejection. This time, the two airlines wanted to make sure this cost was justified and put off their votes until the meetings were clearly needed. Because of this, there was still time to put together a TIA offer.

Conveniently, on that Friday, February 6, our investment bankers tracked me down in Washington, DC, with our first real cloudburst opportunity. John Morgan of Smith Barney pulled me from a meeting of the trustees of the Wolf Trap performing arts center at 2:00 p.m. I have always had a fondness for music and found my Wolf Trap association very rewarding, but on this day, I was distracted. John informed me that Batterymarch, a large Boston mutual fund that had long been a Continental shareholder, was eager to part with its position because of the pending Western merger.

I had previously polled our board on this eventuality and was therefore in a position to respond, but I nevertheless had some real concerns. It was one thing to talk to our directors about a possibly academic share purchase. It was quite another to push the button. I could not imagine what consequences we'd be setting in motion. We knew that acquiring Continental would be a real fight. We had just started New York Air and knew the cash requirements it took. TIA was losing plenty of cash on its own. A dedicated purchase would clearly leave us stretched. But I swallowed hard and gave the go-ahead an hour later. We were off and running. We wound up more than doubling our holdings with two block purchases that afternoon—the first of 420,500 shares at $10.75, made just fifteen minutes before the market closed, and a second of 380,000 shares at $11.25, made only five minutes ahead of the closing bell—leaving us with nearly 1.5 million shares.

We now owned a 9.5 percent stake in Continental and could gain effective control of the airline by making a tender offer for the balance of its shares. I liked our chances, because nearly one-third of Continental equity was held by institutional investors who, we had heard, were unhappy with a Western merger and would likely be delighted to unload the stock. Our investment bankers wanted to price a tender offer, which we planned for Monday morning, at $14 per share, but I was pushing for $12. We had already paid a premium for the bulk of our current position, and I wasn't terribly eager to go over the $11.25-per-share price we had paid for our previous block. We wound up agreeing to a tender offer of $13 per share, which was a 30 percent bump over the market price prior to our purchases.

As a courtesy, I put in separate calls to Six and Feldman that Sunday evening, informing them of our upcoming tender announcement and expressing our hope that a deal could be accomplished on mutually agreeable terms. Both men were cool to me, to say the least, although neither seemed surprised. The following morning, Monday, February 9, 1981, we publicly announced our 9.5 percent position in Continental Airlines and a tender offer for the purchase of up to six million shares, subject to financing, with a planned purchase date of March 6. The completed tender would bring our holdings to 48.5 percent of the company, and with the proxies we would obtain, we would likely be able to defeat the vote on the Western merger.

"Subject to financing," however, was a big concern for us, so that afternoon I flew to New York with Rob Snedeker, our finance head, to meet with John McGillicuddy, CEO of Manufacturers Hanover. We had an initial indication that Manufacturers Hanover believed in what we were doing, so the firm was our principal hope for the financing we needed to complete the tender. It was important that we eliminate the financing contingency in our offer quickly, since the arbitrageurs, so essential in a tender offer, wouldn't go forward and acquire shares if there was a financing risk in place. Our meeting with McGillicuddy and his key folks didn't last long. He really wanted to get a feel for us and our plans; it was there that I learned the meaning of what bankers call a "face loan"—a loan granted largely on the basis of a meeting with principals. After the meeting, Rob and I went back to the small office we kept in New York and received a call to say that the loan had been approved. Great news!

---

Continental management checked in with its objections to our tender offer almost immediately, filing suit in US District Court in Los Angeles later that week seeking to bar TIA from interfering with its proposed merger with Western. The Continental board also voted unanimously to reject our offer, relying at least nominally on the opinion of the

Lehman Brothers brokerage house that the financial terms of our deal were "grossly inadequate." Al Feldman and company also filed a formal petition with the CAB to block us from any further trading in Continental stock until the matter was resolved.

This was all new territory in the airline industry. Bob Six was a product of the old-line brotherhood of airline managers in which rivals behaved like colleagues who left one another to mind their own business. Most of Feldman's airline experience had been with heavily subsidized Frontier Airlines in the years prior to deregulation, where he had been, to a great extent, insulated from the realities of the free market. Continental was still Six's baby, and the Western merger was Feldman's attempt to rescue that baby. Neither one wanted an outsider such as TIA stepping all over their legacies—nor did their board, which supported their position in the public battle that would drag on for the ensuing six months.

On March 2, the CAB approved the Continental–Western merger. It also granted TIA permission to increase its holdings to 48.5 percent and establish a limited voting trust, as we had in the National deal. For both parties to the takeover, it was a good news–bad news bulletin. We had hoped the Western bid would be rejected, as it had been the first time around, because it diminished competition, but the board was convinced that, with each carrier on such shaky ground, the risk to the public was greater without a merger.

Continental immediately scheduled its special shareholder vote on the merger for March 12, which gave us only ten days to gather our votes against the Western deal. Time, once again, was working against us. With the shareholder vote scheduled so soon after our tender deadline, we would have little time to resolicit votes, if necessary. Ultimately, this turned out not to be a problem. Our tender was oversubscribed. We actually collected two-thirds of the outstanding shares, but of course we could only buy up to the 48.5 percent limit approved by the CAB.

Feldman, meanwhile, kept pressing his case wherever he could get a hearing and began a frantic fishing expedition for another investor to top our offer. But no other investor surfaced, and since there were no court orders to stop our bid, after clearing our targeted shares, we went through and closed our tender as planned.

Continental did not exactly hold the door open for us after our purchases. Feldman indefinitely postponed the March 12 shareholder meeting, since it was clear that we had the requisite majority, and sought a preliminary injunction against our takeover in US District Court in Los Angeles. Continental also petitioned the federal court of appeals in Washington to overturn the CAB decision allowing us to purchase our 48.5 percent stake.

We saw these initial moves as garden-variety stalling tactics and remained hopeful that we would complete our acquisition in due course, and on reasonable terms. To this end, I arranged a meeting with Feldman to discuss the possibility of a negotiated merger. Over dinner at the Beverly Hills Hotel, I told him that we were eager to proceed on a friendly basis and suggested that he was an ideal candidate to head whatever new entity might emerge from our acquisition. In fact, he was, in my eyes. Al Feldman had an excellent reputation, and from what I had seen, he possessed a sharp, analytical mind, strong leadership skills, and an innovative philosophy of motivational management.

Regrettably, Feldman refused my overtures, and a few days later, he publicly distorted this dinner conversation to the point where he claimed that I tried to bribe him with a job offer and a substantial salary increase if only he would acquiesce to our takeover. That wasn't the case at all, and Feldman knew it, although in retrospect I suppose I should have waited before discussing the management situation with Continental's chief executive.

---

Not long afterward, we learned the true depths of Continental's desperation and its willingness to virtually destroy the company in an effort to keep us out. Rather than allow us, owners of a majority of the company's shares, to assume control after DOT approval, Continental management proposed a preposterous plan to hand Continental over to its employees by issuing additional shares. Under a scheme hatched with Continental's ALPA union, 51 percent ownership of Continental would pass to its employees in the form of an employee stock ownership plan, or ESOP. Continental employees, in turn, would agree to a 15 percent giveback in salaries spread over the following four to seven years. Continental management helped the ESOP group tentatively arrange for $185 million in financing from a consortium of nine banks and prepared to issue 15.4 million new shares of common stock, which would have reduced our ownership position to approximately 25 percent, thus being a killer to the merger and our stock position because of the enormous dilution in value without anything approaching reasonable compensation.

Don't get me wrong: I believe in ESOPs. We had an employee stock plan at TIA because we believed that there is nothing like the motivation of ownership to increase productivity and boost employee morale. But this particular ESOP, which turned over control of the entire company in one fell swoop in return for a promise of lower salaries and more debt issuance, was clearly an illegal ploy. It had never been done before and was beyond the scope of ESOP legislation that had been previously enacted by Congress.

Nevertheless, we worried that the ESOP might be railroaded through without a shareholder vote, even if it meant that the stock would be delisted from the stock exchange. We fought it on every conceivable front: at the New York Stock Exchange, at the California Department of Corporations, and on Capitol Hill, where a rider in support of the ESOP had been attached to President Reagan's tax bill. Also giving us pause was that President Reagan and members of his cabinet were good friends with Bob and Audrey Six, given their shared Beverly Hills credentials. In fact, the Sixes and other prominent figures were members of an informal group of advisers often referred to as Reagan's Kitchen Cabinet.

We also filed suit in US District Court in Los Angeles against Continental. We sought to enjoin the company from issuing any new stock and charged that CAL's management was in breach of its fiduciary duties and "engaged in gross mismanagement by authorizing the expenditure of substantial corporate funds and the allocation of other valuable corporate resources to the development and promotion of the proposed ESOP." The employee stock ownership plan, we argued, was nothing more than a Continental management protection plan that burdened the company with an enormous amount of debt for little consideration.

At first, we deliberately avoided a shouting match, but then Feldman forced our hand. He took to writing misleading letters to me and releasing them to news services before delivering them to my office. In one such public letter, he derided the resulting debt-equity ratio of a combined TIA–Continental but failed to mention that the vast majority of the burdensome short-term, high-interest debt would be inherited from Continental or that TIA's resources would contribute plenty of cash to the resulting company.

We felt that we had no choice but to respond in kind, and on April 14, I sent a lengthy reply to his charges, which I also released to the press. I concluded:

> I am surprised that Continental management has all of a sudden taken such interest in employee stock ownership. Texas International has had an employee stock ownership plan for some time while Continental has not had a meaningful one. The stock ownership plan currently being promised to the employees of Continental is instead a management protection plan. If successful, the plan will operate to entrench current management, dilute existing shareholders by 50 percent, create a corporate liability on your balance sheet of $185 million, jeopardize the company's ability to finance itself in the future and its status as a New York Stock Exchange listed company, and subject the company and its directors to civil and potential criminal liability. It is a base perversion of the ESOP concept.

At the same time, since we had become very concerned about the risks to us if the ESOP gained approval, we also began the process of talking to Continental through our lawyers about possibly selling our shares back to the airline. In truth, I was really worried about the devastating effect a ruling allowing the ESOP could have on our company. I knew that Continental management didn't seem concerned about how they kept us out and therefore would not let any sane business judgment stand in their way.

The ESOP wasn't the only argument for shedding our stake: revenues were down throughout the industry, and Continental was losing mountains of money. The brief flight attendants' strike of December 1980 and the ensuing turmoil surrounding our tender offer and the potential merger with Western was alarming enough to chase many passengers to other carriers, and resources were clearly spread thin by this transparent management push for employee ownership.

For a time, the most compelling reason to sell our interest had to do with the waffling of the New York Stock Exchange on the ESOP. Word of a Continental deal with the NYSE was so persistent that we were expecting the news to flash across the Dow Jones ticker at any time. I'll never forget the long nervous walk into our general counsel's office for an update on the morning when the frightening word was due to come down from the NYSE. Thankfully, it never came, and the NYSE wound up rejecting the move, but this was only a first-step victory. It might have ended the matter were Feldman and company unwilling to risk delisting from the exchange, but Continental management seemed prepared to flout the NYSE requirements designed to protect the rights and investments of shareholders. Feldman's group also investigated the possibility of relisting on the American Stock Exchange only to discover that a shareholder vote would also be required there; they even looked to trading as an over-the-counter issue.

We could not recognize a reasonable strategy here, because there wasn't one. It was only to allow approval of the stock issued to the ESOP. The delisting of Continental stock would have succeeded in diminishing the value of outstanding shares, eroding investor confidence, and inhibiting the airline's ability to obtain financing, but these appeared not to matter in Continental's all-out quest to keep us out of the boardroom and preserve control.

Once the NYSE ruled against Continental, management looked to the California Department of Corporations to overturn the ruling, but we were heartened to find support for our position there as well. Frankly, as an out-of-state corporation, we weren't expecting a favorable outcome, particularly in a case that on its face appealed to the prolabor positions the state commission had supported in the past. But the rights of shareholders were again judged to prevail over the rights of a puppeteered employee group seeking to simply quash an outside investor.

Next, we had to turn to Washington, where a rider to the Senate version of Reagan's tax bill was being prepared to help the Continental ESOP. If passed, the amended bill might have reversed the California ruling and put the ESOP back in business. The rider was cosponsored by Arizona Republican senator Dennis DeConcini, whose brother-in-law was a Continental pilot, and Senator Russell Long, a Louisiana Democrat, who had long been a staunch proponent of previous ESOP legislation.

I set my sights on Long. Thanks to TIA's service to New Orleans and the Gulf Coast, we were of significant interest to his constituents, and I took advantage of our position in Long's home state to make our case directly to the senator. I met alone with him one afternoon upstairs at the Capitol, in one of the small rooms presumably reserved for confidential chats such as this one. I laid out our situation, careful to emphasize that we had supported ESOPs in the past and stressing that it was only this particular plan—in reality a management entrenchment plan—that we found so objectionable.

"Frank," the senator finally said after hearing me out, "I have to tell you, I'm very supportive of your position, but I'm not very big on taking a shower of shit."

I took the colorful phrasing to mean that our cause wasn't politically helpful to Long. He thought most of his voters could get behind the plight of beleaguered employees trying to improve their situation, but shareholders stood in the minds of most as little more than grubby capitalists. ESOPs, to Long, were apple pie and motherhood, even if this one was just smoke and mirrors, and he made it plain where his best interests lay.

Our own lawsuit didn't quite turn out as planned, either. I honestly thought our attorneys made a strong case against the ESOP, which we charged was in violation of the Securities Act of 1933, the Securities Exchange Act of 1934, and the Railway Labor Act. The plan was simply unconscionable, and I was convinced an injunction would be forthcoming, but it wasn't, because the court refused to block the issuance of new stock.

---

It was during this time that we actively started discussions with Continental about selling our shares back to the airline. Selling would of course have been a major defeat of our plans but would have given us a possibly clean exit from what had obviously become a very complicated and messy situation. Continental's financial results for the first half of 1981 were discouraging, with losses of $34.7 million and growing. Given that there was so much bad blood over the ESOP plan and the calculating way it was "sold" to employees, and given the hostility directed at me personally, I was concerned about our chances for labor peace, assuming we ever did win control. Pyrrhic victories were not on my most-wanted list.

In this climate, I was open to the idea of a buyout, even if it meant taking some loss on our stock position. Continental shares had dipped substantially since our March tender offer, trading down into the $9 range. That summer, I met with Feldman more than once to discuss the sale of our interest, since he was eager to get a deal done. Finally, in mid-July, at the Beverly Hills Hotel, we came to an agreement. In lieu of some of the cash, we would accept an LA office complex Continental was trying to unload. With this arrangement, we could emerge from our position close to whole. Depending to some extent on the price we could get for the building, the deal was worth approximately $12 per share, which left us with a $2 million loss on our investment of around $95 million. All the deal needed was approval from CAL's bankers and the lawyers' final blessing. The projected loss seemed like a small price to pay for getting out from under what had become a highly risky and nearly unworkable position.

A lot of our people were pushing me to take the money and run if we could—particularly Bob Carney, who tended to be the most conservative of our group—and I was finally persuaded to eat the short-term loss, concede the success of the ESOP ruse, and accept Feldman's offer. We even shook hands on the deal and left it to the lawyers to draft the papers.

And that, we thought, was that. I went back to our hotel room to break the news to Sharon, who had accompanied me on this trip. "Let's order up some champagne," I said. "We just sold our shares back to Continental." It wasn't much of a celebration, but I must admit I felt a tremendous sense of relief at the prospect of putting the whole acquisition behind us as quickly as possible.

However, I woke the next morning to learn that the deal was off. Continental's lawyers insisted that the transaction needed to go to a shareholder vote, which was a deal-killer for us. A quick exit was the chief benefit of selling at a modest loss. But we were not about to wait months for a shareholder vote, then risk having the offer rejected, since it was likely that we wouldn't be allowed to vote our shares. Of course, the contradiction in the CAL lawyers' position didn't escape our notice: they apparently didn't see the need for a shareholder vote under the ESOP plan, which would have diluted the company by 50 percent and left it in a much-weakened financial position, but they required one for the purchase of shares from a 50 percent shareholder.

On July 20, the CAB granted our merger preliminary approval, and the only remaining hope for Feldman and the Continental side lay in Sacramento, where California's legislators were actively reconsidering the state's corporations department ruling requiring a full shareholder vote for the ESOP. The ESOP financing also needed final sign-off from the banks that were providing the financing.

I was also back in Los Angeles during the week of August 3, not only to see whether there was any other potential resolution, but also to visit CAL and go over various issues at the company, because we were then expecting the final CAB approval for our deal in the following days. Al Feldman and I spent several productive hours together, talking about some of the aircraft decisions and management moves facing the company. He even offered to drive me to the airport in his years-old Mercedes coupe, which I accepted. I was flying back that Thursday to Nantucket, where my family was spending the summer. The paradox of my relationship with Al was that privately we talked together as friends would while the public perception was very different. On our drive to the airport, he smiled at various times when describing things and was very pleasant.

I will never forget what transpired over the ensuing few days. Back in Nantucket, on Saturday evening, Sharon answered a call from Feldman, who sounded strange to her. When I got on the phone, all Al had to say was that the bank consortium had decided to reject the financing for the ESOP, thus essentially killing it. He sounded really surprised and upset.

The next day, Sunday, August 9, I flew to Sacramento for a Monday morning meeting with legislators. Phil Bakes and I had made plans to lobby the legislature and state our case for shareholder rights and the merger. Although the financing appeared to be dead, we could not be sure that there wasn't some other scheme that CAL's lawyers would concoct, so we went ahead with our plans, although I hated to leave beautiful Nantucket and the family on a Sunday morning.

---

When I arrived at the hotel in Sacramento that Sunday evening, I found a note from Phil Bakes waiting for me at the front desk. "Frank," it said. "Call me; it's important." When I called Phil, he told me that Al

Feldman had taken his own life. For a moment, the truth of this message was too much to take. I would soon learn that earlier that day, while working alone in his office in Los Angeles, Feldman had drafted a press release announcing that the consortium of banks had pulled out of the ESOP bid. He wrote personal letters to his attorneys, to his children, and to his secretary, and then he shot himself.

I could not understand how a seemingly rational man could be driven to such a desperate act in a short space of time, but apparently Feldman had long been distraught over the death of his wife, who had succumbed to cancer just a few months after he took the Continental job. To cope, he immersed himself in his work, protecting his new charges from our unwanted advances. Then, with the loss of financing for his ESOP plan, his will to live seemed to disappear. Faced with defeat in this professional fight, he could no longer distract himself from his previous personal loss—or so it appeared. The long ordeal had, quite literally, taken the life out of him.

Shocked and deeply saddened, I immediately called Bob Six to offer my condolences. Bob and I remained on very good terms throughout the messy takeover, almost as though we were both trying to stay above the fray. He seemed quite moved by the day's events, as could be expected. Privately, my initial impulse regarding Continental was to simply abandon the whole deal. My enthusiasm for it was gone.

The following morning, I woke early and drove by myself to San Francisco. I had no agenda; I just needed to get away from the commotion surrounding the news and reflect on this tragic turn myself. I honestly didn't know what to make of Feldman's suicide, but I didn't feel much like talking to anyone, even to any of our own people, until I had a chance to sort things through in my head.

In the silence of the car, I kept going over the situation to see if there was any key to understanding what would cause a good man to respond to his troubles in this way. I had no clue. As my mind raced over our various conversations, I saw nothing to hint that Feldman was ready to burst. He was always kind of a quiet guy—a little aloof, a little reserved in showing his emotions. But this didn't tell me anything.

Most of the top airline executives I knew were pretty much the same way. So was I.

Then I started to look a little deeper at the aspects of his personality Al did allow himself to reveal, but again, I didn't have much to go on. He was affable, but I had only seen him operate superficially. He may have been loose and friendly in business situations, but I never knew anyone who had a relationship with him on personal terms. I used to think that Al kept a smile on his face but never allowed himself to laugh.

Clearly, Al was a very thorough, rational guy, even in contemplating such an irrational act. It was later reported that he applied for a firearms permit just two weeks before he committed suicide. Then he was made to sit through the state-mandated waiting period before buying his gun. If these things were true, I could not imagine any more telling example of his precise behavior. He was in control of his emotions and his actions until the very end.

As I drove to San Francisco, I also thought back to the 1971 suicide of the Mohawk Airlines founder, Bob Peach. It was strange, almost eerie, thinking about the two incidents side by side. Of course, Feldman and Peach were two very different people, and the circumstances surrounding their deaths were alike only in the result, but I couldn't help linking the two. I had come into contact with Peach during our days pursuing the Mohawk Airlines deal and noted that he appeared somewhat neurotic, to my way of thinking.

I also remembered the suicide of one of my Harvard classmates, a guy with whom I once drove across the country en route to our summer jobs in California and whom I thought I knew well. Two years later, his new wife found him hanging from a curtain rod, and when I heard the news, I had a hard time reconciling it with the balanced, clearheaded, and hard-nosed fellow who accompanied me on that long drive.

It had been ten years since Peach's death and nearly twenty since my friend's, but only ten hours since Feldman's passing. The news was still fresh, and I wasn't sure how to process it. For a long time I felt responsible, telling myself that if we had not made a run at Continental he might not have been pushed to this extreme. I'm not sure that I ever saw any real cause and effect, but it was tough to perceive things clearly. Al Feldman was not just some guy with whom I had done business. He was someone I had known for a good while. He was part of my professional life even before Continental, and now it seemed he would be part of it forever after.

———————————

The final pieces of our deal fell into place following Al Feldman's death. On August 14, 1981, the CAB granted final approval of our acquisition, clearing the way for what we hoped would be President Reagan's rubber-stamp approval, which was needed because international routes were involved. Still, there was some concern among our group that Bob Six's influential friends in Reagan's Kitchen Cabinet would find a way to scotch our deal at the last moment.

Our concerns were unfounded, but it took time to discover that. While our paperwork snaked its way to the Oval Office, Reagan had his hands unexpectedly full with other airline matters—the beginning of the PATCO air controllers' strike, which would hobble the entire industry—and by the time he got around to approving our purchase, Continental's fortunes had taken yet another downturn.

We had already acquired another block of shares, bringing our holdings to 50.3 percent in a symbolic move anticipating the president's endorsement, leaving us to shoulder the devastating PATCO strike on three fronts: at struggling TIA, at New York Air, and at Continental Airlines, of which we were now the principal owners. It was not the best time to be in the airline business, and we were in it deeply.

There was, I noticed, a certain resignation on both sides after Al's suicide, and the gentle treatment of the acquisition in the press may have resulted from it. Our takeover had been big, cliff-hanging news for some time, but after Al's death it was being written about as a fait accompli, and I think Continental management and employees finally began to accept it as such.

As it played out, the PATCO strike presented only a temporary worry. However, we grew even more concerned over Continental's worsening results. Unfortunately, we were also given the cold shoulder by CAL's management when we attempted to get involved. Despite our formal clearances in Washington, the Continental board refused to recognize our majority interest. Normally, in hostile transactions of this type, the new principal shareholders are usually allowed to make immediate appointments to the board, particularly in cases such as ours, given our majority ownership position.

But Continental, which was incorporated in Nevada, where state laws did not require the relinquishing of control until the expiration of the incumbent directors' one-year terms, was effectively legally shielded. It was one thing to be kept from operational control during the waiting period before the terms ended, but quite another to be made to do so without at least a voice on the board of directors.

While there was nothing legally that we could do, we were able to negotiate with Six and George Warde, Feldman's successor, and reached a kind of standstill agreement allowing us to name three directors for the interim period—me; Phil Bakes, who at the time was executive vice president of Texas Air Corporation; and John Robson, the former CAB chairman who had become a trusted friend and adviser. The agreement also set the terms for the acquisition of the remaining Continental shares.

The appointments were significant, because we had some very serious concerns about the direction of the company. At that point, as majority shareholders represented on the board, we would at least be consulted on major matters. Mind you, we still did not have the ability to make changes on our own or to override decisions that went against our best judgment, but our three seats carried a lot of weight, with the force of 50.3 percent of the company behind them.

Our first board meeting, held in Los Angeles in December 1981, produced some very awkward moments, with a roomful of vanquished directors offering little more than tense silences between presentations. The three seats on the board we held were something, but they were hardly enough, given the situation. We needed to know what was really going on operationally, so we pushed for the establishment of an office of the president that would cross corporate lines. Six and Warde weren't about to give up control before they had to, but we were able to make a strong case for placing a number of our guys in key management positions alongside Continental's people. Jay Pritzker proved to be enormously helpful brokering a deal that allowed our Phil Bakes and Bob Gallaway, a longtime associate, to join Warde and Dick Adams, CAL's head of operations, in forming a provisional office of the president—OOPS, as many of our folks called it.

Speaking to employee group on Continental outlook (1982).

One of the first major decisions for the board, after we assumed full control on March 24, 1982, was where to base the combined company. In this, Houston emerged as the logical choice. Continental had a substantial office and maintenance facility in Los Angeles, which, although it was an important city in the system, was hardly one where CAL had any dominance. On the other hand, the strongest markets for our combined operations would be Houston and Denver. The merged company would account for around 40 percent of daily departures out of Houston Intercontinental Airport and 30 percent of flights out of Denver's Stapleton International Airport. It made sense to base our operations in one of these cities, and since we already had our operations base in Houston, the most practical thing to do was to accommodate the additional Continental personnel in that location.

I was conscious of the signal we would be sending to our new employees by uprooting them so soon after taking over. But I knew we had to move one group or the other, and we were of course sensitive to the feelings that the TIA team would have if the decision were to leave Houston. Indeed, as we evaluated our personnel more closely, and as certain Continental executives and middle managers left to pursue fresh starts elsewhere, it became clear that more key TIA people would survive the merger than would their counterparts at Continental. For all these reasons, Houston emerged as the most logical headquarters. Naturally, the announcement of our decision was followed by great derision from the Los Angeles folks.

One of my constant concerns during this transitional period was the attitude of our people. I knew there would be a certain amount of resentment among CAL employees toward me and TIA management, to be sure, but to what extent I couldn't predict. The rank-and-file workers at Continental checked in quickly with their reactions. As a group, led by their union leadership, they remained very much opposed to our takeover, which was to be expected considering their emotional investment in the aborted ESOP, but on an individual level I saw some encouraging signs of welcome. Many were able to appreciate that Continental had been a troubled company and that we just might be the forward-thinking guys who could lead them out of the woods. Their success was tied to ours, so I was given at least some degree of support.

However, employee attitudes toward one another tended to fall along predictable lines. In Houston, TIA people looked on Continental workers as a bunch of flaky, passive Californians, with all the laid-back, New Age baggage that went along with that image. In Los Angeles, Continental employees regarded TIA hands as hicks and bumpkins, unprofessional and unsophisticated in the ways of big-city dwellers. Neither perception was fair, but we were dealing with two drastically different cultures, and it took a while for both stereotypes to fade.

Upon a closer look, we found the Continental franchise in worse shape than we had expected. The company's operations had been neglected in many respects during the Western merger period, even before the takeover battle. Subsequently, management attention had been focused on the ESOP and other defensive strategies to close the door on TIA. One of the real surprises to me was the absence of any real leadership in the airline's upper ranks. Very few of the senior Continental people seemed to be in tune with the realities of the new deregulated airline environment, and the company's service additions to an already weak route system were clear evidence of this. In addition, and most glaringly, the airline had cut back on a lot of its flying in the wake of the PATCO strike and furloughed more than 1,500 employees. Few airlines were performing well, but Continental was hemorrhaging. Net losses for 1981 topped $60 million ($205 million in 2024 dollars).

By January 1982, George Warde implemented a "prosperity plan" aimed at sharply reducing operating costs. We disagreed on a number of specifics, but we fully supported the need to deal with the airline's high-cost structure and to seek wage concessions and work-rule improvements among Continental's employee groups. Without them, we feared the company would be run out of business before we could even get our hands on it.

Warde corralled me one day to complain about his vice president of marketing, Mike Levine, whom he had inherited from Al Feldman's team. "Frank," he said, "this guy's a coconut. He doesn't get along with anybody. He's smart as hell, but I just can't deal with him. Nobody can deal with him." We had known that Mike was something of a bull in a china shop, but we did not want to lose him. He was extremely bright, with excellent strategic judgment, and I felt he could play an important role if we could find a way to accommodate his brash personality. Certainly, Warde wasn't going to put up with him much longer, so the thought occurred to me to bring Mike over to New York Air.

At New York Air, meanwhile, we had a difficult time regaining the momentum we had lost in the wake of the PATCO strike in mid-1981. Its financial results continued to worsen even after the recovery from the strike. If Mike were brought in as CEO, his energy and strategic strength would seem like an attractive answer to a clear problem—although not without risk. If he were given the position, I didn't expect him to last in his new post for any great length of time—two years was my guess—and I told him as much.

He would probably grow bored during that period, I thought, just as our people—and maybe we ourselves—would grow disenchanted with him in the context of New York Air's culture. But in those couple of years he could do some good things and possibly reorient the carrier and redirect its resources. I was also encouraged to learn that Levine's number two would be the more people-oriented Bob Gallaway, whom Levine had gotten to know at CAL and who, we knew, had the capability to smooth out ruffles that might be created by Mike's rougher style. Levine and Gallaway took over at New York Air early in 1982, and by the end of that year, the airline had elevated its no-frills image to that of a full-service, low-fare carrier and was doing better.

---

We initially sought to run TIA and CAL as "sister" airlines—distinct but fully coordinated carriers—but gradually it became apparent that a synchronized operation would never be as efficient as a full-fledged merger. This was an easy decision to reach but a difficult strategy to execute. I hated to lose the Texas International name. TIA was emblematic of our success and a proud reminder of our roots. Continental, on the other hand, was in a sense someone else's airline, but it had a name and logo carrying a rich, proud history. I was also aware that the name had a great deal of meaning for a great many people. For every passenger who might have been unsettled by the trading of the TIA name for Continental, there would be five Continental passengers who had never heard of TIA.

By most outward appearances, the revamped Continental cut an impressive figure. Its fleet consisted of 112 aircraft of only three basic types: thirteen McDonnell Douglas DC-10s, thirty McDonnell Douglas DC-9s, and sixty Boeing 727s. Its revenue passenger miles made it the seventh-largest passenger airline in the United States. Its route system stretched to four continents. All signs pointed toward a promising future.

But outward appearances can be deceiving. CAL faltered further near the end of the summer of 1982, and our financial picture grew darker. We moved swiftly to turn things around by asking our pilots for some changes to their contracts. In our labor negotiations, the pilots were always the hardest bargainers, perhaps because they were our best-compensated employees and so had the most to lose. We always tried to solicit the pilots' support right out of the gate in the hope that a new amended contract with them would prompt the flight attendant and machinist unions to follow their lead.

In August 1982, we reached an agreement with Continental and TIA pilots on a rationalization of their two standing contracts, calling for what was billed as more than $90 million in productivity concessions and wage cuts. This was a key accord, even though we knew at the time that we were accepting a half-baked deal. We needed to raise capital, so we swallowed the deal in order to demonstrate to the financial community that we had won concessions and earned what looked like labor peace.

We also brought in a new president and CEO, Stephen Wolf, which further improved our financial credibility and ability to finance. Wolf was a seasoned industry veteran, a hardworking, diligent guy who had formerly served as senior vice president of marketing at Pan Am. It was not long before he set the tone for our new operation with his tireless focus on the details of the business and his aggressive work habits, which filtered down through our ranks.

Fortunately, we were able to parlay the August pilot concession agreement into a series of successful financings in an attempt to offset our mounting cash losses. We made a public offering of two million shares of Continental common stock in the fall of 1982, which brought in $37.5 million, and we established a $32 million line of credit with a consortium of banks led by Chase Manhattan. We knew we would need plenty of financial resources in the days ahead, so we took advantage of the rise in our stock price and the generally positive atmosphere developing around the company, especially on Wall Street.

We also completed a $40 million note arrangement with the American General Corporation (today, a unit of the American International Group, or AIG), the insurance giant that was located in Allen Center, just down Allen Parkway from our Texas Air office. This financing had an interesting background.

One day that fall, during my lunch hour, I was having a run along Allen Parkway near our office, a route on which I would normally pass the American General Building. This time, the thought occurred to me that American General, a major Houston employer, might welcome the opportunity to help finance the new airline coming to the city. I also had noticed that the tall building had quite a lot of seemingly empty space. Quite excited about this idea, when I got back to the office, I called Harold Hook, American General's chairman—whom I didn't know—and suggested that we have a visit.

He agreed to meet, and during our conversation we discussed Continental's financing and office-space needs. Since the American General Building indeed did have many empty floors and was well suited for our headquarters, a deal with Continental made a lot of sense.

As a result, we got our financing and moved CAL to the American General tower early the following year.

In total, we raised nearly $180 million during this period—quite an achievement at a time when profits were down sharply not only at Continental but also throughout the industry. In the first quarter of 1983, Continental lost $51 million on revenues of $318 million (a negative margin of 16 percent), while the ten other major domestic carriers posted operating losses totaling $516 million.

———————

By January 1983, however, it was clear that the August 1982 concession agreement with our pilots did not provide nearly the savings that ALPA expected it would. The airline continued to hemorrhage. We therefore needed to go back to ALPA and the other unions, explain our results, and ask for greater wage and work-rule concessions. The August concession package with ALPA, which was supposed to realize approximately $90 million in savings over the term of the contract, was only saving the company half that—maybe.

With this new request to our pilots, we didn't feel like we were asking too much. Under federal regulations, pilots were permitted to fly up to eighty-eight hours per month, but our pilots flew barely fifty hours per month, on average, because of onerous and expensive work rules, which none of the new carriers that were challenging us had to face. We wanted pilots to fly just an additional eight to ten hours per month, which really amounted to around two extra flights per month and would have left them flying considerably less than Southwest Airlines pilots, for example. It seemed to us a marginal trade-off for the added job security and was a far more palatable alternative than a further cut in pay. This change in pilot work rules would have provided the company with a 20 percent reduction in pilot expenses.

It's important to note that in negotiations with our various labor groups, we were rarely looking for one-shot quick fixes, as a number of other airlines were. We always tried to take the long view: we wanted to permanently transform our labor contracts and bring our operating costs in line on a lasting basis. After all, it was clear that airline deregulation had permanently changed our competitive position and allowed new airlines, many of which had started in our area, to operate with labor costs dramatically lower than ours. We also tried to explain that we had to buy *permanent* airplanes, raise *permanent* capital, and service *permanent* debt and that we therefore needed permanent changes.

ALPA leaders closed the door on us when we updated them on our situation. Concession bargaining is rarely conducted from a position of strength, and it is unlike any other negotiation. In concession bargaining, you are asking someone to give up something to which you have already agreed.

In addition, we had been involved in drawn-out negotiations with our machinists' union, the International Association of Machinists and Aerospace Workers (IAM). The labor costs specified in this union's far-reaching contract, covering not just mechanics but also commissary workers and other groups, were also far higher than new airlines' costs. Among other things, we were asking for the ability to subcontract work. Our kitchen commissary costs, for example, of which labor makes up the largest share, were more than twice what we would have had to pay to an outside vendor such as Marriott—for equal or better quality and much more flexibility.

In December 1982, both sides in the IAM negotiations petitioned the National Mediation Board (NMB) for assistance. The need for this step, even though the contract had expired and we had been negotiating for several months, reflected one of the glaring inadequacies of the Airline Deregulation Act and offered disturbing evidence that airlines were still being handcuffed by government bureaucracy.

---

Let me pause for a little background. The deregulation law, as written, only addressed the revenue side of the airline business equation. It allowed free entry and freedom in pricing but did nothing to address the legacy of fixed costs that older airlines such as Continental were left with. For example, airline labor negotiations still fell under the provisions of the Railway Labor Act, passed in 1926. The NMB, created by that act, was a three-member federal agency with far-reaching authority to arbitrate disputes between railroad labor and management. The goal was to protect the public against the threat of crippling national rail strikes. When airlines were regulated, in the 1930s, labor contracts were placed under the NMB's purview.

After 1978, as a deregulated industry, airlines should have been lifted from the jurisdiction of the NMB. Our labor disputes should have been handled by the National Labor Relations Board or the independent Federal Mediation and Conciliation Service, just as they would have if we had been a department store, hospital, or any other major employer. Instead, airlines were expected to operate in a deregulated industry with highly regulated labor. Labor leaders all had their officers and lobbyists in Washington, and a major focus for them was making sure they knew who would be appointed to the NMB or to important administrative positions and ensuring that these appointments would serve their best interests. It was a very cozy relationship, one that had an unfortunate impact on airline costs.

Over the years, a pattern to most NMB-regulated negotiations had emerged. Under the board's restrictions, labor and management were bound by the terms as they stood on the last day covered by their most recent contract—until they were released from that contract by the board. This status-quo interval could stretch on for months, even years, after the expiration of a contract. This meant that the unions were almost always eager for a quick release in order to push labor costs higher, while management was usually happy to maintain the status quo and take their time. That was the old days!

Union leaders got wise to these "last-day" conditions and began insisting on a variation of the so-called snapback scenario. For example, the pilots' group might be seeking a 40 percent pay hike, spread evenly over three years, but would happily settle for a more gradual increase, which on the last day would step up, or snap back, to the 40 percent level. In this way, union leaders could sell their membership on the overall package while management could talk up the substantial cost savings over the term of the contract. Sometimes they even negotiated stock payments for the "forgone" compensation. I never sanctioned these kinds of deals because they clearly undermined our position in the long term and provided us with only a short-term Band-Aid to control long-term costs. Yet they were attractive to many airline managers who realized that they themselves might not be in their positions by the end of those three years and did not mind if their successors had to come along and grapple with the new stepped-up compensation level at the end of the contract period.

The NMB regulations were so convoluted that even when the board released both parties from an expired contract, there was still another month to wait before either side could take any action. The release began a formal cooling-off period, which essentially was a thirty-day countdown, at the end of which either party was free to take "self-help" measures. For labor unions, this meant that they were free to strike; for management, this meant that they were free to implement a new contract. Imagine trying to sell airline tickets during this thirty-day countdown period, during which passengers would be aware of the strike threat!

As we headed toward the summer of 1983 and a release from the NMB, it was increasingly clear that we were making little progress in negotiating with our unions. We were getting nowhere with our machinists: the national IAM heads were more concerned with the effect of our bargaining on their negotiations with other airlines. The pilots were unwilling to bend until the IAM yielded, and the flight attendants were waiting to see which way their colleagues would go. Our labor picture was starting to look like it might never come into focus. Yet we also knew that without a serious overhaul in our labor costs, we simply could not compete effectively and survive—too much cash was going out the door. It had also become abundantly clear that these fundamental changes would have to start with the machinists.

During the spring of 1983, we attacked costs on other fronts and attempted to make changes to our route system to stem our losses. Our CAL team worked prodigiously on these efforts. Stephen Wolf was well known for working long hours with our managers and was frequently seen going home at 9:00 or 10:00 p.m., attempting to identify the changes that had to be made at the company. Costs were not the only avenue for improvement, although they were the most obvious and most important.

The team worked diligently to rehub the airline largely around Houston, a big potential asset of ours. As competition took hold, particularly from low-cost new entrants into the market, CAL's "point-to-point" routes were losing their financial viability. The most important of these was the Chicago–Los Angeles route, which had been a major cash cow. CAL's corporate offices contained huge displays of the elaborate Asian and other "glamorous" meal options provided on this and other routes. The company was well known for having the best in-flight service, a major competitive advantage. However, the ball game changed with airline deregulation. Low costs, traffic from feeder routes, and dominance (i.e., constituting maybe 25 percent or more of departures from a hub) were the new requirements, and CAL lacked all three. With both ends of the Chicago–LA route without feed—Chicago and Los Angeles both being dominated by American and United, with their great amount of feed traffic—CAL, and its big DC-10 airplanes, held an untenable position in the market.

———————

With the reworking of the hub structure, quite a few new cities were added to Continental's routes. I recall noting in early May that the team had decided to add six new cities to feed the Houston hub—all to begin on the same day. Being very concerned about our financial risk, I was alarmed at embarking on such a large undertaking at once, particularly since new routes generally require some time to spool up and generate net cash. But Stephen Wolf felt he had to move rapidly to stanch the long-term bleeding.

And there was plenty of bleeding to stanch. When Stephen joined the company in late 1982, the monthly losses were averaging nearly $20 million. Six months later, as we approached our June directors' meeting, the losses were still running at $20 million monthly, even after the improvements that had been made and after the pilots' contract's supposed cost improvements.

At that June board meeting, the directors were brought up to date on our lack of progress in the labor negotiations, the impending confrontation with the IAM, and our progress on other fronts. We also carefully outlined our delicate financial position and limited remaining flexibility. This led one of the directors, John Robson, to ominously say, pointing at me, "Frank, I'm coming to believe that the answer to CAL's dilemma does not lend itself to traditional solutions." His well-chosen and soon-to-be prophetic words echoed in my ears after that.

July was spent in heavy late-stage negotiations with the IAM and in preparing for the strike deadline the IAM had set for early August. Another sadness about this whole period was that although we were able to reach an agreement with the local IAM district president, Lanny Rogers, a tough but realistic old mechanic from Braniff, the national IAM headquarters refused to accept it. Lanny was aware of our very stark competitive environment, because he had personally witnessed the fall of Braniff. National IAM leaders told him, "Lorenzo is a strike target. It's time to teach him a lesson. Go back and plan a strike." Rogers refused, claiming there would be no support among the CAL rank and file for a strike once the terms of our final offer were made known. But not long afterward, he was dismissed as chief negotiator, and his replacement, perhaps more focused on his own job, refused the deal we had negotiated with Rogers.

We had known all along that our negotiations were being manipulated by IAM's national office. Under their structure, the home office in Washington (known as the International) could step in and overrule the local district regardless of the latter's desires. This unusual situation would become a factor in Frank Borman's subsequent last-ditch effort to save Eastern Airlines.

We never realized the extent to which the IAM national office wanted to prevent our local from setting some kind of national precedent by accepting terms substantially different from those in place at other large airlines—even though, unlike us, most other airlines were not yet dealing with competition from new low-cost airlines.

Because of this refusal by the IAM to bargain with us in good faith, and because of the pilots' union's refusal to consider an arrangement that would have provided its members with a substantial equity interest in the company, Continental entered a dark era of labor turmoil that cost the machinists and other workers thousands of jobs but wound up transforming the US airline industry.

# CHAPTER EIGHT

# The New Continental

*Creating a Way Forward*
*1983–1984*

W E WERE fully prepared to keep our planes flying on August 13, 1983, when Continental's machinists walked off the job. Just 150 of our 900 mechanics reported for work that day, crossing the picket line, but we quickly brought in 250 replacement mechanics who had been lined up for us by an outside contractor. Our flight attendants, mindful that we had begun training more than 600 replacement flight attendants in midsummer, withdrew from their pledge to support the machinists and turned out in full force. By the end of the first week of the machinists' walkout, our daily schedule was at 93 percent of its prestrike level.

At that point, the machinists' strike was effectively broken, but not without the airline getting quite hurt. Despite our ability to keep flying, the publicity surrounding the IAM strike had scared off Continental passengers. Load factors were down to less than 40 percent, and we were burning money like jet fuel—and August was usually our best month. The only thing our numbers folks didn't agree on was *when* we would actually run out of cash.

Throughout this period, I actively discouraged our people from ever speaking the words "bankruptcy" or "Chapter 11." I was deathly afraid that if people outside the company suspected that we were even thinking in those terms, passengers would take their business elsewhere. We would experience what would be essentially a "run on the bank." Now that I've had the opportunity to reflect on it, such caution may have hurt us, in a sense, because it never fully allowed management to express our financial circumstances with complete candor.

The year before, Braniff had filed for Chapter 11. The CEO at the time, Howard Putnam, left the same position at Southwest to take on the enormous task of trying to save Braniff from collapse. Putnam had joined Southwest from a mid-level officer's position at United. Neither position prepared him for the financial mess Harding Lawrence's growth craze had created or for the turmoil brought on by deregulation. Braniff became the first airline to seek bankruptcy following deregulation. Putnam and his executive team did not believe passengers would fly a bankrupt airline, so his strategy was to ground the airline and attempt to reorganize it before restarting operations. Eventually, Jay Pritzker bought Braniff, and operations restarted in 1984 with an entirely different business model. But as we internally debated our options, Braniff was still on the ground with no assurances it would ever reorganize.

Sure, our negotiators were out there using all kinds of "drastic measures" language in labor discussions, but I suspect their talk of "pushing the company to the brink" or whatever words they used may have sounded somewhat hollow to the unions. Perhaps the imminent threat of bankruptcy might have jarred them into a compromise. Of course, it might have also found its way into the newspapers and made the prospect a self-fulfilling prophecy. In 1983, the traveling public was not nearly as used to talk of bankruptcy as it would later become. We were keenly aware that consumers had not been exposed to the idea of flying on a bankrupt major carrier up to that point.

Bankruptcy certainly wasn't a strategy concocted to escape our labor contracts or pare back our operations, as the unions contended from the outset. To me, bankruptcy was failure, pure and simple. It was something to be avoided at all costs. We looked on bankruptcy only as a last-ditch alternative, a "making-the-best-of-what-you-have" type of move. No airline had ever survived it up to that point, and I did not have to look far for a compelling argument against it, with Braniff just up the road in Dallas.

To me, bankruptcy was the kiss of death, and no bankruptcy expert could convince me that filing would signal anything less than complete failure. Still, we retained the services of specialists at the law firm of Weil, Gotshal & Manges, led by the bankruptcy impresario Harvey Miller, and took our first tentative steps to prepare for the worst. We soon learned that there was a great deal about bankruptcy that even our expert advisers couldn't tell us. For example, we were advised that we could "probably" alter the terms of our labor contracts under Chapter 11 immediately on filing, but we later learned that there was a case pending before the US Supreme Court that might prevent us from doing so.

My greatest concern, though, were bankruptcy issues that were specific to the airline industry. Even if Chapter 11 is technically a reorganization of debts owed to creditors, I knew that the news of our bankruptcy would not be reported as "Continental reorganizes." The headlines would say CONTINENTAL GROUNDED or CONTINENTAL GOES BUST. I thought there was a good chance that an airline might not survive such a public relations blow.

The other problem was that once travel agents and various institutional accounts became wary of our ability to stay in business, we might face potentially ruinous cash-flow problems that not even Chapter 11 could protect us from. Already we saw some evidence that travel agents, because of their fear of our potential demise, were "plating away" our bookings to other carriers. Travel agents were required by federal regulations to pay for tickets within seven days of booking, even if the scheduled flight was three or four weeks—or more—away. As agents grew concerned that Continental might suddenly stop flying and not honor tickets, they tended to reduce their clients' exposure by still booking Continental flights but writing the tickets on another airline's account. This way, their clients wouldn't lose money if Continental were to suddenly cancel flights. For us, though, this plating away meant a sharp drop-off in cash flow, dramatically reducing our working capital. Instead of getting cash within seven days of booking, we had to wait thirty days or more as some of our payments flowed slowly through the airline payments system, in many cases after we had actually flown those paying passengers.

At this point, in mid-August, I was second-guessing the Continental takeover. I blamed myself for setting in motion the sequence of events that had landed us in such dire financial straits. A number of things had not broken our way. Continental had turned out to be in far worse shape than any of us had thought; the unions were far more intransigent than any of us had feared; and the merger of our separate operations had not gone as smoothly as any of us had anticipated. All these disappointments provided me with plenty of reasons to stay awake.

On August 31, we ended another month of crippling losses at Continental by requesting more than $150 million in wage and work-rule concessions from pilots, flight attendants, machinists, and nonunion employees. In return, we proposed that employees receive ownership of approximately one-third of the company. These calls for concessions were just as difficult to make as they must have been to hear. There is no easy way to ask an employee to cut off one of the rooms in his house or to stop feeding one of his children. Surely that was how our people must have heard our appeals. Employees had their own fixed costs, and it was a very tough thing to ask them to go backward, so I took pains to present our situation in human, personal terms.

After outlining our plan to union leaders, we presented it to our pilots' union negotiators with a proposal that would allow all employees, including the pilots, to acquire a 30 percent interest in the ownership of the airline, a request that the pilots' union had at various times asked for. But this deal, to the best of my knowledge, was never presented to the pilots themselves.

We then set about visiting concerned employees in meetings throughout our system. During one such session in Denver, a flight attendant, a former union leader, stood up and dispassionately endorsed our plan. She said that what we were asking for was terrible but added that she saw no way around it.

"We don't have any power," she told her assembled colleagues. "Employees only have power when the company they're working for is making money. Continental is clearly not making money and may well not be around without some relief. We have no choice."

The response of this flight attendant was typical. She was not a particular friend to management, and she didn't throw hugs and kisses at us for proposing to slice her paycheck and increase her work hours. She even said that she "barfed" when she first saw our plan. The truth is, we all nearly barfed when we saw the concessions required in the plan. It was a heck of a way to build employee morale, although the stock ownership plan was of some help. For a long time, I had held that in the service business, management could not afford *not* to have a healthy esprit de corps, but that had become a luxury beyond our diminishing means.

---

As the days wore on in September, it was clear that we were careening headlong into bankruptcy. In evaluating what we would need and how we should operate in order to successfully get through this period, I came to the conclusion that there would have to be one distinct hand at the tiller. I had been chairman and chief executive of the company throughout this period, while Steve Wolf served as our very capable president and chief operating officer, responsible for the day-to-day activities of the company. He would be the one charged with the difficult hiring and firing decisions we were soon to face—and with figuring out which routes to continue flying, what fares to charge, how much cash risk to take, and so on. But I began to realize that with my long experience in these areas, I was the logical person for the job, although it was not one that I was enthusiastic about at all.

This was no slight to Steve. After all, flying the airline through bankruptcy was not exactly the job he was hired to do. Rather, my decision was based on my belief that I needed to maintain full control of our operations during the very trying times that lay ahead. If this was to be our last and only chance, I wanted to call the shots. I never did believe that having two hands on the steering wheel was a good thing.

I also discussed the management situation extensively with our board and found the directors to be in unanimous agreement. On Tuesday, September 20, just four days before we planned to file, I sat down with Steve and informed him of our decision. I told him that it was the most troubling management move I ever had to make, and it remains so today. I explained that the directors and I felt we had no choice but to ask him to step down and let me run things, given where the company stood. Steve took it like a pro. He understood my concerns. He was very service-driven, famous for sweating out even the smallest details. He was also a tireless, dedicated worker. My admiration for him has continued, and I have followed his career in the years since. But we desperately needed an entrepreneurial approach coming right from the top.

I left it to Steve to decide if he wanted to step down before we filed or just after and to put his own spin on the move. As it played out, the press interpreted his "resignation" as the last straw in a clash over our dealings with labor and our pending bankruptcy. They surmised that Steve was prolabor and I was not, but that was not at all the case. That was classic union propaganda once again.

Rather, Steve and I parted on extremely amicable terms. There was not a moment of friction between us. We both were in full agreement on our concession proposal and the steps we had taken with the unions. I remember stepping into Steve's office as he was cleaning out his desk, and from our pained small talk it was clear that neither one of us wanted to end our association, even if we both knew it was the right move. When he reviewed the draft of the press release about his departure, one of his comments to me was that it made him "sick to see."

We tentatively scheduled our filing for Saturday, September 24, late in the afternoon. We chose a Saturday for obvious reasons: it was the quietest day of the week, with our lowest frequency of flights—meaning that it would necessitate the fewest passenger disruptions—and it fed into the quietest news day of the week, which meant that most of the gloom-and-doom headlines would have to wait an extra day, until Monday. Hoping for a near miracle, we also scheduled a meeting with the pilots' union for that Saturday in a last-ditch attempt to avoid bankruptcy. They didn't show up.

But choosing when to file was not the only decision we were facing. We had to determine what to do after our filing, and as we counted down to that date, we were still looking at a number of options. Most of our people were pushing for a complete shutdown of operations, giving management ample opportunity to cut back, implement new labor arrangements, and make the necessary layoffs, then resume flying in a week or ten days. Another option was to pare back our operations and staff immediately after filing and continue flying at around 50 percent of capacity.

There were advantages and disadvantages to each operational plan we considered. Shutting down for a week or so would give us more time to catch our breath and assess which of our key labor groups would support us in bankruptcy, but it also might send the wrong signal to the financial community and the flying public. The longer our planes remained grounded, I feared, the harder it would be to get them back up in the air. The notion of trimming back our system-wide operations and continuing to fly Continental's most profitable routes with virtually no interruption was appealing on its face, but it, too, presented a problem. We would never know how much of our schedule we could maintain until we learned how many pilots would be available to fly our planes and how many mechanics there would be to service them.

The path we chose, a blend of those options, was to furlough our entire workforce on the Saturday evening of our bankruptcy filing, then rehire a fraction of them on Sunday and Monday at competitive levels. We would ground all our domestic planes for two days late on Saturday afternoon, then reopen for business on Tuesday morning with a dramatically reduced schedule of flights. This way, at least, we would have the balance of the slow weekend, and all of Monday, to face the monumental task of reducing the workforce and trimming domestic flights to a manageable level.

Our international operations, largely in the Pacific, had to be handled differently. We were forced to maintain all our scheduled international flights, which accounted for 20 percent of operations, because there are no Chapter 11 protections from creditors abroad, and we could not endanger our valuable international route rights by not flying them. We would plan to cut our domestic flying drastically—by 75 percent—which meant that our revenues would fall by a corresponding amount, assuming the old fare levels.

Chapter 11 bankruptcy draws a curtain through your entire financial house. All your liabilities are kept on one side of the curtain, and all your assets are left to stand on the other. Whatever revenues you generate are either paid out to meet your operating and payroll costs or effectively held in trust for your creditors. A bankruptcy judge is assigned to earmark all receivables and determine how much cash goes toward each. In a sense, bankruptcy of this kind ties one hand behind your back (preventing you from selling off assets, for example) while leaving the other hand fairly free to conduct business as usual.

Bankruptcy offered us breathing room by suspending interest payments on more than $650 million in long-term debt. Also, and significantly, bankruptcy released CAL from its labor contracts (and from most of its other contracts), leaving us free to negotiate updated terms with new and returning workers. At the time, although it was being challenged in a case before the Supreme Court, bankruptcy laws did not distinguish among labor, bank, and vendor contracts. Given that more than 35 percent of our costs were going to labor, the ability to establish acceptable work rules and wages offered us tremendous relief in the short term and would soon give us a fresh outlook on our long-term plans.

I didn't sleep at all the night before our filing day. I had no experience managing an airline through such a critical period. No one did. As I lay awake, I tried to envision how we might navigate Continental out of the rough patches ahead. I tried to balance how aggressively we should work to achieve labor peace against what might be seen as the more pressing obligation of meeting our reduced payroll costs and maintaining some semblance of a flight schedule.

When I arrived at work early Saturday morning, I was met with the unsurprising news that the pilots had canceled our scheduled last-ditch meeting. Consequently, we dispatched our lawyers that afternoon to the US Bankruptcy Court for the Southern District of Texas, in Houston, where they formally filed for protection from creditors under Chapter 11 of the bankruptcy code. It was not necessary for me to appear personally in court, but I did have to put on a public face later that afternoon at a press conference near our Allen Center offices. I choked back tears as I made the announcement.

"There is no halfway solution to our problems," I told the roomful of reporters and employees. In one of the most widely quoted lines from this somber occasion, I added, "There is no chapter five and a half."

Under our plan, I cut my own salary from $267,000 to $43,000, matching a senior captain's compensation in our bankruptcy-adjusted pay schedule, and vowed not to allow a raise for myself above this level until the company became profitable. It was a gesture of support for the sacrifices of our returning workers—"founding employees" of the New Continental, as they were soon known in-house. The rest of our officers took modest cuts of 15–20 percent. Of course, since the majority of our employees had been let go in those early days, for what we hoped would be a temporary period, the remaining employees were very happy to be staying with the company.

The risks of filing were several and had to do mostly with matters that bankruptcy laws placed beyond our control. For example, the unions could, and most likely would, seek to have their contracts upheld in the courts and sue us for damages if they could prove that our weak financial position had been exaggerated or that we had filed for bankruptcy simply as a way to slash wages. Another risk was that creditors could persuade the judge to oust current management and leave the job of overseeing our day-to-day operations to a court-appointed trustee. Or, perhaps even more of a legal stretch, we could be left wide open to claims that the separate assets of Texas Air, the airline's parent company, should be used to satisfy creditor claims at Continental.

We had good relations with most of our creditors, including the major airports as well as our caterer, leasing companies, fuel suppliers, and advertising agencies. We truly were in this together, as we explained. They relied on our continued business, and I expressed to all of them my hope, indeed our goal, of offering favorable terms of repayment. As I explained, our debts to them were not the cause of the company's problems.

It was an awful afternoon, the darkest (and scariest) moment of my career. Part of me felt like I was giving the eulogy at the funeral of a dear friend, while another part, perhaps more realistic, recognized that the press conference was probably our best and only opportunity to present our bankruptcy in a positive light. I also used the occasion to proudly announce the birth of the New Continental, as I called it—a low-cost airline offering our trademark reliability and service at competitive prices, matching those of other low-cost carriers.

The headlines the following morning were not as bad as some of us had feared, buried as they were on the Sunday news pages. On Monday, most reports included some "expert analysis" of our situation, and the tone of these accounts was generally far more sympathetic than we had any right to expect, although some of the commentary characterized our filing as a strategy for abrogating our collective bargaining agreements. One of the most conspicuous early examples was prominently displayed on the front page of the *Wall Street* Journal, where an unnamed executive at another major airline offered the following assessment: "If the idea works, why not use it?"

I cringed at lines like these, but we came upon them with such frequency that I eventually stopped paying attention. As we discovered, most of these claims flowed from back-against-the-wall union leaders eager to preserve their positions at all costs, but I was distressed at how quickly reporters picked up on such a one-sided perspective and how easy it was for them to find "anonymous" competitors to repeat the charge.

Following the Saturday news conference, we had two days to reinvent our company from the ground up. We asked each department head to sit down with our officers and go over how to run their operations on a bare-bones budget. With our entire workforce technically furloughed, our department heads (themselves fewer in number) were free to examine their employee files and offer jobs only to their best people. Within seventy-two hours, we needed to cut our workforce down from 11,000 to around 4,000. The alternative would have been to hemorrhage red ink.

Phil Bakes supervised a lot of these sessions for us, and he did a remarkable job. I did not have the stomach or the heart for it. I would see an employee's name cross my desk and immediately picture his face or the faces of his family—a throwback to my first days at Texas International, when I would often meet employees at the annual company picnic. I had gotten to know some of our people so well over the years that I was too emotionally invested to make some of these hard decisions. Phil could be as emotional as anyone, but because he had only spent a few years with the company, he was better able to take the direct, rational approach that this delicate situation required.

With the labor equation in Phil's good hands, I escaped the office on Sunday to work on marketing and pricing strategies and map out the changes in flying schedules that I thought made the most sense in our stripped-down condition. I asked our planning folks to do the same thing on their own, and very early on Monday morning we returned to the office to compare notes. This, too, was key. Without approaching the problem from varying perspectives, we wouldn't have our employees' full confidence or the buy-in we needed to move forward, but with a consensus operating plan, we could reopen for business knowing we had collectively put our best cards on the table.

———————

Not surprisingly, we all came back with the same basic operating strategy: fly only our busiest routes with increased frequency and at drastically reduced fares. We cherry-picked among our most successful markets, obviously paying attention to what kinds of routes made sense, and wound up selecting the twenty-five cities we would continue to serve. (The scheduling cuts meant that we only needed to deploy around 40 percent of our 107-aircraft fleet.) Of course, it was not enough to simply sustain service in our strongest cities. We had to also play to our strengths and increase the frequency of our flights in those markets. Instead of maintaining our pre-bankruptcy schedule of three or four flights per day at regular fares, we might go to six or eight flights with our new, lower fares; we might even institute hourly service along our heaviest routes. In this way, we hoped to reduce costs, stimulate traffic, and increase our market share dramatically.

The powerful impact that hourly service can have on the marketplace has always been astonishing to me. People tend to fly more when there are more choices, and airlines with a large number of flights tend to draw additional passengers from connecting airlines. I knew that if we could find an economical way to add some sensational fares to our stepped-up frequencies, there would be a better-than-even chance that we would get passengers back onto our planes. The trick was to arrive at a formula for maximizing revenues consistent with our costs, and to reach that equation, we went through a classic pricing exercise.

I sat with our pricing experts around a big conference table and tossed out a series of numbers. "What would happen if we priced every seat at $9?" I asked. The answer, naturally, was that every seat would be filled. "What about at $19?" I asked and got the same answer. We kept on working upward until we reached the threshold where we believed that the chosen price and likely load factors would maximize our revenues. At that time, we were thinking we needed to fly a 70 percent or so load factor in the weeks immediately following our filing, which would have placed us at the industry's high end—and well above the sub–40 percent load factors we'd been averaging going into Chapter 11. So we determined that we could do so starting at $49 system-wide. From there, we felt we could build our fares back up to $69 or $79 without a significant drop in our loads.

All these developments sent shock waves throughout the airline community. On the afternoon of our bankruptcy filing, Frank Borman released a taped message warning his 37,000 Eastern employees that they, too, must consider meaningful wage concessions or face following Continental into bankruptcy. The Western Airlines president, Dom Renda, also made some bankruptcy noises of his own. For the first time in memory, airline executives pointed openly to the decline of another carrier as proof that the industry could no longer afford its runaway labor costs.

Over the course of that black weekend, my worries drifted from marketing to labor, and at that critical juncture there was no way to anticipate employee support for our filing. The machinists were still out on strike, and our pilots, flight attendants, and nonunion workers were justifiably disenchanted with the emergency work rules and salary cuts we announced.

ALPA's master executive council initially instructed its members to fly under protest, which left us to assume that there would be more than enough pilots to fill our reduced schedule. That would change later in the week, when the council ordered a strike to commence four days into our resumed operations, and the immediate waffling on the part of the union was either a telling indication of the lack of direction among union leadership or a sign that the national ALPA in Washington had reversed a local union position.

From what we saw, the pilots had no idea what to make of Chapter 11. These ALPA guys in Washington were always a day late and a dollar short, and I do not think they fully grasped what was happening to Continental or to their members. Even after we had filed for protection, they seemed to think our troubles were an elaborate bluff, a negotiating ploy to keep their salaries down and break the union, and it took another few days before they finally took our claims seriously.

However, on that Tuesday, September 27, as we came back flying again, the pilots were still with us, and the New Continental emerged as leaner and far more efficient than any major carrier on the national scene. Our counters were jammed with passengers eager to snap up our $49 one-way fares. Our planes were flying at near capacity, with only minor disruptions, and there were news cameras positioned throughout our system to corroborate our claims that the airline wasn't dead just yet. I have always been a firm believer in first impressions, and Continental made a great one on its first day back. We were down, but we were not out, and there seemed to be a ready market for the value-driven, full-service product we hoped to offer in the months ahead.

The "New Continental" announcement ad (1983).

With our 2,025 pilots set to strike on September 29, once again we were faced with an uncertain equation. Even at approximately 40 percent of normal capacity, including international operations, we could not be sure that enough ALPA members would cross the picket lines to pilot our planes. The union had put together a substantial strike fund, assessing members between $70 and $300 per month and offering strike benefits comparable to our reduced pay. When captains were receiving $3,800 per month against average salaries of just $3,600 per month—$43,000 annually under our new structure ($134,000 in 2024 dollars)—there was little financial incentive for them to return to work.

We had only offered continued employment to around half our pilots, given our improved efficiency and the fact that we were operating just a couple of hundred flights on our daily domestic schedule, but we were still deeply concerned over what a pilot walkout would do to our pace of recovery. We had hoped that labor peace would enable us to bring the company back far more quickly than we could ever hope to do under strike conditions. But with pilots joining the machinists on strike, we were at odds with our two biggest and most essential employee groups. That would mean our return to full strength would take much, much longer.

For a time, it even appeared that the pilots' union would take the strike industry-wide. The ALPA chief, Henry Duffy, briefly threatened a walkout of all his 34,000 members, effectively grounding the entire domestic airline industry "as a protest to the government that this industry is not working and needs fixing." Duffy's warning was mostly bluster, but we saw it as a clear indication that our situation had struck a nerve. ALPA leaders were undoubtedly concerned over the domino effect our bankruptcy would have on other airlines. To ALPA leaders, 2,000 pilot jobs at Continental were nothing when weighed against 34,000 jobs industry-wide. They were quite prepared to see Continental go down the drain if it meant preserving the existing wages and work rules for their members at other carriers.

In addition, it was becoming clear that the pilots' union was

Well-paid, striking Continental pilots unhappy with their wages (1983).

taking its fight international. Continental was able to continue operating its profitable Australia–New Zealand routes with some of its available pilots, much to the consternation of ALPA. These routes were important to the company because they generated a lot of cash and because a stoppage could cause us to lose our federal route authority. One morning in mid-October 1983, I received a call from our director of Asian operations, Paul Casey, informing me that he had heard from the head of the airport fueling company, who claimed that his employees were not going to be able to fuel our airplanes. It seemed that the fuelers' union had been visited by ALPA representatives from the United States, and the fuelers planned to honor the ALPA picket line.

Our options were limited, naturally, because we were 8,500 or so miles away. However, I had an ace up my sleeve in the person of Lindsay Fox, one of Australia's most successful entrepreneurs. I had met Lindsay when he chaired the YPO meeting in Melbourne two years before. (YPO, formerly the Young Presidents' Organization, is an association of young chief executives from around the world.) I had recently invited Lindsay to join Continental's board, too: it seemed to me that we should have representation from the Asia-Pacific region given that it was such a valuable route for us. Anyway, I called Lindsay after hearing from Paul Casey; I explained the problem to him and asked if he could help.

Lindsay, a classic entrepreneur, had a very interesting background. Starting as a driver, and later with a rig of his own, he built a thriving trucking company, Linfox, which went on to become the largest logistics company in Southeast Asia. His several thousand trucks could always be recognized on the road by the message written on the rear: YOU'RE PASSING ANOTHER FOX. He certainly knew his way around and was friendly with a great many of the union leaders. In any event, Lindsay said, give me a little time, and I'll see what I can do.

A few hours later, Paul Casey called back to say that the problem had been solved. It turned out that Lindsay had found his way to the general secretary of the transport truckers union and told him—in his always friendly way I'm sure, at least initially—that he hoped the truckers would fuel our airplanes, because if they didn't, his drivers would. Done and done!

Lindsay remained a critical director during my time at Continental, invariably offering sound advice—even though it was not always what I wanted to hear.

———————————

During the ALPA strike, our ability to fly depended upon our ability to persuade pilots to cross their own picket lines. The best way to do this, we determined, was via a direct, one-to-one appeal, so we set up a room in our headquarters with a bank of phone lines, and we all took turns calling the pilots to explain our position and ask them to return. It was a real boiler-room operation, and our pitches were as intense as any sales call. I was in there with the rest of our group, working my way down the list, talking to pilots about what we were trying to do, what we saw the union trying to do, the positive direction we thought the company was headed in, and our commitment to taking it there.

Most of our calls took place in the evenings, after the dinner hour.

With our pilots scattered in time zones all across the country, we stayed on the phones well into the night. It was challenging, frustrating work. Not only were we attempting to address some very valid concerns (increased hours, reduced wages, questions over seniority, and the legitimately suspect financial health of the company), we also had to counter an extensive union program of misinformation. ALPA leaders had their own bank of phone lines, and they were matching us call for call. It is only now that I can fully appreciate the absurdity of the situation. Imagine two groups of people, each holding diametrically opposed views, waging a long-distance tug-of-war using individual pilots as the rope. On some calls, I had to undo a whole lot of damage before I could get the pilots to really listen. It was often a futile exercise, but we had to go through it anyway.

For all our efforts, there were some nights when we could only persuade a dozen or so pilots to return to work. There were barely enough pilot turnarounds to keep us in business. On October 1, the first day of the ALPA strike, 120 pilots crossed the picket line, and we were forced to cancel 15 of 118 scheduled domestic flights. By the following week, after a few dozen more pilots had come over to our side, there were no strike-related cancellations, and we started to think we'd dodged a bullet.

It was no easy thing for our pilots to cross the picket lines and fly our planes. ALPA leaders and strikers were not exactly known for their subtle ways, and some of their methods bent the law. This was an all-out economic war, and if ALPA could not win the battle by conventional means, its leaders seemed perfectly willing to fight it out in the trenches. And they fought dirty. They terrorized our non-striking pilots in a manner that I could hardly believe, following them to their hotel rooms on their overnight assignments and trying to persuade them to desert their aircraft the next morning. They threatened their homes, their families, and their future livelihoods. They told these pilots they'd be blacklisted—that once Continental buckled to ALPA demands (and until that time, airlines had *always* ultimately buckled to ALPA demands), they'd never get another job with the union. We got a lot of last-minute calls during this period from pilots asking to be pulled from the schedule, and no doubt most of those calls resulted from union pressure.

Two notorious incidents added weight to the persistent ALPA threats. One involved a non-striking pilot in Denver who reported that a stuffed elk was thrown through his living-room window by striking colleagues. It was like a scene out of a movie, but it sent an emphatic message throughout pilot ranks. The other incident was even more disturbing. At a roadblock set up to stop drug trafficking in the area, San Antonio police stopped two striking Continental pilots allegedly on their way to bomb the home of at least one non-striking Continental pilot. In their car, the cops discovered bundles of dynamite and road maps highlighting the locations of non-strikers' homes. On further investigation, it was revealed that these two pilots were out to exact revenge on their working colleagues, and they wound up serving prison time for their intended crimes.

We saw labor peace as critical to Continental's recovery, so we continued to negotiate for an agreement with the pilots' union even as these threats and reports of violence persisted. I could think of no way to reason with unreasonable people, but there was no way to avoid trying, either. However, after reading what was going on in the newspapers and listening to the horror stories brought in by our loyal pilots, we concluded that it was impossible to pursue negotiations.

One of ALPA's favored ploys was to announce that our planes were unsafe without its pilots at the controls. This was nonsense, but it is the standard union line during any airline work stoppage. Regrettably, it was sometimes effective, because Americans look at airline pilots in much the same way as they look at doctors, attorneys, and other highly trained professionals. When any such group declares that the public is in danger, people take these warnings very seriously. ALPA took advantage of this whenever possible, presenting itself as an authority on matters of public safety just as, say, the American Medical Association does. I always thought that even its name, the Air Line Pilots Association, was chosen to reinforce that image of responsible, educated professionals when in fact ALPA is a labor union just like any other—except with much more money.

----

After so many years of practice, the union—which was formed in 1931—had elevated its brand of self-serving propaganda to an art form. One of the most devious ways ALPA leaders did this was to establish an internal "safety committee" that ostensibly monitored the standards and practices of airlines. In reality, the committee appeared to have little interest in investigating those airlines with which the union enjoyed good relations, thanks to a compliant management team. Somehow, the only reports issued by this body had to do with airlines whose management was trying to keep labor costs in check and respond to the competition brought about by airline deregulation. The committee was promoted as a body for ensuring public safety when all it really safeguarded was ALPA members' benefits, work rules, and wages—and, most importantly, the union's security and continued existence.

ALPA's safety inspectors worked overtime to take every incident out of context and trumpet it to the press, thus feeding the strike and undermining Continental's reputation. They ran full-page newspaper advertisements dramatizing the most innocuous everyday occurrences. Naturally, every airline has incidents during operations, but only a fraction of them present a problem of genuine concern.

Unfortunately, we suffered one serious but ultimately harmless infraction of air safety procedures just a few weeks into the pilot walkout, giving new ammunition to ALPA's claims. By coincidence, I was flying from Houston to Denver on a Continental DC-9 helmed by a senior pilot named Mike Woods. I had known Mike, ironically, as an ALPA regional leader and a very vocal opponent of management. In fact, the last time I'd seen him, we were in discussions with the union over the start-up of New York Air, which he opposed. I was somewhat surprised to see that he had crossed the ALPA picket line, and when I found out he was piloting the plane, I made a point of paying him a visit in the cockpit.

"Mike," I said when I went up for a chat, "I'm glad to see you supporting the company."

"You've taught us, Lorenzo," he said. "You've given me religion."

"How so?" I asked. I was curious to hear what part of our message had resonated with him.

"I'm finally realizing that the company needs change," he allowed, "and we're not going to get it from ALPA."

We spoke for several minutes, and when we began our landing approach into Denver, I excused myself and returned to my seat. I never wanted our pilots to worry about my presence as we came in for a landing, a time when pilots are very busy, but I was in the cockpit long enough to see the sun shining brightly off the fresh snow at the airport. It was a beautiful clear day. Mike put the plane down gently and rolled to a stop, and there was no indication that anything had gone wrong.

After the flight, I had to run to a tightly scheduled editorial board meeting at the *Denver Post*, at which I planned to update the editors on the New Continental. So I charged off the plane and headed for the newspaper's downtown offices. By the time our meeting broke, some ninety minutes later, there was a handful of reporters milling outside on the street in front of the building, wanting to know about the landing incident on my flight into town. "What're you talking about?" I asked in the text-message-free environment that existed then. I honestly had no idea. As far as I knew, it had been an uneventful flight on a bright sunny day.

I learned later that only two of Stapleton's three runways had been clear and operational that day, thanks to a heavy snowfall the day before. The runways were about 900 feet apart, and each was about 120 feet wide. A taxiway, at a width of 75 feet, ran between them, and this, too, had been cleared of snow. Mike had been told by controllers to land on the "middle runway" as our plane approached, but no mention was made that Denver's third runway was concealed, covered with snow. So Mike landed the plane on what appeared to be the middle runway—the cleared taxiway between the two visible runways.

By the following morning, ALPA's well-oiled public relations machine helped ensure that the story of this accidental yet obviously very improper landing, no matter how understandable it was, was making national headlines. No one had been hurt, no damage had been done, and no one at Continental was proved negligent in any way, but the union turned it into a big story just the same. To be sure, an incident of this kind requires an FAA investigation, if only to ascertain why the air traffic controllers used such imprecise language while providing runway instructions. However, the amount of play this story received was out of all proportion to what happened, and the finger was pointed far too quickly at our pilot. Even the *New York Times* termed the incident "a special embarrassment" to Continental.

Henry Duffy, ALPA's chief, had a field day with the misadventure. "We have maintained from the beginning," he said in a statement, "that the work rules imposed upon those pilots still flying for the new Continental and the immense pressure they are operating under would unquestionably cause a serious and rapid degradation of safety. This isolated incident at Denver is only a further example of why we have been warning passengers not to fly on the new Continental."

What was so infuriating about Duffy's remarks was that he neglected to acknowledge that strong-arm tactics by his own union forces were largely responsible for whatever pressures our pilots were under. He also failed to mention that until a short while before, Mike Woods had been one of ALPA's most loyal leaders. Just because Mike had committed the cardinal sin of working despite a union job action, he had not been transformed from a competent pilot to an incompetent one. It was astonishing to me how quickly the union would sell out one of its own.

The negative attention from the Denver landing died down soon enough. The FAA found insufficient grounds to sanction Mike, and Continental, in our examination of the incident, also decided that Mike's mistake did not warrant punishment. But ALPA did achieve its goal of stoking passenger fears and putting a dent in our reputation.

I honestly believed that Continental was the safest airline in the skies in those days, because in my view (which was also shared by aviation experts), pilot complacency is one of the biggest enemies of airline safety. Our pilots had few reasons to be complacent. With their striking colleagues and union pilots in other airlines watchdogging their every move, they needed to stay sharp. Furthermore, our operations and maintenance facilities were on high security alert, so vandalism and sabotage were never a serious concern. I have always said that if ALPA really considered safety its number one concern, then perhaps it would not be so quick to defend some of the most egregious instances of pilot error.

---

On November 23, 1983, the birth of our son offered a welcome respite from all these struggles. This would be our fourth trip to the delivery room, and I thought I had it all figured out. That day, I arrived with a video camera and tripod, because I did not want to miss a thing, but Mother Nature had other plans. After Sharon experienced some irregular contractions, our fourth child was delivered by cesarean section in a room from which I was excluded. I was just thrilled that mother and child were healthy.

We named our son Timon, a family name on my mother's side, a discovery that Sharon and I made on that years-ago trip to the cemeteries in my parents' Galician village. For his middle name, we chose Francis, after Sharon's grandfather (and, happily, after the English version of my birth name, Francisco). I never really thought all that much about having a son or a male heir. If I thought about it at all, I just assumed that the baby would be a girl. After three beautiful daughters, I did not know anything else, and I could toss a baseball around with my girls just fine.

After Timon, though, I could not imagine life without a little boy. He was a wonderful surprise and an incredibly easy baby, even from the very beginning. The girls were captivated by their baby brother. He was like a little toy to them at first, but as they all grew up, it was quite heartwarming to see the way they looked after him. We took him on a transatlantic flight to London before he was two months old, and he did not give us a peep of trouble—he slept in his straw basket, which we had gotten in Mexico, just next to our bed at the Connaught Hotel. All our kids were terrific travelers at early ages. I suspect they got that from me.

I still look back fondly on the 1983 holiday season for many reasons, including the fact that Timon's arrival coincided with the first signs of life at the New Continental. Even after we ended our special promotional fares, our load factors continued to outpace those of the competition, at 67 percent in November and 63 percent in December. Scheduled flights climbed to more than 50 percent of our pre-bankruptcy level, and our cash position improved significantly.

Continental fares remained a bargain, with two-digit price tags throughout much of our system. The new pricing strategy called for a simplified two-tier fare system modeled on Southwest's highly successful fare structure, which was also being adopted at People Express and the rejuvenated Braniff, which finally returned to the skies in 1984, after its 1982 bankruptcy. We went with a straightforward peak/off-peak plan and shunned the complex yield management pricing system used by most carriers to this very day.

Back then, yield management systems were not nearly as sophisticated as they are today, but they had already become a source of some controversy—and the bane of most travelers' existence. When seats in coach class on a single flight are priced at, say, $320, $249, $199, and $110, consumers find it very difficult to comparison shop. The low come-on fares are saddled with so many restrictions that passengers never really know if they qualify for them, assuming they can even find them.

Simplified fares were very much in line with our new basic service philosophy, and they helped reinforce what we hoped had become the airline's new image as a value-driven carrier. Rather than arriving at an average $69 fare for a given flight by charging $199 for some seats, $99 for others, and $59 for most of the rest (with perhaps half a dozen at $39), we just went ahead and charged everyone $69. Alternatively, we could get to the average of $69 by charging $79 during the week and $49 on the weekends. It was, we thought, a dignified, rational way to separate ourselves from the competition and reward our passengers without insulting their intelligence.

Of course, this has all changed now. Computer algorithms determine fares, which may change by the hour or time of departure based on demand and other factors. Airlines, particularly the large carriers, generally avoid advertising their prices. When they do, they usually announce something like "as low as . . ." instead of a specific fare.

In addition, as we approached the 1983 holiday season, we began adding new flights so frequently that we were running short of pilots. For the first time, we were forced to make permanent pilot hires from outside our ranks, enrolling forty new pilots in our training program. We had no other choice if we ever hoped to return to our pre-bankruptcy schedule and build the New Continental. Our talks with ALPA had reached a total impasse. Although many claimed that these forty hires constituted our attempt to bust the union, we were continuing our plan to bring back Continental and respond to market demand for more flights, fulfilling our obligation to pay our creditors and making it possible to bring *all* our furloughed employees back to work.

With these outside hires—who had the option to join the union but who usually decided against it, seeing as how the union wanted them out—negotiations with our pilots came to an effective halt. Predictably, ALPA insisted that in the event of a settlement, we should furlough these new pilots immediately, but we couldn't agree to that. The only way we could persuade these outside pilots to cross ALPA's picket line and sign on was to make a commitment to them. We guaranteed that their jobs would survive any settlement, and we couldn't afford to go back on our word simply to satisfy another in a long list of demands by our striking pilots' union.

These outside pilot hires created several potential complications (involving seniority rankings, for example), but we could not hold so many jobs open indefinitely. We needed to increase our number of flights to generate cash flow and prevent our lessors from taking back their idle aircraft. As far as I was concerned, if a striker tired of the fight and wanted to return to work, we would gladly have him, but only if there was a job available. We refused to displace one of our new hires to make room for a striking pilot who had suddenly "gotten religion," as Mike Woods might have put it.

On January 17, 1984, the courts delivered good news that clarified our labor outlook. The federal bankruptcy judge in Houston who was handling our case, Judge R. F. Wheless Jr., declared that the airline had not acted in bad faith when it filed for protection from creditors. This was an extremely critical decision for us. Had we lost this case, we would have had to offer back pay to strikers and reverse the steps we had taken to improve the survivability of our operations.

Then, on February 23, the US Supreme Court delivered a narrow 5–4 decision in what was widely called the *Bildisco* case, which upheld the right of bankrupt employers to set aside existing labor contracts and impose new wages and work rules. The court's decision, in a highly disputed case not directly involving Continental, effectively neutered the labor unions' last remaining chance to invalidate our new contracts.

But the unions didn't stop there. They pushed hard for legislation in Congress that would not only prevent changing labor contracts in bankruptcy but would also apply this legislation retroactively to any bankruptcy cases then outstanding, including ours. I remember getting a panicked call from our Washington-based lawyer, Clark Onstad, asking me to fly to Washington and meet with our Texas senators as well as with my business-school classmate John Heinz, Republican senator from Pennsylvania, and others in an attempt to head off an amendment to a bill that was moving through Congress. This amendment would have provided the retroactivity that the unions sought. Fortunately, our congressional representatives were able to see through this, despite the unions' intense lobbying. I have very fond memories of a wink I got after the committee showdown on the bill from Lloyd Bentsen, the highly respected Democratic senator from Texas's Rio Grande Valley, as he was walking down the stairway from the committee room. It was all clear on that front for a while.

On the ground and in the air, the New Continental exceeded our most optimistic projections for recovery. Even in the press, where liberal journalists castigated management and portrayed me as an enemy of organized labor, there was no denying our turnaround. A lead editorial in the February 17, 1984, issue of the *Denver Post*, written in response to a push from labor groups seeking to amend the laws after Judge Wheless's decision, offered perhaps the best example of the way in which our comeback was being reported: "Free enterprise isn't supposed to be a popularity contest," the editors wrote. "We'd rather have rough, abrasive Frank Lorenzo playing the game by the rules and saving consumers money in the process, than watch [others] rewrite them at public expense."

---

Of course, we could not always rely on such favorable reports. I much preferred to let our performance speak for itself—and it did. In the first quarter of 1984, we posted a small operating profit, and by the second quarter we were able to point to a net profit of $10.4 million. By April, Continental had rebounded to the point where I felt I could comfortably relinquish the day-to-day controls, and I tapped Phil Bakes to succeed me as president and chief operating officer. I remained as chairman and chief executive, but I left it to Phil to guide the airline in its operations, a role he had been exposed to since the bankruptcy.

In addition to focusing on marketing and legal issues, we focused heavily on our relations with employees. We felt it was critical to reward those who had taken substantial pay cuts in the wake of the bankruptcy, so we offered them direct grants totaling one million shares of the company's stock, stock option opportunities, and a well-received profit-sharing plan. We also formed employee councils and encouraged employees to participate in the management of the company, a move made possible by the elimination of the layer between management and employees that was usually occupied by union representatives. We even established a motto: "Every employee who wants to participate in management can."

We had planned to restore the airline to 90 percent of pre-bankruptcy capacity by midsummer of 1984, but we were pleased to be able to reach that level in early May—barely eight months after our bankruptcy filing. Our costs per available seat mile had fallen to less than 6.5 cents compared to pre-bankruptcy costs of 8.5 cents. That decrease may not sound like much, but whacking nearly 25 percent off our operating costs was huge. Our labor costs at that point constituted only 21 percent of operating costs, in line with our lower-cost competitors—down from 35 percent at the time of our filing. By midyear, we were carrying more passengers than ever before while serving only half as many markets, and our load factors continued to lead the industry.

In October 1984, when our third-quarter results were reported and we achieved a profit of $30.3 million on operating income of $43.8 million, we really knew we had achieved something extraordinary. Our available cash and equivalents had soared to $126.8 million. Within one year of our filing, Continental had accomplished a complete turnaround in its fortunes. Steady, continued growth had brought us back to a workforce of more than 10,000 employees, while labor costs had been reduced by an astonishing 45 percent. We were operating 120 percent of our pre-bankruptcy seat miles. Though still in bankruptcy, Continental had been reborn, not only as the industry's largest and most popular low-cost carrier but also as the only low-cost carrier with a long-established reputation that provided a full-service product.

However, we knew we had to continue to increase the breadth of our operations organically while the opportunities still existed. To do that, we needed additional aircraft. But the unions fought us at every turn. We went to Boeing and placed an order for twenty-four 737-300 aircraft, which were to be leased, to fill out our hubs. This required approval from the bankruptcy court, although since the planes were to be leased and the company was doing so well, the creditors—other than the unions—didn't have any complaints.

In addition, we bought four DC-10 aircraft to increase our international service, and the unions tried to stop this, too. One of the aircraft was to be used for a new route from Houston to London, replacing Pan Am, which had lost the route. The unions tried to stop us in the courts and in Washington. The pilots' union even went to London and attempted to get the heavily unionized London companies to refrain from servicing our aircraft. The fight to build Continental internally through aircraft acquisitions, while still in bankruptcy, was so unusual that Harvard Business School wrote a case for its students describing the situation. When this case was taught, I was invited to speak to the class.

CHAPTER NINE

# Seeking Critical Mass

*The Struggle for TWA*
*1985*

S CONTINENTAL returned to strength, we were eager to spot our next opportunity for growth, so we were once again on the lookout for troubled carriers. Continental had still not formally emerged from bankruptcy, but as we entered 1985, we could see the airline gaining momentum as a profitable, streamlined, and very competitive yet modest-sized company. However, there was a shared sense throughout our ranks that if we hoped to maintain that momentum in an increasingly competitive environment, we might need to merge with another carrier and expand Continental's base. This would give us what we increasingly viewed as the essential critical mass needed to survive in deregulation.

We had several areas of weaknesses—including marketing, networking, and facilities—that could be addressed by the acquisition of another airline. First, simply put, we lacked the marketing muscle that other larger carriers enjoyed. In addition, we lacked a significant East Coast presence and had few international routes. Finally—and crucially, given the computer age we were entering—we lacked a state-of-the-art computer reservations system with a travel agency interface, a competitive feature then viewed as essential and that most major carriers already had.

But most other carriers were slow to learn from our cost-cutting example and the realities of the deregulated environment. As a result, they were losing money, which meant the industry remained full of companies ripe for turnaround. Beginning in 1984, we devoted significant amounts of time to assessing some of industry's perennial money losers: Eastern, TWA, Western (before its acquisition by Delta), United, and USAir. By early 1985, we had set our sights (again) on TWA.

The airline had been spun off from its parent company, Trans World Corporation, and had yet to find its way. From our outsiders' perspective, the airline's management still seemed to be running the business with a loss-leader mentality. A January 1985 *Fortune* magazine survey listed TWA as one of the least-admired companies in America for the second year in a row, and the ranking was probably justified. There was no direction, no clear strategy, and certainly no esprit de corps. The airline was operating on autopilot, with few concessions made to the new competitive environment—or so it seemed from afar.

TWA was clearly vulnerable to outside investors, but it was uniquely attractive to us because it provided several major strategic strengths and some great assets that nicely offset its trouble spots. The TWA brand, for one, was probably one of the most recognizable airline brands in the world. The carrier itself might have fallen on hard times, but the name still was very powerful from a marketing perspective. Further, it had a significant network of European routes, most notably to Paris, Frankfurt, Rome, and beyond, which would greatly enhance the value of Continental's sole European route—from Houston to London—and mesh with our New York aspirations and our service to Mexico and Canada and our modest Asian operations. We believed this would give us a very marketable international franchise.

The airline also featured a graying but nevertheless extensive fleet as well as a burgeoning domestic hub operation in St. Louis. Its New York operation was based at JFK, where it controlled the airport's iconic Eero Saarinen–designed terminal, which would have augmented Continental's and New York Air's LaGuardia and Newark airport presence. Also, its east-west flying complemented our north-south orientation well. It was, we thought, a very recoverable airline franchise, and with a stock price far below the company's net asset value, it was one we thought we could afford. At the minimum, it would be a sensible investment.

The size and variety of important destinations served by carriers was becoming strategically important in those days, in part because of the fast-growing nature of frequent traveler programs—which, as I mentioned, were first introduced in the late 1970s by Texas International. The more routes and destinations a carrier offered, the greater the attractiveness of stockpiling miles in its loyalty plan, as frequent-flier programs were called.

One of the most attractive of TWA's assets was its PARS computer reservations system, which trailed only American's SABRE and United's Apollo systems as the largest in the industry. At the time, we were extremely eager to beef up Continental's reservations system to the level of the other majors, and marrying our framework to TWA's seemed a natural way to do that. Since passengers were increasingly looking to travel agents for their ticketing needs, and since travel agents almost always relied on one reservations system or another— much as passengers looked to their loyalty plans when determining airline selection—it was crucial at the time for an airline to install its own reservations system in as many agency offices as possible.

Back in 1985, long before the age of internet reservations, this was doubly important, because despite public pressure to the contrary, there was still a significant bias built into most airline reservations systems. For example, TWA could program its PARS system to ensure that its flights were listed first on an agent's screen, irrespective of whether they were the most direct, the most frequent, or, critically, the most economical. Placement was key: more than 90 percent of travel agent bookings were pulled from the first screen, so the benefits to the patron airline could be quite substantial. Other carriers had to pay a fee, usually $1.75 to $2.00, for each reservation made on another airline's equipment, so there were benefits to the host airline even when bookings went to a competitor.

Continental had its own internal reservations system in place, but we had not yet invested in the programming and other resources necessary to achieve the sophistication that travel agents demanded. As a result, our penetration beyond our core markets was insignificant. Even in Houston, Denver, and Los Angeles, where we enjoyed a substantial market share, we barely registered as a blip on the screens of local travel agents—not a great long-term position to be in, we thought. TWA's computer reservations system, by contrast, had the state-of-the-art software that was so attractive to travel agents. It offered excellent penetration in the St. Louis market and along the East Coast as well as pretty good penetration in California. We were intrigued by the thought of adding the underlying strengths of Continental's route network, thus extending our reach even further.

The more we looked at the numbers and the fit, the more we thought a move for TWA made tremendous business sense, and the depressed price of the airline's stock in early 1985 provided the ultimate attraction. Since the spin-off from Trans World Corporation, completed the previous year, TWA shares had been relatively flat, trading in the $8–$10 range. It really was a dormant company in every respect, and the market consistently reflected that.

We finally launched a modest buying program in early 1985, quietly collecting small blocks of TWA stock while figuring out our next move. We still were not sure which way we wanted to go with our investment, but if the lackluster activity in the market was any indication, it appeared that TWA would be there for the taking. Or so we thought.

---

Every spring in the 1980s, Michael Milken, Leon Black, and the rest of Drexel Burnham Lambert's high-profile investment bankers presided over their annual conference in Beverly Hills. These "predators' balls," as they came to be known, tended to be lavish affairs, typically frequented by financiers, power brokers, chief executives, and financial analysts, and the March 1985 gathering, at which I was present, was no exception. New York investor Carl Icahn, one of the most conspicuous corporate raiders on the prowl throughout the early 1980s, was among the leading members of the financial community in attendance. Like almost everyone else at one of Drexel's gatherings, he was no doubt fishing for takeover or investment targets.

During the 1985 conference, Icahn listened to a presentation given by TWA's chief financial officer, Robert Peiser, at which he outlined some of the airline's woes and prospects. This was standard fare at Drexel conferences: client companies would offer analysts an inside view of their operations without divulging any nonpublic information in hopes of sparking investor interest. Those present at the TWA session reported that Icahn was listening with rapt attention, although Icahn himself claimed that his interest in TWA preceded Peiser's talk.

Whether spurred by this presentation or acting on his own impulses, Icahn began buying TWA stock in the weeks after the Drexel conference, and on April 29 he crossed the 5 percent ownership threshold, giving him ten days to publicly file with the SEC. After a flurry of buying during that ten-day window, he announced a 20.5 percent stake in the company, surprising the financial community, alarming the airline industry, and putting TWA management and directors on the defensive. The airline issued a press release that same afternoon, May 9, declaring that Icahn's interest in the company was unsolicited and unwanted.

In retrospect, the TWA board might have been open to a friendly deal with another airline at that time, but such an aggressive pursuit by a guy with Icahn's predatory reputation was probably the last thing the directors wanted. If Icahn's past accomplishments were any indication, they must have thought he would either strong-arm them into buying back his shares at an inflated price or swoop in unchecked and sell off assets. Either way, he was a problem. Even TWA's unions voiced strong objections to Icahn's maneuvering, labeling him the enemy of organized labor and a menace to the long-term job security of TWA employees. Loyal members of the pilots', machinists', and flight attendants' unions began wearing STOP CARL ICAHN buttons to broadcast their concerns.

In our own offices, I didn't quite know what to make of this development. Certainly we could not help but notice all the recent activity in TWA stock, even if we hadn't known who was behind the buying. Icahn's reputation as a greenmailer did not exactly suggest that the airline would elude our grasp, only that it would cost us more money to acquire it than we had originally anticipated.[4] Most of Icahn's public activity had been more wheeling than dealing, and there was no reason to think his interest in the airline industry in general, or in TWA, ran to anything more than turning his investment into a quick profit. Already, TWA stock had jumped to the $14–$16 range, and given that Icahn was in at the lower levels, he probably felt there was still a good way for the stock to go.

After digesting the news, I put in a call to the TWA chairman, Ed Smart, the man who had rebuffed my overtures six years before following the National deal. It was only a matter of time before Smart and company would be out looking for other investors to fight off Icahn's advances, we figured, and we wanted to be sure they considered Texas Air in their search. It would be a lot easier for us to reach an amicable merger agreement if the initial inquiry came from the other side of the table. "Ed," I said, trying to help our chances along, "if there's anything we can do, just feel free to let me know."

He thanked me for the call and said that the board was still considering a number of defense strategies. Icahn, for his part, continued buying stock as the price of TWA shares continued to climb. We chose to sit back and wait, feeling that there was too much uncertainty for us to go forward at that point. We maintained the just-under-4-percent

---

[4]    Greenmail is the practice of buying enough shares in a company to threaten a hostile takeover so that the target company will instead repurchase its shares at a premium.

stake in the company that we had accumulated while we waited for Icahn's next move—and TWA's.

The investment banking landscape surrounding this deal, and our representation in it, was interesting as well. Drexel's Michael Milken, with whom we had done several financings, designated Leon Black, in the New York office, to work on the TWA deal with us. (In later years, Black would go on to found the very successful Apollo Global Management firm.) Black played a pivotal role in the negotiations that followed, ostensibly as our investment banker, although I was never entirely sure where his allegiances lay. In the past, Black and Drexel had worked on deals for TWA and as a banker for Icahn as well as for Texas Air.

Drexel was a fascinating place in the mid-1980s, and a lot has been written about it. My own take didn't stray from that of most other accounts. From what I could see, it was mostly Michael Milken's show. He was the one who popularized all the junk-bond trading that was going on at the firm at the time, the guy whom everyone went to with their deals and who raised all the money. He sat at a desk in the center of a large trading floor at Drexel's Beverly Hills office, usually from five in the morning to five in the afternoon California time. He was one of the easiest guys to reach on the telephone because he was always at his desk. He was a tireless, high-energy worker who was also incredibly intense. When he became interested in a deal, he was all over it.

The principal player at TWA was its chairman, Ed Smart, who had been brought into Trans World by my former TWA boss, Charles Tillinghast, in the 1960s to oversee the company's external activities. Both men had taken turns at the law firm of Hughes, Hubbard & Reed, which had coincidentally had represented us in many matters over the years. Smart was always the non-airline guy, and when he finally assumed control of the flagship airline operation, it was apparent that his focus remained with some of the company's other businesses, perhaps most particularly Hilton. As best I could see, he never had any great interest or confidence in the airline side of the business.

Smart was eventually succeeded as CEO at TWA by C. E. "Ed" Meyer, whom I had known since the two of us had worked together many years earlier at Eastern. Meyer was a rising financial executive there, with a public accounting background, and we kept in contact over the years. In fact, Meyer had grown up near Sharon's family, so we would hear of his comings and goings through her neighborhood grapevine as well as through the usual industry sources.

I do not think Icahn particularly liked the airline business, either—or that he even thought much about it—until he happened upon TWA. However, once he focused on the company, everyone at TWA was frantic. In his typical way, he very quickly assembled more than eleven million shares, nearly 33 percent of the company (acquired at between $12.50 and $16 per share in the space of just a few weeks), which put him in a commanding position. TWA's negotiators were able to get him to voluntarily agree not to buy any additional shares pending a preliminary injunction in an action they had filed in federal court, but at this stage it really didn't mean a lot. Icahn was in the driver's seat.

In the meantime, he submitted an all-cash $18-per-share offer to the TWA board on May 21, 1985, seeking the balance of shares. In his proposal, Icahn stated his intention to continue operating TWA as a major domestic and international carrier, praised current management for its efforts, denied speculation that he would sell off key assets, and disavowed his prior greenmailing activities. But with the carrot came the stick, because he also threatened to push for the removal of the TWA board unless his bid was quickly put up for shareholder approval.

However, we did not believe him. We simply did not believe that Carl Icahn wanted to own an airline. Drexel Burnham and Leon Black also felt that way, and they certainly knew him well. But it did not matter what we thought. Smart, Meyer, and the rest of the board thought his interest was genuine, and so did Wall Street. Shares of TWA common stock instantly jumped to Icahn's new $18 level.

———————

It is important to be aware that throughout the extended negotiations that followed, we and Carl Icahn played by two different sets of rules.

The rules we had to live with stipulated that we needed considerably more time to close the deal than Icahn did, because we were an airline and had to get government approval for the acquisition. There were, after all, antitrust issues to consider. Icahn, on the other hand, as an individual, had no such restriction. Although this difference in regulatory treatment would not have been our choice, it was, very ironically, our own doing.

Here is where our position on the issue of deregulation came back to haunt us. As I wrote in chapter 4, in our lobbying for deregulation legislation in the mid-1970s, we pushed to remove the so-called any-other-person amendment from the Federal Aviation Act. At the time, we believed it was important to open up the airline business to outside capital, and one of the ways we thought to accomplish this was to insist that the burdensome Department of Transportation requirement covering the sale of one airline to another did not apply to persons not involved with any phase of aeronautics, i.e., "any other person." Little did we know at the time that this change would give Icahn a big edge seven years later. Also, ironically, you may recall that it was none other than Ed Smart of TWA who had unsuccessfully asked us to give up on our push for this provision.

Our decision to go after the airline was ignited by a call from Smart and Meyer together. They had apparently determined that accepting an offer from a "white knight" suitor was the best way to sidestep Icahn's bid, and they wanted to solicit our interest, which of course we already had. As a result, on May 24, just three days after Icahn's $18 offer, we informally floated the idea of a friendly transaction at $20 per share, thinking that at this level we might at least get Icahn to rethink his goals. Our Drexel advisers also thought that at this level, which probably would not be the final price, Icahn could at least realize an immediate significant profit without the risk.

We put no formal offer on the table, but we hoped to have one in short order. Already, Icahn was sending signals that he would not vote his shares against any other realistic offers. TWA had also received an overture from Resorts International, the hotel company, which had a long interest in airlines. On June 8, Resorts made a tender offer at $22 per share, with a cash component of only around 60 percent. It was not the most enticing offer in the world, but it was something—a start.

Icahn's initial strategy for running TWA emerged in early June. Just as Meyer and the directors had feared, he planned to cut back on TWA's domestic flying and eliminate most routes that did not feed the airline's St. Louis and JFK hubs. In addition, he was said to be exploring the liquidation of certain severable assets (such as, perhaps, the PARS reservations system and the airline's lucrative foreign routes) and looking at ways of reducing costs—including, most likely, extensive layoffs and the reopening of standing labor contracts.

At this juncture, TWA's labor unions remained strongly opposed to an Icahn takeover. Employees were still sporting their STOP CARL ICAHN buttons and lobbying legislators to block the deal. Icahn threatened major cuts across the board. While he did not exactly declare that he would strip the company bare, his message was nevertheless clear: TWA's assets were fair game, and nobody's job was safe. He might be open to the idea of continuing to run the airline, he indicated, but only if it returned a consistent profit and only if he were able to "reinvent" the company. From what we could gather, and from what TWA's union leaders could tell, the two goals were mutually exclusive.

More than ever before, the TWA board was in desperate need of what business reporters had taken to calling a "least-bad-case scenario." TWA employees, too, were despondent over their prospects under Icahn. The trouble was, the best least-bad-case offer, the one from Resorts International, was also suspect and did not remain on the table long, because Resorts was unable to finance the transaction. This opened the door for us to finalize our offer for TWA and proceed to an agreement with their board.

---

On June 11, one day after the hasty Resorts bid fell apart, we formally offered more than $20 per share for TWA. We knew we were not where we needed to be in price, but we felt we had improved on the only other non-Icahn bid to date. We also indicated that we were willing to be flexible. After two days of round-the-clock negotiations, we reached a deal with TWA, and on the morning of June 13 we signed an agreement calling for the acquisition of all outstanding TWA stock for $23 per share—$19 in cash and $4 in preferred stock. The $23 price didn't come out of the blue, because Leon Black of Drexel had told us that, based on his conversations with Icahn, he knew $23 was his number.

The completed purchase, valued at almost $800 million, would have created the country's second-largest airline network, with 40,000 employees, almost three hundred aircraft, more than $5 billion in revenues, and a very balanced route network. The agreement, unanimously endorsed by the boards of both companies, was subject to a vote by TWA shareholders, the completion of satisfactory financing, and government approval. As a hedge against Icahn, TWA granted Texas Air an option to purchase 6.5 million shares at $19.625 per share, which would have combined with our existing position to balance Icahn's stake and dilute his control.

As anticipated, Icahn responded to our agreement by vowing not to play the role of spoiler in any TWA acquisition and declaring that he had no plans to counter our offer or buy additional shares at that time. We had no reason to doubt him at that point—but no reason to believe him, either. At our price, he stood to make approximately $60 million on his investment, which wasn't half bad for such a short period of time. But I was not convinced that he would bow out until he was sure he had maximized his return.

The agreement made front-page news across the country, and most of the accounts cast Texas Air as an "attractive alternative" to the likely liquidation facing TWA under Icahn. Trading in TWA shares was halted for most of the day, pending our announcement, but the stock managed to close above $20 for the first time since Icahn surfaced with his position. For many, our planned acquisition signaled a new era of price competition and dramatic fare cuts for the consumer. In a *Wall Street Journal* report, Henry Rosenblum, president of one of Houston's largest

**Friday
June 14, 1985**

# Houston Chronicle

## Texas Air purchases TWA for $793 million

Trans World Airlines Inc. will be acquired by Texas Air Corp., Houston-based parent of Continental Airlines and New York Air, for $793.5 million.

Under an agreement approved by both firms' boards Thursday, each of TWA's 34.5 million common shares would be converted to $19 in cash and $4 of a new issue of preferred stock in TWA.

The companies said that while TWA would become a wholly owned subsidiary of Texas Air, TWA would retain its identity and its present management. The combined operation would employ 39,000 workers, and its 1984 revenues would have been $4.03 billion.

TWA has been up for sale for several weeks as an alternative to a hostile takeover attempt by Carl C. Icahn, the New York investor.

Icahn's investment group bought up 11.2 million shares, or 32.8 percent of TWA's stock, and offered $18 for each of the remaining shares. Texas Air was one of the original bidders for TWA, with a cash and securities offer of $20 a share. In recent days, however, it raised the bid by $3 a share.

The Icahn group stands to make $78.6 million from the Texas Air agreement because much of its stock in TWA was bought for between $12.62 and $16 a

### TEXAS AIR AT A GLANCE

| | Continental* | New York Air** | Trans World Airlines |
|---|---|---|---|
| Headquarters | Houston | Flushing, N.Y. | St. Louis |
| No. employees | 11,000 | 1,379 | 28,000 |
| Major operating hubs | Houston, Denver | New York | St. Louis, New York |
| Revenue passenger miles*** | 10.9 billion | 937 million | 28.3 billion |
| 1984 revenue | $1.2 billion | $176 million | $3.7 billion |
| 1984 earnings | $108.1 million | $6.8 million (loss) | $29.9 million |

\* 84% owned by Texas Air
\*\* 70% owned by Texas Air
\*\*\* One passenger flown one mile

share, according to filings with the Securities and Exchange Commission.

In trading Thursday, the stock rose 37½ cents a share to $20 on the New York Stock Exchange. Texas Air's stock fell 50 cents to $13.37½ a share on the American Stock Exchange.

The deal, represented a coup for Frank Lorenzo, president and chief executive of Texas Air. Lorenzo, who

made an abortive run at TWA in 1979, is known as a master of the unregulated airline market and as very tough on labor. After acquiring Continental, he took it into bankruptcy to escape costly union contracts.

Texas Air made offers for Muse Air and Frontier Airlines earlier this year.

## Lorenzo turns 'white knight'

### TWA purchase latest in airline industry odyssey

By BARBARA LONGEWAY
Houston Chronicle

In late 1979, so the story goes, Trans World Corp. Chairman L.E. Smart stalked out of a breakfast meeting with Frank Lorenzo, then president of Texas International Airlines, when 39-year-old Lorenzo began proposing that his tiny airline acquire Trans World's ailing giant, TWA.

Frank Lorenzo returned to Trans World Airlines Thursday as a "white knight" to accept its board's blessing of a Texas Air Corp. $793.5 million acquisition that could place the country's second-largest airline in Houston.

Lorenzo is now president of TAC, a holding company which controls both Continental Airlines and New York Air.

Texas International was merged into Continental after a bitter takeover fight gave Texas Air control of Continental in 1982.

"What Frank was proposing in 1979 was what Trans World eventually did (in 1984), which was separate the airline from the holding company," said a former Texas Air employee involved in the pitch. "Everybody knew the airline was for sale — it's just Lorenzo was the first to make a pitch."

Since 1979, Lorenzo has been on an

Lorenzo

odyssey through the U.S. airline industry that has resulted in the rethinking of many of the industry's assumptions on both the financial ratios and the labor relations needed to operate an airline.

"With this acquisition, Lorenzo showed that he's continuing to push the edge of the envelope," said former Continental pilot Bob Lavender, who was part of a group of Continental employees that tried to buy that airline to keep Lorenzo's hostile takeover effort from succeeding. "He's the kind of person who will always test the outer limits of what can be done — legally and operationally."

A TWA Employees Committee announced Thursday an effort to take

*Houston Chronicle* announces TWA deal (1985).

travel agencies, declared that "[Frank Lorenzo] will do everything within his power to make TWA a low-fare carrier. If I were a member of the traveling public, I'd be dancing in the streets."

But there was no dancing in the Texas Air boardroom on this morning after. There was still the matter of negotiating an Icahn "peace" agreement, and I was more than a little disappointed by this turn. Leon Black telephoned on the morning of our announcement to report that Icahn wanted to be paid a kill fee, or "tip," in exchange for giving up his controlling position. This took me completely by surprise, although such a payment was not out of the question in deals of this type.

"It's just to cover his expenses," Black explained. "I don't think it's unreasonable."

"How much are we talking about?" I wanted to know.

"Maybe six or seven million," Black said, "somewhere in there."

I told Black that we could probably work something out at that level. The justification was clearly that Icahn was not like a typical TWA shareholder in that he had incurred certain unique expenses—lawyers, analysts, and so on—and was therefore entitled to a modest premium in return for his agreement. Besides, we were looking at a deal size approaching $1 billion, so another $6 or $7 million would not be meaningful if that was all it cost to buy Icahn's support. But he didn't stop there.

After an all-night negotiating session, Icahn's $6 or $7 million rose to more than $18 million. In addition, and most importantly for us, Icahn would not agree to vote his shares for our deal if another bidder—perhaps another airline, which I saw as a real possibility—came in with a higher offer. In the end, and after much back-and-forth, we didn't come to an agreement with him.

While we and TWA prepared the proxy statements needed to proceed with our merger without Icahn's endorsement and made the necessary filings with the Department of Transportation, Icahn decided to aggressively renew his efforts to acquire the airline and took his fight to TWA's labor unions for support. It was a clever strategy. Ever since launching New York Air separately from unionized Texas International in 1980—and, in the early 1980s, successfully bringing Continental's cost structure into line under Chapter 11—Texas Air management had been vilified by airline labor unions, particularly ALPA, and most of that hatred was directed squarely at me.

Icahn seemingly recognized that we were perhaps the only potential owners less desirable to TWA's unions than he was. After the public announcement of our merger deal, the awareness that we were "back" transformed Icahn from the leading enemy of the airline's pilots and machinists to their most viable savior. True, he was an unproved manager, with a history of stripping assets from his companies, but in the eyes of the pilots' union, still smarting from the 1983 Continental strike, he looked good by comparison.

Icahn entered a series of backdoor negotiations with ALPA and IAM representatives, ultimately winning wage and work-rule concessions amounting to approximately $500 million annually. With the promise of such drastic cuts in labor costs—26 percent from the pilots and 15 percent from the machinists—Icahn claimed that he was finally convinced that the company could be run at a profit. Nothing close to those concessions had ever been offered to TWA management, nor would they be negotiable with Texas Air, given the anti-union reputation that we shouldered, especially with ALPA. TWA's unions would do everything to keep us from acquiring a controlling interest in the airline, and if the concessions to Icahn were any indication, they were about to do just that.

We continued to persist in our pursuit of TWA, despite Icahn's saddling up with the pilots' and machinists' unions. One evening in late June, Leon Black called me to say that Icahn was willing to discuss another truce with us. Black said that the two of them were having dinner at a restaurant on Manhattan's Upper East Side and wanted to know if I could meet with them later that evening. He said that Icahn had shown him a press release he planned to issue the next morning, announcing a tender offer of $24 per share, and that we would do well to keep him from making the announcement, whatever it took. Icahn's tender strategy would at the very least push up the price of our merger agreement by another $30 million, but it was also potentially a killer for us in that it was not subject to shareholder or government approvals, as of course ours was.

---

I agreed to meet at Icahn's place at 11:00 p.m. because of the importance of this phase of the deal, although I hated these late-night sessions, which Icahn seemed to relish. His rather austere apartment was at the northwest corner of Seventy-Ninth Street and Madison Avenue. We met there for several hours and reached a loose agreement: Texas Air would pay Icahn a $25 million bonus fee, or tip, for his agreement. However, unlike our abandoned deals, this one would have real meaning in that he would also grant us an option to buy his position at $23 per share. This would ensure that we would win the company if some other bidder emerged during our approval process. Here Icahn was willing to give us something of true value, and we were willing to pay for it. The option on his shares, combined with the TWA option in the merger agreement and our own toehold position, would give us effective control, all but guaranteeing our success.

We ended our negotiation at three o'clock in the morning, and as Icahn walked me, Leon Black, and the others to the door, he extended his hand to me and said, "Well, then, I guess we have a deal." Then he checked himself and added, "Of course, I'll have to have my lawyers review it in the morning."

"Wait a second," I said. "I thought we had a deal. This is fairly straightforward. You never mentioned anything about your lawyers looking at it tomorrow morning."

Sure enough, Black telephoned me the following morning to report that Icahn had informed him that his lawyers had advised him not to do the deal. According to Black, the attorneys feared that the option portion of our agreement would trigger a short-term sale rather than a capital gain, given the required holding period, but I had no doubt that the about-face concerned something else. In my mind, what really happened was that Icahn just wanted to push the price of his support even higher. He probably went to bed thinking that if he was able to get us to pay an additional $25 million, there was no reason to stop there. There were several ways we could have structured the deal to avoid any tax issues, but it seemed to me that he was clearly using his lawyers as an excuse.

The late-night session in Icahn's apartment did produce one sort of victory for us, however: he did not issue the press release to which Black had referred. He was not tendering for control, at least not yet. He was, however, pursuing his own union concessions. On July 1, ALPA formally agreed to 20 percent wage cuts under an Icahn-controlled airline and productivity changes that would have brought the savings to around 26 percent. In exchange, he offered a "generous" profit-sharing and stock ownership plan and a promise to keep the company out of our hands. The beauty of the union cost-cut deal for him was that it was with him alone and did not extend to TWA management or to any other party that might ultimately gain control of the airline.

In later years, the TWA unions and employees would learn that Icahn's stock deal was hardly as generous as it appeared. While he granted the unions a slice of the common equity—which would have been difficult for us, since we were intent on merging TWA and Continental together—he made most of his own investment in preferred stock. This clever financial move allowed him to largely earn back his acquisition cost in later years through preferred dividends, outsmarting the unions, who insisted on "ownership" (common equity) in the airline and trumpeted it to their members as an "accomplishment" in their agreement to lower pilots' and machinists' pay. In actuality, the existence of preferred stock, with dividend rights paid ahead of the common stock, made the equity given to the unions and employees of limited value, given Icahn's control.

Despite this early accord, ALPA and other union officials were not entirely convinced that Icahn offered them their best prospects, and they hired their own investment banker to lead the search for another suitor. That search took the unions, for a time, to my old friend Jay Pritzker, the Hyatt chairman, who had helped with our original deal for Continental and who had since gone on to purchase the resurrected Braniff International Airways.

Talks with Pritzker, who was always interested in airlines, apparently progressed beyond the exploratory stages, but time and circumstances were running against him. To the unions, it gradually became clear that Icahn offered the best shot at closing the door on Texas Air. However, to Icahn, Pritzker's sudden interest in the carrier validated his own position and, alongside the heavy union courting, likely pushed him to thinking, as we understood it, that perhaps these airline investments were not so crazy after all.

After the Pritzker courting, I believe Icahn also started to think for the first time that his deal with TWA might be a very good one—one that could be far more lucrative than his trademark bluffs or traditional stock play. A pared-down TWA under Icahn-only labor terms started to look extremely attractive in projections. Accordingly, he stepped up

Cartoon depicting fight to acquire TWA (1985).

his efforts to acquire full control of the airline. He made no immediate move to buy additional shares on the open market, but the fact was that he could do so at any time. With his estimated $500 million in labor savings, Icahn had managed to turn TWA from a money-losing operation into a projected break-even or modest-profit concern.

On August 5, Icahn bested our offer for TWA by $1, offering $19.50 in cash and $4.50 in preferred stock for all outstanding shares, and he resumed his aggressive buying. Two days later, he owned more than 45 percent of the company, and on August 8, we were so convinced of his chances for success that we sat for a third time to negotiate a peace with Icahn's lawyers. This time, however, it was Icahn asking Texas Air to drop its bid and clear the way for his deal, but we did not come to an agreement. There were significant benefits to us in our deal with TWA, and we were not going to negotiate them away.

---

In the end, Carl Icahn won control of Trans World Airlines. The airline's directors wanted to end the fight and realized that with his 45 percent position and the ability to buy more shares and close very quickly, the airline was his. There was a great deal of eleventh-hour dickering— over certain provisions, granted to us by TWA and challenged by Icahn, providing us with acquisition exclusivity—but these differences were settled. Ultimately, we and TWA, with Icahn's blessing, reached a termination agreement on September 13 providing an $18 million breakup fee, a $28 million gain on the options granted to us, and another $10 million from the sale back to Icahn of our original position. While we clearly weren't looking at TWA as a source of short-term profit, the $56 million we gained in four months was a nice consolation prize.

But things did not quite work out as the TWA board expected. As Icahn had promised, he helped move the termination deal with Texas Air along. However, with us out of the picture and no one really watching, he never completed his buyout of minority shareholders at $24 per share in cash and stock. He wound up rejecting the merger in favor of simply assuming control of the airline and installing himself as chairman on the strength of his majority position.

Although no longer relevant to us, what happened to TWA under Icahn was a great sadness. Like many financial people, Icahn had a particular focus on cutting costs. He was not prepared to take risks and did not seem interested in building the company or expanding its route structure domestically to take advantage of airline deregulation. Under his control, the airline apparently would not invest in any new airplanes, a "strategy" that eventually left the carrier with one of the industry's oldest fleets. The airline was also left dependent on St. Louis and JFK while his competitors reached into new markets. He cut routes and ultimately sold off the rights to London's Heathrow Airport, which the company had long held and which had been far and away TWA's most important and valuable international franchise.

By January 1986, TWA shares had returned to the $14 level they had been at almost a year earlier, when we all first entered the picture, leaving Icahn's $300 million investment worth approximately $200 million. But through the asset sales and dividends on his preferred stock, he came away in pretty good financial shape over time, despite the grim deterioration of the airline itself. Ultimately, TWA was sold in bankruptcy to American Airlines. The pilots' union, which engineered the Icahn takeover, had their members' seniority largely eliminated when they were placed at the bottom of American's pilot seniority list—"stapled to the bottom of the list," in industry parlance.

Personally, because I had been a TWA admirer since my teenage years, this outcome left me quite saddened. I have been pleased at least to see the Saarinen terminal at JFK and the TWA brand reincarnated by an entrepreneurial group as the TWA Hotel in 2019. But it's no substitute for an airline that should still be flying.

---

One of our consolations over the loss of TWA, and the enormous critical mass the company would have provided, was the heating up of our ongoing discussions for Frontier Airlines. We had been quietly pursuing the Denver-based regional since April 1985, around the same time that Carl Icahn first surfaced with his TWA position. We believed that the struggling Frontier would nicely bolster our presence in the Denver market, where we were the number two carrier. A hub was often a losing proposition for a number two carrier if the number one carrier had a much larger route system and a much larger presence in the hub, as did United. But Continental's very competitive cost structure was also a huge advantage. The possibility of linking up with the number three carrier, particularly one with many short-haul routes, would have put Continental in a much-improved position. At the time, Frontier served fifty-three destinations from Denver—thirty-six of which had no Continental service—and had 117 daily departures. Continental flew 131 daily flights from Denver, while United led the way with 163.

Frontier had performed very well in the 1970s, but seemed to have lost its way when dealing with deregulation in the 1980s. It had suffered from Continental's and United's buildup of the Denver hub, a market probably only able to support two players over the long term. In many ways, we went after the airline as a defensive strategy. Earlier in 1985, Frontier had sold five planes to United to raise cash, and the transaction left us concerned over United's growing strength in the region as well as its future intentions. Because of Denver's importance to us, if United went out and acquired Frontier, it would just clobber us there—or so we thought.

Frontier had been in play since December 1983, when RKO General, the controlling shareholder in the closely held parent company, Frontier Airlines Holdings, considered selling its stake in the holding company. Ever since, the airline had been tangled in a series of thwarted employee buyouts and takeover attempts, and the continued uncertainty suggested that there might be an opportunity. I got to know the chairman of RKO General, Tom O'Neil, scion of the General Tire and Rubber Company family, and visited with him on a few occasions. However, he was not a very easy person to read or with whom to negotiate.

After some encouraging discussions, on April 4, 1985, we offered $185 million for the airline but were rejected by the board. When that deal soured, and after further discussion with O'Neil, we returned on May 23 with another bid, this time for $230 million, only to be set aside again when the board decided to sell half the airline's fifty-plane fleet to United to help finance an employee buyout they had agreed on. This deal would have had United owning half of Frontier's fleet, although with a leaseback arrangement from United.

Our ongoing negotiations with Frontier went largely unnoticed in the press, just as our side-by-side maneuvering at TWA was making headlines. Obviously, TWA was a huge deal, international in scope, but the bid for Frontier was also important to us. We did not see the two deals as mutually exclusive; we were simply trying to further strategically position our company while it was still possible. With Frontier, we hoped to solve our Denver competition problem, while with TWA, we sought the enormous critical mass it would have provided. Both deals would have left us stronger and better positioned for growth.

As the summer wore on, and as our TWA deal looked increasingly in jeopardy, we continued our pursuit of Frontier. In August, Frontier's unions finally agreed to wage and benefit concessions to help finance the still-simmering employee buyout, and we moved quickly to counter the employee bid before the October 30 shareholder vote. In September, we proposed an all-cash, $20-per-share tender for up to seven million shares of Frontier stock, bringing the value of our bid to approximately $250 million. The offer, again made in consultation with the Frontier board and O'Neil, called for the airline to continue to operate under its current name, as a sister airline to Continental.

Unfortunately, this too did not shake out as planned. Frontier's unions, not surprisingly, reacted negatively to our topping bid, and the airline's parent company was soon scrambling for another offer. Don Burr, my former associate, had reportedly been eager to expand in the West and envisioned the creation of a western hub in Denver. He probably also wanted to outbid and "beat" his old friend. Hence People Express, controlled by Burr, surfaced in October with a $24-per-share bid that knocked both Texas Air and the Frontier employees' deal clear out of the sky. Burr's offer amounted to 20 percent more than ours. As we saw it, there was little economic justification for People Express's share-price offer, and it made no sense for us to compete at these seemingly irrational levels. Consequently, we withdrew our tender, happy for the small profit we were able to make on the 800,000 Frontier shares we had previously accumulated and relieved that the carrier would at least no longer be available, in whole or in part, to our Denver rivals over at United.

Little did we realize it at the time, but we would visit Frontier again in a different form six months later.

# CHAPTER TEN

# Eastern Airlines

*The Final Union Standoff*
*1985–1990*

I N THE fall of 1985, our unsuccessful run at TWA made us more aware than ever of our need for an advanced computer reservations system. If we wanted to be able to fully compete with the major carriers, we would require a sophisticated modern system that would give us direct access to travel agents across the country. When TWA's PARS system passed into Carl Icahn's hands, I set my sights on the only workable alternative that remained—Eastern's System One. Although System One was not as technically advanced or as popular as American's SABRE or United's Apollo system, it was an enormous improvement over what we had, and there was a chance that it was up for sale. The airline's well-known labor troubles had pushed Frank Borman's company to the point where raising cash through an asset sale loomed as an important option. Selling System One, with Eastern staying on as its major client, seemed like it was possibly in the offing.

To follow up, I arranged a meeting with Borman in New York on November 20, 1985. When I arrived, I felt like I was retracing my steps as I entered the Eastern offices where I'd worked twenty years earlier. The offices at 10 Rockefeller Plaza, overlooking the famous skating rink where I had proposed to Sharon thirteen summers before, were as unassuming as ever. Even the secretaries looked familiar, and I smiled in recognition as I strolled the halls to the chairman's office.

Despite the rumors of a potential asset sale, it was clear from the outset that Borman wanted to talk about more than Eastern's computer reservations system. In the years since Apollo 8, he had understandably aged just a bit from the way I remembered him from the news accounts. His hair was somewhat thinner and turning white, and he didn't hide his wrinkles. He quickly steered the conversation to Eastern's overall financial situation. The airline had lost nearly $1 billion over the previous seven years, and it looked like 1985 would see more losses. By year's end, Eastern would carry more passengers—and lose more money—than any other airline in the world.

Borman was looking for a merger partner to help Eastern avoid bankruptcy, which he saw as getting ever closer. Apparently, he thought Continental might fill the bill. I was surprised he solicited us for a deal, even if it was out of desperation, and was intrigued at the turn the meeting had taken. Still, I was flattered and said we would be pleased to have a look. I did not know it at the time, but Borman and his bankers had already been to nearly every other major airline with the same pitch. The only interest seemed to have come from Don Burr, even though his airline, People Express, had just swallowed Frontier and was faltering on its own.

After the meeting, Borman and his team supplied us with a mountain of financial data, and along with a couple of our key managers, we analyzed the numbers back in Houston. Clearly, the biggest drain on Eastern was its out-of-control labor costs; Borman's persistent inability to make progress in this area was well documented. Eastern's baggage handlers, for example, earned an average of $48,000 ($138,000 in 2024 dollars) plus benefits, nearly what fully trained mechanics made in the same union. At American, in stark contrast, CEO Bob Crandall's newly implemented two-tier wage structure allowed the airline to hire

TXI introduces peanut fares (1978).

TXI flying peanuts, background from ad (1978).

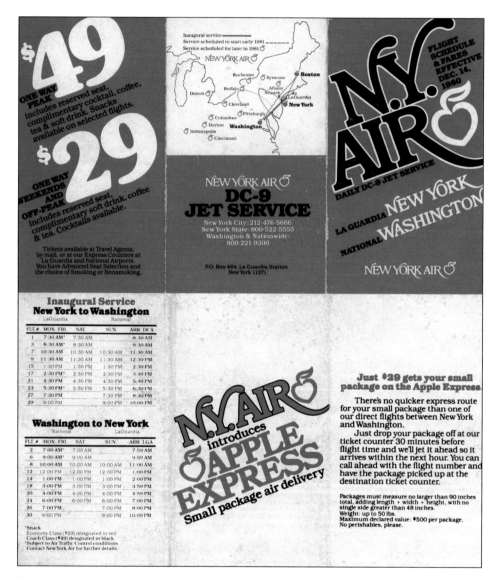

New York Air Service literature (1980).

Unions target me with threatening mail (1983).

In our boardroom with our three girls in front of peanut ads (1986).

With Continental's 1980s logo in the background (1988).

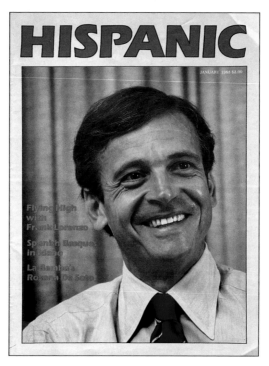

The Hispanic audience was tuned in to what was going on (1988).

At the beach with Timon, Mercedes, Nicole, and Carolina (1989).

With Phil Bakes and US Secretary of Transportation Sam Skinner (1989).

Ed Stein's cartoon poking fun at Continental debt (1990).

Dinner with Jun Mokudai, head of Continental Japan (1990).

Timon and my mother after visiting the la Madeleine restaurant, our first deal after Continental (1990).

Longtime assistant Millie Jones (left) and Sharon at Boys and Girls Club fundraiser at our house in Houston (1990).

With Timon at Barbara Walters interview (1993).

Steve Kolski (right) and myself presenting new ATX airline to New York governor Hugh Carey (center) and Stephen Berger (sitting), director of NY/NJ Port Authority (1993).

Skiing at Zermatt (1994).

Trip to rain forest in Ecuador with family (1996).

My mother at Harmony Creek Farm (2006).

My children in more recent years, from the left, Timon, Nicole, Mercedes, and Carolina (2010).

Timon shaking Dean Hubbard's hand at graduation from Columbia Business School (2012).

Sharon and I with our Vespa in Nantucket (2018).

Sharon driving the twelve-meter *American Eagle* off Nantucket (2019).

At our fiftieth-anniversary dinner in New Jersey (2022).

Donald Jr. and Trump on the *Trump Princess*
(1988).

Trump, Timon, Nicole, Sharon, and Fred Trump at formal lunch (1988).

Trump with me in the main cabin of the
*Princess* (1988).

All four of us on the deck (1988).

Trump speech at shuttle sale with Phil Bakes, Eastern's CEO, and me (1988).

Nicole, Trump, Ivanka, Sharon, and me on Aspen Mountain (1989).

Ivanka Trump and our daughter Carolina at dinner (1989).

With Trump and Sharon at dinner (1989).

All of us having a toast (1989).

Toasting with Trump (1989).

baggage handlers at around $16,000 ($65,000 in 2024 dollars), which was the going rate in the "outside" world at the time for this type of work.

Even when Borman had been able to win short-term concessions from his unions, as he had with a twelve-month wage freeze earlier that year, he did so simply by agreeing to the sorts of snapback provisions we had always rejected in our own negotiations, since they specified that everything at the end of the contract would return to the way things were before the agreement plus the wage increases and other provisions that had been negotiated for the period on productivity. On January 1, 1986, when the freeze lifted, Eastern employees would automatically receive a 20 percent salary bump, wiping out the savings of the one-year freeze in just a few weeks and putting the airline back on course for financial ruin.

It was alarming to see just how many facets of Eastern's business were unprofitable. On a route map, Eastern had a great franchise. There was the Atlanta hub, in competition with Delta. Eastern "owned" Florida, and it had a solid north-south franchise along the East Coast. There were focus hubs in Philadelphia and Charlotte. The shuttle was considered a crown jewel by employees and by many outside Eastern. And there was the midcontinent focus hub in Kansas City.

But the fancy route map was deceiving. Florida was more of a low-yield leisure market than a high-yield business market. Orlando, where Disney World is located, is a huge family vacation market. Miami is, to this day, a huge cruise ship destination, another vacation market. Eastern's positions in Philadelphia and Charlotte were okay but not great. The Kansas City hub was developed more as a package-freight connecting point, perfect for its big Airbus A300s, than as a true passenger connecting hub.

The best part of Eastern, other than the shuttle, was its Latin American route system. Borman had bought the system from a failing Braniff even as the latter carrier was hours from shutting down in bankruptcy. Since deregulation, most of the airline's profits outside the shuttle came from selling off assets. Nevertheless, we initially determined that Eastern still had net assets (total assets, minus debt and other liabilities) of more than $2 billion compared to an equity market value of only $400 million. The airline's underlying financial asset strength was so substantial that we thought we could ultimately use it to finance part of our acquisition and gain a great amount of financial flexibility in case it took longer than we anticipated to effect the needed change in labor costs.

Eastern had many attractive strategic assets, too. In addition to its shuttle operation and computer reservations system, it had the most landing slots at LaGuardia and Washington National Airports. It had the largest route network in South America of any US carrier, and it boasted some of the most attractive airport space, particularly in its key Florida markets. Most important, as far as we were concerned, was the fact that Eastern's system did not substantially overlap with any of our core operations except New York Air's lucrative shuttle markets, thus making antitrust clearance more straightforward.

We could not afford to let this one get away. With both TWA and Frontier behind us, Eastern was the only remaining airline deal that could provide us with the critical mass we desperately needed to grow to the next level—the long-term-survival level, as we saw it. It was also available at a seemingly affordable price. To follow up on our New York meeting, I arranged a dinner meeting with Frank Borman at a hotel in Fort Lauderdale in early December.

The small one-bedroom Marriott suite where we met had a rectangular conference table. When Borman arrived, he sat himself at its head. I took the seat at his left elbow. Because he said he was pressed for time, we bypassed the entrées on the hotel menu and ordered only sandwiches and soft drinks.

The colonel's demeanor was wary, almost cold. I had the feeling that his lawyers had told him to proceed with extreme caution. He began with a short speech, which sounded rehearsed. "I'm only here to listen," he said, "and to answer questions. I'm not interested in hearing any specific merger proposals, and I'm assuming that whatever passes between us will stay in this room." Of course I agreed.

Then, once we were done with the formalities, I ignored Borman's prepared speech and laid my cards on the table. I told him we were prepared to consider the purchase of Eastern Airlines at a premium meaningfully above the market, and of course we knew that Eastern's stock had fallen a lot in prior weeks given the company's problems. Borman's mood brightened almost instantly. Disregarding what was likely his legal advice, and moments after warning me that he didn't want to hear a specific proposal, he asked about a price. I told him that we would have to study the numbers and market information, but it would probably be similar to the substantial market premiums common to other acquisitions.

As we talked on, Borman's apprehension faded, and so did his heroic mystique. I realized that there was nothing cunning or calculating about the man sitting next to me. Borman seemed utterly without guile. While perhaps this is not always a good trait in a chief executive, it's a welcome characteristic in someone with whom you're negotiating, particularly in this type of situation. I didn't think Borman had it in him to lie about his intentions. If he did try to misrepresent something, I doubted he'd be very smooth in concealing it. The way he reacted to the general price discussion told me that we were getting somewhere.

We concluded our brief meeting with a handshake at the door. Borman said he'd need some time to sort through his options, then he headed home in his pickup truck. I got the impression that he was not yet resigned to selling Eastern. The flight commander in him still wanted to succeed in the primary mission of saving the company. But for Borman, Eastern might well have been beyond saving. For too long, its union leaders lacked the resolve to make desperately needed changes to the company's cost structure. Eastern's labor contracts, with their impossibly rigid work rules and high pay scales and benefits, had made it impossible for the company to run profitably on routes that had low-cost, low-priced competitors. In the previous few years, most of Eastern's profits had come from selling off assets. Whether Borman was ready to accept it or not, the day of reckoning was near.

I went downstairs to pay the bill—$321 for the room, $50.80 for dinner—and hopped in a taxi back to the airport. The whole time I was thinking that it didn't matter whether we merged Eastern with Continental or continued to operate each one separately. The overall size and scale of the Texas Air group, aided by System One, was what mattered. In my view, every carrier faced a simple choice at the time: hunt or be hunted. The advent of airline deregulation had made that an inevitability. A shakeout was already underway, and not everyone would survive.

We waited to hear back from Eastern through the holidays and into early 1986.

Borman faced two critical deadlines in February, either one of which could force the board to sell the company. February 26 was the date on which Eastern's 4,600 pilots and 7,000 flight attendants threatened to go on strike unless they had a new contract, and on February 28, Eastern faced technical default on $2.5 billion in loans unless it could obtain significant wage concessions from its unions. Those were Borman's points of no return.

Eastern shares reached new lows in January as Wall Street appeared to lose faith in Borman's ability to turn the company around. In fact, the stock was trading so low that it was attractive on its own, even without a deal. We began to consider acquiring a toehold stake in the airline. I didn't think it made sense for us to sit on the sidelines without any stake if there were to be a deal of some kind without us and the stock took off.

In early January, having heard nothing more from Eastern, we began purchasing Eastern stock in modest blocks, at just over $6 per share, being very careful not to disturb the trading market, and kept buying until mid-February, when our nearly three million shares put us at the 4.9 percent ownership threshold. However, on Sunday, February 16, Jeffrey Berenson, an investment banker engaged by Eastern, tracked me down in Acapulco, where I had escaped with the family for the Presidents' Day vacation week. It was eleven o'clock in the morning, and I was sitting with a book on the balcony of our two-bedroom suite. Sharon answered the phone, and when she told me it was Berenson, I asked her to tell him I was out. I wanted some time to think things through before talking.

I didn't know Berenson terribly well before these talks. We had only spoken twice on the telephone regarding our interest in Eastern, but I was comfortable dealing with him, because he seemed like a competent banker. He seemed to be a straight shooter who knew how to keep his mouth shut—a rare feature, I was finding, in the investment banking community.

When I called Berenson back, he told me that the Eastern board was planning to meet on Friday. "There's a chance the board will call on you to make a formal offer," he said. "I need to know if you can put one together by that time."

"We certainly maintain our interest," I said. "If you call us on Friday, we'll see where we stand."

I was not being coy or playing hard to get. There was general consensus among our group that a bid for Eastern made sense, if made on the right terms, although Phil Bakes—Continental's president, a director of Texas Air, and a close confidant of mine—had initially expressed reservations, comparing Eastern's union situation to a cosmic black hole from which we might never return. (Little did Phil know then how right he would be.) But his views had evolved to the point where he saw a lot of value in the deal. Still, we were a long way from structuring any kind of offer.

I cut my Mexican vacation short and flew back to Houston, where for three days we turned the conference room at Texas Air's corporate offices into a command center. There we looked at every aspect of the deal from every angle. On Friday, as we expected, Berenson called from Miami to say that he had been directed to seek a proposal from Texas Air. He waited until four o'clock, after the stock market's closing bell, before placing the call. Eastern shares had ended the day at $6.375, and with the market closed for the weekend, this figure would stand as the market price for the balance of our negotiations.

We didn't know it at the time, but Eastern's directors had heard some alarming reports at that day's board meeting. The airline's January losses totaled $48 million, and projections for February showed a loss of more than $58 million. Without an infusion of outside cash, it was only a matter of weeks before the airline would have to file for protection from its creditors under Chapter 11.

As soon as I hung up with Berenson, I sat around our walnut conference table with Rob Snedeker, Charlie Goolsbee, our general counsel, and Bob Ferguson, our top dealmaker, to go over the specifics. We were joined on the speakerphone by Gerry Gitner, who had worked with us in the early days at Texas International and had left with Don Burr to form People Express, only to return as Texas Air's president after growing disillusioned with Burr's quirky management style. We also sought advice over the telephone from key board members Carl Pohlad, Rob Garrett, Jim Wilson, and Lindsay Fox. Bob Carney also gave us his views.

We discussed our various options for around an hour. We considered a deal for 80 percent stock, then one for 80 percent cash, then one for 50 percent of each. We tried to look at each alternative from the perspective of the Eastern board and anticipate their concerns while still leaving us some room for negotiation. Then we debated the actual price of the deal, using the closing stock price as our guide.

Finally, with a framework for a deal in place, I called Berenson and told him we were prepared to make a formal proposal under which Texas Air would acquire Eastern Airlines. There was, however, one important condition: our offer would be open only until midnight on Sunday. By 12:01 a.m. on Monday, I told Berenson, we would walk away from the table, deal or no deal. "If you can live with that structure, we'll call you later with a specific proposal," I said. "Otherwise, we can just end it here."

It was a potential deal-breaker, I knew, but the short deadline was essential for us. As it was, our bid would become public once our offer was formally presented to the Eastern board. One of the trade-offs Borman had granted the unions in return for earlier concessions was the awarding of four seats on the board to members of Eastern unions. Those four directors were not going to sit on the news of any potential buyout, especially not news of an offer from Frank Lorenzo's Texas Air.

"I think we can live with that," Berenson replied. "I'll be expecting your call."

An hour later, with the approval of our board, I called Berenson back and outlined our deal. We would pay $9.50 per share—three dollars in cash and the balance in stock—bringing the total value of our bid to around $600 million. The price was nearly 50 percent more than Eastern's market value at the time but still far below the $2 billion in net assets we had estimated in our review.

At this point, I was eager not to make the same mistakes we had made with TWA. If the Eastern board voted for our deal, as the board at TWA had done, I wanted to make it extremely difficult for someone else to take control of Eastern's shares in the marketplace. So in addition, Texas Air would immediately purchase 12 percent of Eastern stock (the maximum amount the board could sell us in one block), which would combine with our toehold position to effectively block an outside investor. Texas Air would also be entitled to a $20 million fee, in cash or stock, whether we ended up with the airline or not. Such a large breakup fee would make Borman reluctant to use our bid merely to strong-arm his unions.

Berenson did not choke on our terms, which I took as another good sign. But I could not wait around with the rest of our team to hear Eastern's counteroffer. It was Friday night, and I had promised to take Sharon and our daughters to the movies. Too often, I have found, the easiest appointment to break is the one you make with your family. But on this night, we would have all been better off if I had taken a rain check, because I was not much company. *Out of Africa*, with Robert Redford and Meryl Streep, simply couldn't hold my attention. I probably made a half dozen phone calls from the movie theater lobby, where there was a pay phone, each run disguised as another popcorn or soda trip, to check and see if there was any news. There was none. I should have relaxed and enjoyed the movie.

At seven o'clock on Saturday morning, Berenson woke me up in Houston to pass along the word from his board. "The proposal is too light," he said. "There's not enough cash in it."

"What are you looking for?" I asked. By this point, I knew Berenson as a no-nonsense guy, and there was no reason not to get straight to the point.

"I'm looking for Eastern's shareholders to at least get the current stock price in cash," he said. He also said we needed to bump up the overall price of the deal. We had left some room in our initial bid, expecting the investment bankers to come back and seek a little bit more. It was a clever approach, and I was inclined to see it his way.

"We might be willing to go to ten dollars per share," I said, "and increase the cash component to six dollars and twenty-five cents. But that's it. We're not prepared to do any better."

Berenson said our counteroffer was "responsive," which I understood to mean he thought he could sell it to Borman and the board.

Next, I called our guys in Atlanta, where it was almost nine o'clock in the morning, to bring them up to speed. Snedeker and company, who had traveled to Atlanta in the evening, reported that they now felt we were being used. They had just arrived at the law offices there but already had reason to believe that Borman was selectively informing the unions that we were prepared to bid for the airline and trying to use our interest for maximum leverage at the bargaining table. They pressed me to seriously consider abandoning the talks, but I was not convinced we should just because we thought they might be using us.

On Saturday morning, Borman also called from Miami to report that he was finally going to tell the unions that Texas Air was a potential buyer. I wasn't sure he hadn't done so already but took his comment at face value.

"What about our agreement?" I asked, referring to Borman's pledge to keep our bid off the union table.

"Look, Frank," he said. "I have to tell them. You understand that.

And when I do tell them, I expect it will put added pressure on them to reach a settlement. In that respect, yes, I suppose you're being used. But if I don't achieve full agreement with all the unions on all our proposed concessions, I plan to recommend to our board members that they accept your proposal."

As the morning dragged on, our Texas Air group met with Eastern's attorneys to go over the fine points and put the deal on paper. They used the hundred-page agreement we had signed with TWA the prior summer as a kind of boilerplate: under our tight deadline, there was no time to start with a blank page. The TWA contract was a good one, even if it had not stood up to Carl Icahn, and there was no reason not to use it as a foundation.

By Saturday afternoon, word of our proposal had leaked to the media—spread, most likely, by union officials hoping to marshal their members against us and stir up public interest in the plight of Eastern workers—and my phone started ringing off the hook. But I kept my promise to Borman and would not talk to the press.

Eastern, too, successfully avoided these outside inquiries, and we were later able to trace most of the leaks back to the various union camps. Indeed, IAM's Charlie Bryan, president of the IAM local, was directly responsible for at least one story: he told the *New York Times* that he would rather see a Texas Air takeover than reopen his IAM contract. "I can work with Frank Lorenzo," he was quoted as saying, suggesting that he could no longer work with Frank Borman. It was a line he would have to eat a year later.

At this late stage in Borman's labor negotiations, the pilots and flight attendants were still willing to bend, but Bryan was intractable; his contract still had more than a year to run, and he saw no reason to bail out Borman by reopening it. Eastern had its top negotiators working around the clock on the machinists, but there had so far been no movement. As it happened, the national IAM leaders were in Miami that same weekend for their annual convention, and Borman took advantage of their proximity to press his case directly to the national IAM president, Bill Winpisinger, and vice president, John Peterpaul, but neither man would help turn Bryan around—which they could do under the IAM structure and which Borman claimed he had a promise from Winpisinger to do as a last resort.

Despite the distractions, that Sunday was no different from most. I went out for a run, played in the backyard with the kids, and did some repairs around the house. At two o'clock, I went to my study and waited for a conference call with our board of directors. We were all spread out across the country, and it was impossible to get together in person on such short notice, so we made do by telephone. The board knew in general terms what we were proposing, but this was the first chance we had to brief them in detail. We spent around an hour going over the specifics of our planned acquisition, and the conference concluded with the board's unanimous and enthusiastic approval.

---

In *Countdown*, his autobiography, Frank Borman recalled his thoughts at that time, comparing the situation to the space missions he had flown two decades before. "It's the same thing," Borman wrote. "I've never gone into a mission without at least three alternatives. If the primary goal cannot be attained, you go to an alternate mission. If that's out of reach, you abort, which is a failed mission but at least you're alive. This time fixing the airline is the primary mission, selling it is the alternate mission, and Chapter 11, God forbid, is the abort."

Borman still had not given up on his primary mission, even at that late hour. By ten o'clock in the evening, only two hours before our midnight deadline, Snedeker called from Atlanta to say that he and the rest of his team were convinced we were being jerked around. They had not heard from their counterparts in Miami for the previous couple of hours. The board's full attention seemed to be on its labor contracts—an ALPA agreement was reportedly ready for signature, and a pact with the Transport Workers Union of America, which represented the flight attendants, was near completion—and our guys were now convinced that Eastern had involved Texas Air as part of one big ruse.

"They're using us, Frank," Charlie Goolsbee insisted over the phone. "I'm surprised you don't see it."

This time, after much discussion, I finally agreed, and I instructed Goolsbee to withdraw our offer for lack of good faith. If Borman was so focused on his labor equation that he could not see clearly the alternative that we had offered, then that was his business, but I was not about to let him string us along any longer just so he could accomplish his goal.

Borman called me at home a few moments later, in just about the time it took for word of our withdrawal to travel from Atlanta to Miami. "Frank," he said, "don't do this." He sounded exasperated, almost desperate.

"My guys tell me we're being jerked around," I said. "They don't think you're operating in good faith."

"I can certainly understand that," he said, "but I give you my word. The directors are looking very sincerely at your offer."

"What about the unions?" I asked.

"We're still talking to the unions," he allowed. "I won't lie to you. Fixing Eastern—that is my first priority. If we cannot fix it, we will sell it. If we can't sell it, we'll tank it."

"All right," I said, relenting. "I'll put the offer back on the table." And we did.

Meanwhile, as the midnight hour approached, I received a call from Eastern director Jack Fallon, chairman of the airline's executive committee, who wanted me to accept what he was calling a hell-or-high-water clause and extend our deadline by four hours. Basically, he wanted us to commit to acquiring the airline even if it was forced to declare bankruptcy before we could close the deal.

This was a relatively easy concession to make, since this was largely a net-assets deal and I felt we had to concede something. If you truly want to acquire a property, it is difficult to keep your options totally open and still get the lowest price: in order to get the best deal, you often have to give the strongest commitment—this was my belief. In most of our negotiations, I tended to offer big deposits up front to persuade the other party of our strong interest and decrease their financial risk. Even if the deal we offer is comparatively modest, it is always a real deal with a high probability of getting done. Here, I knew, the offer we had placed on the table for Eastern was not especially rich, considering its assets, but the board seemed willing to go ahead with it, provided I could offer reassurance that we were fully determined to proceed even if Eastern's operations took a turn for the worse. The specter of Chapter 11 did not trouble me. I had already been through it with Continental and lived to tell the tale. I was convinced that the asset values of Eastern were sound and that those assets would not evaporate in bankruptcy. Besides, I thought bankruptcy could be avoided, at least until closing.

After briefly discussing the issue with our legal team, I got back to Fallon and told him, "Have your people add it to the contract. We'll sign it, and we'll agree to four more hours."

This was easier said than done. A hell-or-high-water agreement was apparently so rare that none of the high-priced lawyers on hand were sure how to word it. Finally, someone came up with a draft that was acceptable to both sides.

Back in Miami, Borman and company put their four-hour stay to full use. A number of Eastern employees had begun to mill about the lobby of Building 16, the company's headquarters and the site of the after-hours board meeting, awaiting the verdict. Inside, the directors were playing their final hand. Borman left the room to let the board freely consider Bryan's latest proposal, and he later wrote that he used the time to stroll to the memorial fountain outside the building, honoring the company's founding spirit, Captain Eddie Rickenbacker. He read the plaque beside the fountain. "I kept looking at it," he wrote. "I just couldn't stop looking at it. Standing there alone in the moonlight, never had I felt so close to this tortured, troubled airline. Never had I wanted so badly to save it."

But it was out of his hands. Charlie Bryan stubbornly rejected every counteroffer and compromise the directors presented, and in the end, there was nothing to do but put the sale to a vote. Just after three o'clock in the morning, the directors voted 15–4 in favor of selling

Eastern Airlines to Texas Air—the nay votes were cast by Bryan and the other three union directors.

Cartoon poking fun at takeover of Eastern (1986).

I was on a plane to Miami before breakfast, still reeling in the wake of the weekend's events. This was the critical mass we had been seeking for so long. Eastern would provide us with a strategically critical computer reservations system, a strong, sophisticated management team, and unmatched facilities throughout the country. In fact, those facilities showed their value quickly, since with Eastern's domination of Newark International Airport's Terminal B and Continental's domination of Terminal C, we were able to keep the other large carriers from creating a competitive hub in that city. We knew American wanted to get into Newark in a major way. But more on that later.

Texas Air would also soon be flying more planes than anyone else in the world with the exception of Russia's state-owned Aeroflot. In 1985 figures, the combined Texas Air fleets would fly nearly fifty-one billion revenue passenger miles, nearly tripling our current traffic. We would be responsible for 57,000 employees. Born as a somewhat suspect little holding company, Texas Air had been transformed into one of the most formidable, forward-thinking investors in the domestic airline industry—or so we hoped.

It did not take Wall Street long to declare the Eastern purchase a great deal for us. For $607 million, half of which would come out of Eastern's own bank account, we stood to acquire a company with more than $2 billion in net assets. Eastern stock, which had traded as low as $4.75 in prior months, climbed to the $9 range within a week of our announcement. For years, the uncertainty over Eastern's union contracts had acted as a mortgage on the company's assets. With this deal, investors hoped that Texas Air would be able to liberate the operation from its skyrocketing labor costs, and Texas Air stock soared on the news. Normally, the market drives the shares of an acquiring company in the opposite direction, anticipating the debt or equity dilution resulting from the takeover, but by the end of that first week, our shares climbed from $17 to $28.50.

In the short time since we were asked to put together an offer for Eastern Airlines, our focus had been on acquiring the prize. None of us had time to consider what we would actually *do* with the airline once we bought it. For the time being, at least, we would not do anything. We could not. The deal was still subject to shareholder and government approval, and it would be several months before the Department of Transportation would make its ruling. The only potential complication we could see was the possible antitrust implications of operating the New York Air and Eastern shuttle markets alongside each other, but we thought we could work that through with the regulators.

As we did in most of our other deals over the years, we took things one step at a time. At that point, we intended to run Eastern separately from Continental and New York Air, although we would certainly look to consolidate operations in some areas down the road. Borman, as part of our agreement, would remain as chairman and chief executive until the deal was closed, although we would look to install some of our own people in top management positions to help with the transition and ensure that our interests were being served during the interim period.

No other deal of ours had ever generated so much attention: indeed, it was difficult to think of *any* other airline deal that got so much interest. Maybe it was because in just two days we had grabbed one of the country's largest airlines for a little under one-third of its asset-rich net worth. Maybe it was because everyone sensed that there was a shoot-out destined to take place between us and the combative unions that had held Eastern hostage for so long. Maybe it was because people were curious to see if we could succeed where others couldn't.

Our original intention was to simply fly Eastern as a separate carrier, apart from Continental, for the foreseeable future. Four or five years down the road, we envisioned some sort of combined Continental–Eastern fleet, but it made no sense to consider any sort of merger until we had gotten Eastern's losses under control and brought Eastern's cost structure closer to Continental's. This process could not begin until we received final DOT approval. In the meantime, Borman and the Eastern president, Joe Leonard, were still in charge, although they dealt with us in a transparent manner by opening their books as well as their board-room doors. Predictably, Eastern's management was hit by a wave of exits, and Borman and Leonard were very good about putting some of our people into these open spots.

They even consulted us on the significant operational decisions they were pondering. Around a month after we had announced our deal, Leonard told us that Eastern was planning to pull out of its Kansas City hub. Borman had created the hub in the early 1980s, thinking that Eastern needed a western presence, but it never made any money, and Leonard figured it was high time to cut Eastern's losses there.

We didn't see it that way, however, at least not initially. We thought we could develop a number of smaller regional hubs and manage these alongside two or three giant centers. Eastern had a number of these regional hubs throughout its system—in Charlotte, Philadelphia, and New York, for example—in addition to its dominant operations in Atlanta and Miami. Our team was not prepared to close the door on Kansas City before we had a chance to make our own assessment. Two years later, when we finally decided on our own to close Eastern's Kansas City operations, the unions wailed that we were stripping the company, not realizing that we had given the four thousand affected jobs an effective two-year stay of execution back in 1986.

---

Eastern started 1987 stronger than anticipated financially, but despite that, there were other markers that showed that the airline would be on a slow slide to insolvency without changes in its costs. The labor concessions that Borman had won in his last-ditch bargaining with the pilots and flight attendants in 1986 were due to expire in the months ahead. The machinists' contract was due to expire even sooner, and those negotiations would set the tone for the airline's immediate future.

Charlie Bryan had tried to pull the rug out from under us from the very beginning. Immediately after our February 1986 acquisition announcement, he began beating the drums for another buyer to come in and force us out of the company. He even pushed in vain for an employee buyout.

I had no dealings with Bryan myself during my Eastern days, which Bryan probably took as an affront. We believed Borman had made a big mistake in getting directly involved in labor negotiations. A local union leader lives his contract day in and day out. He knows every detail, every nuance. The only way management can negotiate a labor deal responsibly and effectively is to match labor leaders with executives who are also able to devote their full attention to the matter. Eastern had such a person as its chief negotiator. In addition, Phil Bakes was Eastern's president and CEO, and I certainly did not want to undercut him. Phil was full-time in Miami at Eastern and was highly regarded by us back in Houston. He relinquished the same posts he had held at Continental when taking over as CEO of Eastern. I remained in Houston, focused on Continental, and was consulted only on major issues, not on a day-to-day basis.

It was not that I was totally opposed to direct union relations or meetings when it seemed appropriate. For example, I did have personal dealings with the head of the national IAM union, Bill Winpisinger, who flew to New York from Washington once to have lunch with me as we attempted to break the Eastern–IAM logjam. On another occasion, I met with the head of the Eastern pilots' union at New York's University Club for a drink.

For years, Bryan played Borman like a pipe organ. He never put his real demands on the table until the deadline drew close because he knew he could draw Borman into the negotiation, where his involvement could cost Eastern dearly. During one negotiation, Borman extracted certain economic concessions from Bryan in exchange for something much more costly in the long term: he gave IAM the right to represent the mechanics' first-level supervisors. Making workers and supervisors members of the same union was in reality a recipe for a breakdown in workplace authority. We were told that Bryan, after this concession was agreed to, went out to the main machinists' area at Miami International Airport, stood up on a ladder, and proudly told the workers that the union now represented all their bosses. The rank and file erupted in cheers, while the supervisors stood silent, knowing they had effectively been stripped of their authority.

Unsurprisingly, I had been made the flash point for the coming battle with the Eastern unions, and it would not be long before my reputation and integrity were under full-throttle attack by the unions' heaviest artillery. During the discovery phase of one of the many lawsuits with the unions, we uncovered a strategy memo prepared for the unions' public relations people by an outside PR consultancy that was headed, "Make Frank Lorenzo the issue—avoid discussing airline deregulation." The Eastern deal may have been a steal, but if these early turns were any indication, it would be far more difficult than I bargained for.

---

Negotiations had to start somewhere, so in October 1987, we asked the machinists to accept nearly $250 million in concessions and to allow management to hire part-time workers under certain conditions. Anything much less would place the airline in real jeopardy, we thought, and anything more would likely incur the wrath of the IAM. As it was, I feared we were pushing the envelope a bit with this opening offer, although it was similar to what Eastern had been seeking before our purchase.

If we succeeded in convincing the machinists that the only way they could preserve their job base was to relent on their wage and benefit demands and to splinter the IAM's skilled mechanics from its unskilled members, allowing us to establish two different wage scales, then we had a shot at reinventing Eastern as a vital, financially viable carrier for the long term. If we failed, and caved in to the IAM's absurd and inflexible demands, we would be pushed right out of business, because this would lead to our getting few if any concessions in bargaining with the other unions, who were anxiously waiting to see if a concession precedent was set. However, those other unions had nothing to fear, because Bryan countered by demanding 10 percent pay increases over each of the next two years, and if we had held out any hope that the machinists would finally see the light, it was dashed by his response. We were not even on the same page.

Eastern's management looked on Bryan's proposal as a bad joke, something he could float to his members and back away from at a later date when the need arose. It was not based on any real economic assumptions. It was based on wishful thinking, his own politics, and the union's apparent desire to force our hand. I had long thought that Bryan was on a kind of power trip, and the beginning of these formal talks confirmed it. He had just been elected to an unprecedented fourth term as head of Eastern's IAM district earlier that month by an overwhelming margin, and he seemed eager to flex his new muscles. Our offer was difficult for him to accept, we knew, but it reflected an honest need to sharply reduce Eastern's cost structure, bearing in mind the fare competition with which Eastern was surrounded.

We did not think we could accomplish this on the first pass, but we had at least hoped that Bryan would come back with something that might have acknowledged Eastern's critical need. While he could well have been realistic, considering the position of the company, he instead came back with these absurd and totally out-of-touch numbers. This left us too far apart for any serious negotiations and forced us to consider a general downsizing of the company—a de-risking, so to speak—and the attendant sale of certain assets.

It also forced us to call on the National Mediation Board to break the standoff. Here again, our hands were tied by the ancient mediation rules established by the Railway Labor Act. Recall that regulations required a thirty-day cooling-off period prior to any work stoppage or unilateral changes to a contract. The NMB could declare an impasse at any time, at the request of labor or management, which would set the thirty-day clock to ticking. After that, labor was free to strike and management was free to impose new terms, but absent a "release" by the NMB, both sides were bound by the terms in force on the last day of the old contract.

Traditionally, airline management was only too happy to have the terms of labor contracts frozen at their expired levels. The unions, seeking a pay increase, would push mediators to quickly recognize an impasse; the airlines, looking to hold down costs, would sit back and let the process unravel at its own, usually leisurely, pace.

But this was no longer the situation, at least not at Eastern. Borman's labor contracts reflected the shift in industry practice and called for certain snapback provisions prior to the close of term. The 20 percent concessions granted by the pilots in early 1986, for example, would be given back at the end of the contract, and the pilots would be rewarded with a pay hike substantially above their pre-concession levels. Under this scenario, the interests of labor and management in mediation were completely reversed, and it was up to us to ease the stalemate. The unions were not about to give regulators any cause to imperil their hard-won gains.

---

Both sides braced for a strike. A walkout would be a miserable turn of events, but it would not be a killing one, we thought. We had flown through work stoppages before, and we were confident that Eastern could survive a strike by its machinists, provided—and this was essential—that we could get the pilots to cross IAM picket lines. We formulated a strike insurance plan, drawing on some of the resources of Continental, and looked to the NMB to start the thirty-day countdown. We had to get this negotiation, which was not going anywhere, behind us.

And so, beginning in January 1988, we waited. And waited. And waited. Every day, we all went into the office thinking we would have a ruling from the NMB, and every day we went home wondering what we had to do to convince the board that we were too far apart to make any headway in negotiation without a deadline. Months went by as Eastern's losses mounted. We lobbied extensively in Washington, hoping to be released from our old contract, but the machinists countered our every argument. Bryan contended that we were out to break the unions and claimed we were pushing for a strike. In reality, we were pushing to get this negotiation behind us and didn't think that Bryan and the IAM would be realistic until they were forced to be. What we were truly seeking was a resolution to this conflict.

With the labor situation at a slow boil, Phil Bakes and his team turned their attention to day-to-day concerns. They pared back some of the airline's operations and reduced service in markets where we no longer liked the profit potential. We also trimmed some fat in our management ranks and cut our overall workforce by around 10 percent. We looked to beef up our service record, and even in the middle of these labor wars managed to improve our on-time performance rating, as measured by the DOT, to an industry high.

One of the first major steps we took to position Eastern alongside our other holdings was to transfer its computer reservations system to the corporate level, where it could independently service each of our sister airlines—and other outside airlines—away from the din of the labor fights at Eastern. Under this shared arrangement, we projected that System One's reach would be significantly enhanced, as indeed it was. Eastern's management had long sought such an outcome.

Eastern PR department cartoon (1988).

While it was a sound, even logical, move and certainly within our rights, since we owned the company, it generated a swirl of protest. Months later, the unions would point to the transaction as proof that Eastern and Continental were being operated as a single carrier and that Eastern's assets were being stripped for the benefit of Texas Air. Texas Air paid an equitable market price for the system, a number reached through the independent assessment of investment bankers at Merrill Lynch, and we made sure that Eastern's leaseback expense would never exceed the operating costs it had previously been paying to maintain the service. With more than two thousand employees, System One bore enormous labor costs, and Eastern simply traded its wage and benefit outlay for a comparable monthly service charge. In exchange, the airline received an infusion of cash and increased penetration into Continental's base. Continental, too, greatly benefited from the alliance with Eastern and System One's increasing market share. Just as importantly, System One services now could be sold to other airlines, resulting in a greatly reduced perception that it was run by the marketing departments of our airlines.

It was, I thought, a good deal all around, but we took some heat for it, as we would for most of our efforts at consolidation, which were second-guessed by the unions. We were challenged on our merger of the Eastern and Continental sales and marketing forces, our creation of a central fuel purchasing unit, the alliance of Eastern's and Continental's frequent-flier programs, and the sale of excess aircraft from Eastern to Continental. The deals were contested in the courts and in the press, even though such arrangements were not unusual—even among unaffiliated carriers—and even though they reduced overhead and increased productivity. In our case, since the carriers were affiliated and under full common ownership, the benefits of these moves were even more obvious.

Eventually, the pilots got in on the act. Beginning in late 1987, ALPA launched what it called the Max Safety campaign. For the following two years, it registered an endless stream of fabricated complaints directly with the FAA. Pilots were instructed to fill out PRIA (Pilot Records Improvement Act) forms for all sorts of perceived or imagined equipment violations. At the end of each month, the FAA was inundated with thousands of write-ups that they were obliged to check out. ALPA then issued press releases recording the number of safety complaints filed against Eastern by its own pilots.

Although there was a long rivalry between Eastern's ALPA and IAM leadership, here it seemed that Jack Bavis, the pilots' union head, and Charlie Bryan had found a common enemy in Texas Air. Max Safety was a blatant attempt to smear airline management and damage Eastern's reputation with the flying public. It also included a good old-fashioned slowdown of operations. Pilots were instructed to exercise extreme caution on the ground as well as in the air, and our planes were taxiing the runways of some of our busiest airports at only one or two miles an hour. Our on-time performance levels sagged, and public confidence in the airline sank to new lows every day. The crisis was rapidly coming to a head.

Eastern was clearly a failing carrier, obvious for all to see, but closing the deal for Eastern wasn't smooth. Although the Reagan administration would greenlight mergers in October and December 1986 between Northwest and Republic Airlines and between TWA and Ozark Airlines, each of which had competing hubs in the same cities, Reagan's Department of Justice and Department of Transportation balked at our deal. DOJ and DOT viewed the bundling of New York Air and the Eastern shuttle under one "roof," so to speak, as anticompetitive. This complication would cause us great angst. We eventually decided to sell New York Air's slots at LaGuardia and Washington National Airports to Pan Am, which started its own shuttle service in competition with Eastern's. Stripped of its highest-value, highest-profile asset, New York Air would eventually be folded into Continental. It was a painful decision, given the entrepreneurial spirit of Texas Air and our memories of starting New York Air and competing with Eastern. We were backed into a corner from which we had to decide whether to sell the crown jewel, the Eastern shuttle, or much of New York Air (the full story of this agonizing decision will be told in the next chapter).

Our inability to reach an agreement with the unions eventually led to a strike. Initially we tried to fly through it, but ultimately operations shut down. Despite our desire to keep the airline flying and keep the jobs that went with it, we reached the point where the next move was to consider selling Eastern. The situation could possibly threaten the entire Texas Air group.

---

By the spring of 1989, Eastern was bleeding lots of cash. We could not get operating costs even close to where they clearly needed to be, and the unions remained unmoved, refusing to renegotiate their contracts.

The strike continued as well. We finally put Eastern into bankruptcy on March 9. Even so, we received significant interest from potential Eastern buyers, most of whom had been approached by the unions. These buyers basically felt that they could extract major union cost relief, which we and Colonel Borman could not obtain, and thus benefit from ending the strike and, with any luck, gaining labor peace.

In addition, it was believed by potential buyers that we were under financial pressure to sell. The deal that got the furthest was a potential sale to a group led by Peter Ueberroth, the Major League Baseball commissioner, whose term had just ended and who was well known for his handling of the 1984 Olympics in California. Carl Pohlad, the Texas Air director and owner of the Minnesota Twins, had been with Ueberroth at a baseball owners' meeting in Fort Lauderdale in early March 1989 when Ueberroth approached him with his interest. Carl contacted me and said that Ueberroth's group would be a logical buyer and that we should try to negotiate a deal and sell Eastern to him. Ueberroth had already been having discussions with the unions, with our approval, and the unions were, unsurprisingly, very interested in seeing him buy the airline.

After much negotiation, we came to an agreement with Peter and his group and announced it on Thursday, April 6, 1989. They were to buy the airline for $464 million, subject to approval of concessions by the airline's unions. Peter claimed he had already negotiated a deal with the unions, so it was assumed that this condition would be met. In addition, the deal was subject to creditor and bankruptcy court approval—which would be easy with union accords, although there was no assurance on financing.

We were very skeptical of what the unions would really agree to and feared that Ueberroth, and probably Pohlad, were somewhat naive about what in reality could be put in writing with the unions. Because of our doubts that the deal could be consummated, and because of the disruption that a sale causes, we put a seven-day fuse on it, requiring union approval by midnight the following Tuesday, April 11. Peter thought that would allow sufficient time for his approvals. These were heady days for Ueberroth, who was set to become the operating head of the airline, and the announcements were accompanied by mammoth amounts of publicity, which he did not appear to discourage.

But the Eastern union approval never happened as it was supposed to, and the deal fell apart on the following Wednesday. The unions, cagily, announced that they would be agreeable to Ueberroth's cost cuts, but only on the condition that we allow the immediate appointment of a trustee to take over our ownership position. This requirement was obviously absurd, because it would have allowed the airline to be taken from us without any assurance that Ueberroth could raise the money to buy it. The union's lawyers undoubtedly would have made it clear to their clients that we could not possibly give up permanent control of the airline before we received payment for it. However, Ueberroth was publicly disappointed, and in walking away from the deal he told the bankruptcy judge that he would not be willing to come back and revisit the purchase.

Carl Icahn, who wanted to merge Eastern with TWA, and my old friend Jay Pritzker and the Hyatt group, always interested in airline deals, were also circling around and publicly declaring their interest. Icahn was the most aggressive in pursuit, although I knew that his style was to push hard on a deal, see how low he could get the price, and then walk away.

Nevertheless, I agreed to have dinner with Carl one evening, although I was confident it would go nowhere. I felt it would show that we were casting a wide net in attempting to settle Eastern's ownership issue, which we in fact were. Carl and I met at a small Italian restaurant, a favorite of his, on West 56th Street in Manhattan—Il Tinello. Knowing that the singer Karen Akers, one of Sharon's and my old friends (she was then the wife of a Columbia fraternity brother, Jim Akers), was performing that evening at a small cabaret on West 27th Street at 9:15 p.m., I arrived for dinner with Carl at 7:15 p.m. and told him that I would be leaving at 9:00 p.m. at the latest because I had a commitment downtown. He then gave me twenty questions on what I was going to be doing, and when I told him that I was headed for some fun with an old friend who was singing in a cabaret, he asked if he could join me. The sight of two formally dressed businessmen sitting in the back of the tiny, informal space (Carl is quite tall), having martinis, must have been a sight to behold. As it turned out, the evening was enjoyable and gave me a view of Carl's "other side," but it certainly did not advance the prospects of an Eastern sale.

---

Unable to move forward, we continued with our efforts to rebuild Eastern as a small airline focused on the Atlanta hub. To accomplish this, Eastern began hiring pilots, although many of the company's pilots were coming back. In the second week of August alone, 250 pilots returned, and we temporarily stopped hiring.

In addition, we looked at assets to sell in order to raise cash, the most obvious being the New York–Boston–Washington shuttle (I cover this sale in the next chapter). We also looked at selling other assets to prepare for the reorganization plan, which would allow us to pay our creditors and get Eastern discharged from bankruptcy. A package of assets valued at $1.5–$1.8 billion, which we knew could be readily sold or already had been sold, was planned for the reorganization. The biggest additional piece was the sale of Eastern's South American routes, largely encompassing Brazil, Argentina, Chile, and Peru.

The sale of the South American route was put in place with a phone call I made to the farsighted Bob Crandall, CEO of American Airlines, whom I knew well. Our planning group had long considered the near-term value of these routes to us, since we knew they would likely be a cash drain for the foreseeable future. Crandall and I agreed on a juicy $500 million number on the phone, higher than what our planners thought we could get. But the sale took a long time to complete, given the union fights that ensued and the myriad details involving aircraft, personnel, liabilities, and so forth that needed to be sorted out. We also continued to have doubts as to whether we needed to sell the routes as part of our reorganization plan, since we were aware that we were selling a network of routes with future promise. But the route sale did get completed and approved by the bankruptcy court in early 1990.

At that stage, we were putting the finishing touches on our reorganization plan, although the unions were continually scrambling behind the scenes to sabotage it. They had a major advantage in that they were members of the creditors' negotiating team, even though the pilots and flight attendants had ended their strike and many members had returned to work in the fall of 1989.

In February 1990, we reached agreement with our unsecured creditors on a plan to discharge Eastern from bankruptcy that would have returned fifty cents on the dollar for unsecured creditor claims. But only a month later, we had to go back to the creditors and admit that the plan would not work, since Eastern's results had worsened. In the negotiations that ensued, in late March, we were unable to come to an agreement, because the unsecured creditors, spurred on by the unions, were holding out for a blanket guarantee from Eastern's parent company, which we had always held apart from Eastern. Texas Air was willing to make a major contribution in cash and notes, but it was unwilling to be responsible for Eastern's liabilities in total. So on April 10, 1990, the creditors asked the court to appoint a trustee to take over the ownership of Eastern, replacing Texas Air, a request that was granted on April 19.

The court's decision to remove Texas Air and appoint a trustee tolled the death knell for Eastern. It meant that Texas Air—with its airline, its financial resources, and its deep management strength—was to be replaced by an individual. A very difficult decision to reconcile with reality. But it shows the continued influence of the unions on the creditor committee.

As it happened, in place of our management, the trustee appointed by the court was Martin Shugrue, whom we knew well because he had briefly served as president of Continental in the 1980s and had been with Pan Am. The unions dropped their picket lines under Shugrue, and the airline was brought back at a reduced size. Marty also embarked on an expensive advertising campaign in the summer of 1990, in part featuring himself. It seemed, according to our folks, that he never really understood Eastern's weaknesses. Sadly, the carrier, also struck by the rapid increase in fuel prices after the invasion of Kuwait, ran out of cash later in 1990. In January 1991, Eastern, well known as the Wings of Man, stopped flying and was liquidated.

"Unions tried to tell Eastern employees that they won the Lorenzo war."

It is easy to blame ourselves and look at the Eastern purchase as a bad deal that shouldn't have been done. Certainly, it was a bad deal in terms of our financial loss and our lost time and energy. However, it is also realistic to acknowledge that things would have been quite different for Continental without the purchase.

For starters, Frank Borman said that Eastern would (or had to) be placed in bankruptcy if the unions didn't agree to new contracts and if Texas Air didn't complete the purchase. While it's of course fruitless to speculate about who would have purchased Eastern's assets, we had already seen that there was interest on the part of other carriers in establishing a Newark hub. If we didn't acquire Eastern, Continental probably wouldn't have been able to build its massive and very profitable hub at that airport. Instead, Newark would have been a two-carrier hub, which usually entails more competition and less attractive economics. In addition, Texas Air still owned Eastern's System One, which served as the backbone of Continental's computer reservations system for years.

But still, all things considered, Eastern was a deal that we should have passed on.

# CHAPTER ELEVEN

# The Shuttle Sale

*From the Wings of Man to the Wings of Trump*
*1988–1990*

THE DECISION to sell the Eastern shuttle, which we reached in 1988, was difficult because it was a valuable asset that was considered by employees and many others to be one of the crown jewels of the company. The factors that went into deciding to sell it are complex. Indeed, the first sign of trouble in our Eastern acquisition was one we had not fully anticipated: the divestment of New York Air landing slots and gates because of antitrust concerns on the part of the Reagan administration. As I mentioned in chapter 10, Reagan officials refused to approve our purchase of Eastern, claiming that by adding Eastern's shuttle service to our New York Air operation, we would damage competition in the heavily trafficked Boston–New York–Washington corridor.

While we had been concerned about the antitrust aspects related to the shuttle and New York Air, the ruling nevertheless caught us by surprise because the federal government had been routinely approving mergers and acquisitions in the airline industry in the 1980s, as I've mentioned. We had counted on using Eastern's shuttle to complement

New York Air's commuter service and had been looking at increasing our combined frequency to half-hourly departures. As it was presented to us, we had to divest ourselves of one or the other in order to secure government approval of the purchase.

At that point, it really was not an option to hang on to New York Air and sell the Eastern shuttle. Eastern employees regarded the shuttle as a proud company symbol, and from a human relations standpoint, there was no way we could sell such a high-profile asset just as we were taking ownership of the company. Shareholders would not have been happy either, because the shuttle was probably one of the most well-known, most prestigious, and most consistently profitable operations in the airline business and clearly had a greater value than the New York Air shuttle operation.

As much as we hated to lose the shuttle part of New York Air—the guts of its business—on May 13, 1986, after negotiations with several parties, we agreed to sell most of New York Air's shuttle landing slots and applicable gate space to Pan Am for $65 million. When DOT officials deemed the sale inadequate (we suspected they were likely pressured by behind-the-scenes lobbying from Pan Am), we were forced to sell Pan Am an additional fourteen slots for $9.8 million.

The sale of the original core of New York Air was a very painful move for us, since we all were so intimately involved in the birth and nurturing of the company. Indeed, an airline operation at LaGuardia had always been a somewhat hazy dream of mine. Also, we had gotten to know many of the NYA employees right from the start, and most of them had an entrepreneurial flair, given the start-up nature of the company. It was a difficult decision for us to have to implement, and it decreased, at an early stage, the value of Eastern for us.

---

By 1988, the situation at Eastern had grown so dire that the company eventually had to resort to the sale of assets just to stem the flow of losses. Phil Bakes had one of his senior people draft what would become a controversial memorandum examining the impact of various asset sales against a standard set of criteria. The memo was known internally as "Chunks" for the way it broke the airline down into its component parts and considered the consequences of shedding virtually every severable aspect of our business—which was how the Eastern shuttle ended up on the chopping block.

To the public and to employees, the shuttle stood at the heart of Eastern's business, but in truth, it represented only 5 to 6 percent of the airline's revenues and had a stated book value of less than $50 million. After more than twenty-five years, given new competition, Eastern's grip on the shuttle market was no longer what it was. Ridership was declining as the Pan Am shuttle gained market share—as had New York Air itself in the early years after we started the airline in 1980.

The Eastern shuttle was also such a Spartan product that there were many in management who felt that it gave the rest of the airline a bad image, despite its popularity and historic but declining profitability. Indeed, our research suggested that a commuter accustomed to the shuttle's bare-bones service was not likely to consider Eastern's full-service operations to Florida. The Eastern shuttle was also a poor feeder because it was not particularly integrated with other routes. Nobody flew from New York or Boston to Washington on the shuttle in order to connect to Florida, because there were plenty of nonstops between New York and Florida and Boston and Florida.

But the most compelling reason to pursue a sale of the shuttle was that Eastern needed the cash as losses from the rest of the airline's operations continued to mount. Nonetheless, we had enough misgivings about shedding the shuttle, perhaps mostly psychological or employee attitude–driven, that our first move was to explore a kind of hip-pocket transaction through our Jet Capital holding company. That proposed deal, valued at $250 million, would have kept the shuttle operating under the Eastern name and largely under Eastern control. Effectively, Jet Capital would have put together a group of investors, and a large bank loan, to purchase the shuttle business without any of its airplanes. In this way, we thought, we could do a fair deal that would bring Eastern a lot of cash and at the same time keep the shuttle in the family.

By all independent accounts, this was a sound move, a reasonable investment benefiting both Eastern and Jet Capital. But the deal was quickly greeted by a firestorm of negative reactions from the company's unions, which we fully expected—and from Wall Street, the media, and Eastern employees, which we had not expected, at least not to such a degree. It looked like Jet Capital was trying to steal the shuttle from Eastern at a distress-sale price. This was not at all the case, as the ultimate sale would bear out.

And so, in February 1988, we retained Merrill Lynch to evaluate the shuttle and scout the marketplace on our behalf. The investment bankers set an estimated price tag of between $350 million and $425 million for the shuttle, including eighteen Boeing 727 aircraft, which we saw as a validation of our $250 million price tag on the proposed Jet Capital deal. After all, the Jet deal didn't include the airplanes and parts and instead anticipated an attractive-to-Eastern lease on the equipment, which would have netted a further $75 million or so to Eastern. In addition, Merrill assumed that other airlines would be our most likely buyers, which we knew would inflate the value of the deal by at least $50 million. In these terms, the value of the Jet Capital deal was around $375 million, which placed it right in the middle of Merrill's valuation range.

While we were waiting on the Merrill Lynch report, I had drawn up a list of potential buyers, and somewhere near the top was New York real estate developer Donald Trump. Trump had originally been contacted by our bankers about being part of the group of investors buying into the shuttle with Jet Capital. Other names were Jack Kent Cooke, who owned the Washington Redskins football team and whom Barry Simon, Eastern's general counsel, had previously worked for, and Jay Pritzker, the Chicago financier and hotelier who had alerted me to the Continental opportunity ten years earlier.

While we were focusing on potential buyers, we were severely distracted by a DOT investigation stirred up by the unions. With all the falsely created pilot reports, ALPA and IAM succeeded in convincing

Jim Burnley, secretary of transportation, to launch an investigation of the safety and management of Eastern Airlines and the Texas Air group, even though it was a totally partisan and unreasonable request and clearly just a public relations stunt and an effort at harassment, since airlines are continually monitored by the FAA. This investigation was unprecedented for a major carrier and spoke to the enormous political power of unions, even during a Republican administration.

On Wednesday, April 3, 1988, Burnley announced a thirty-day inspection program. The evening news and newspapers put our "examination" front and center during the entire review period. Although we received a clean bill of health from the DOT on May 31, 1988, much public relations damage had been done to our airlines' reputations, which was not repaired by the Friday-afternoon "all clear" news release from the government.

---

However, despite this hostile environment, and even because of it, we pushed on with the possible shuttle sale. The ideal buyer, to our thinking, would have to be an independent non-airline buyer. If we were going to lose the shuttle, we did not want it to end up with one of our major competitors. We also wanted to attach a number of restrictions on the sale, which included long-term prohibitions on its resale to other airlines and the right of first refusal in any resale transaction. And we wanted to ensure that Eastern's frequent-flier program remained the shuttle's principal incentive program after the sale.

Trump was the perfect suitor, I thought, because the shuttle was the kind of high-profile property that he seemed to crave. Most important, he appeared eager to do deals. He appeared to be flush with cash and banker friends, although we were not sure which was more likely to be backing up his commitment. He had casinos, hotels, apartment buildings, office towers, and plans to build more of the same. His purchase of a giant luxury yacht from Adnan Khashoggi, the Saudi arms dealer, sparked an international photo opportunity after it was refurbished somewhat and rechristened the *Trump Princess*. It was at the time the largest private yacht in the world.

I approached Trump personally in April 1988 at the wedding reception for Jonathan Tisch and Laura Steinberg, scions of two of New York's best-known families. The affair was held in the Great Hall of the Metropolitan Museum of Art, completely redone for the occasion, of which the father of the bride, my old friend Saul Steinberg, was a major benefactor and of which the groom's uncle, Larry Tisch, was an active trustee. The wedding did more than unite two of the city's most socially prominent families: it also provided me with the opportunity to float the idea to Donald Trump that he might want to consider adding the Eastern shuttle to his vast holdings.

I was not all that subtle about it, because I had the feeling that subtlety was not Trump's strong suit. During cocktails, I walked over, drink in hand, to where he and his then wife, Ivana, were standing. (As I approached, it occurred to me that the fabulous emeralds Ivana was wearing could have easily have been worth as much as the shuttle down payment.) When Trump and I were left alone, I let it slip that the shuttle might be for sale. "It's the kind of thing that might make sense for you someday," I said as matter-of-factly as I could.

From the look on Trump's face, I could tell he had interest right away. One thing he did not have was an airline, and no matter how much money airlines can lose, or what a nuisance they can be to run, there is something sexy about owning an airline. (That is, until you own one.) Trump, I sensed, wanted to own one. I knew, of course, that he had just paid more than $400 million for the Plaza Hotel, so I compared those apples and oranges at my first opportunity. "The shuttle is our Plaza Hotel," I said, appealing to the side of him that clearly coveted these showcase properties, "but I'm not sure the board wants to sell. It's probably premature."

"Well," Trump said, in what I took to be an effort not to sound too eager, "if you and your board are ever interested in selling it, let me know." He and Ivana then had a photograph taken of the four of us and made a toast, and off into the illustrious crowd we went.

Just after this encounter, on the following Tuesday—an indication of his immediate interest—Trump called and wanted to follow up on our conversation, which we did around a month later during a breakfast meeting. We would have met sooner, but I was only in New York every few weeks, and this was the first common opening in our busy schedules. Trump suggested we meet at the Plaza, in the Edwardian Room, and I happily agreed. I figured that going there as Donald Trump's guest would be an experience.

Trump met me at the hotel wearing a deep blue suit and a yellow tie, which was standard attire for him. He was looking a little flabby, which I guessed was attributable to lack of exercise, although after we sat down to breakfast, I figured his diet was a factor, too. It certainly was not designed by a nutritionist. For this first breakfast he ordered eggs and bacon and all the trimmings. I had my usual—hot cereal and fruit—and I don't think the contrast was lost on either of us. It led us right into our first bit of small talk, about health and nutrition. He was clearly sensitive to the fact that his diet and exercise habits left something to be desired, particularly in the face of my avowed interest in nutrition—plus, he had heard about my marathon running.

Amusingly, in our subsequent breakfast meetings, also at the Plaza, Trump's eating habits improved while mine worsened. I doubt whether he was consciously aware of it at the time, but he gradually switched to lighter, more healthful fare as I gravitated toward the heavy artillery. I guess I was trying to make him feel more comfortable with what he was eating and to come across as less of a health freak, while he may have been looking to show more self-control than his taste buds had been used to.

Once, after a long run in Central Park before one of our breakfasts, I decided to treat myself to pancakes, which I enjoy on rare occasions, particularly when I "earn" them, as I had that morning. When I sat down at the Plaza, I ordered a stack, figuring my guilty pleasure would be mitigated by the fact that he would at least be able to feel good about what he was eating. But Trump aced me out of my consolation by ordering a bowl of hot cereal. The moral of the story: people do strange things when they're sitting across the table from each other trying to do a deal.

Breakfast with Trump in the Edwardian Room often turned out to be quite a spectacle. After we were seated at the corner window table, with a grand view of Central Park, he would usually say hello to a number of people who passed by. For a guy with a reputation for being somewhat insensitive, he was very courteous and gracious with his guests—and with me. Once he finished playing Mr. Hotelier, and after we had dispensed with our pleasantries, it was usually fairly easy to get down to business and keep his attention.

At our first meeting, I told him how I saw the deal. I cautioned him that the board had not yet decided whether to actively pursue a sale and that I myself was still unsure of the best course of action. But I let on to him that our price, if we were to sell, would be $425 million for the entire operation, including the planes. (I had sent him a copy of the Merrill Lynch study noting the $425 million valuation prior to our meeting, so he had some idea where I was coming from.) He seemed to choke a little bit on the price. Maybe "gag" is more like it. I was really aiming for $400 million. I knew that if I went to the board with that offer, I could truly say that it was an excellent price.

Of course, I had some lofty expectations, but I knew I had the leverage of selling to one of our competitors or other investors to fall back on. Clearly, the shuttle was worth more to American or United than it ever would be to Donald Trump. He and I both knew this. What Trump probably did not know was that there was no way we would ever consider a sale to another major airline except as a last resort. He came back with a lowball indication of $250 million, which was the price of the proposed Jet Capital deal. I told him I could not imagine our doing a deal at $250 million or anything close to it, and he promised to take another look at the numbers and get back to me if he wanted to continue talking. It was, I thought, a pretty good first meeting. His price was lower than I thought it would be, but he was clearly interested. And I got the definite impression that his interest was not going away anytime soon.

After our hour-and-a-half breakfast and discussion, Trump took me on a grand tour of his historic hotel, which he was very eager to show off. There was, I suspect, some braggadocio to this turn, but I also had the sense that he was genuinely proud of his hotel and enthusiastic over its prospects. He was absolutely determined to make the entire operation over in his first-class image. He was very animated on our tour, very energetic, like a boy showing off his newest and most expensive toy. He showed me the various changes he was making to the already magnificent lobby area, such as adding gold leaf to the stunning ceilings. At one point, he led me right into a dress shop at the southeast corner of the hotel, picked a moderately priced garment off the rack, and said, "Look at this cheap stuff. I'm going to bring some real quality to this place." He had an equally low opinion of Trader Vic's, the restaurant downstairs, which he seemed to think was a well-worn tourist trap. He hoped to replace it with a high-tech, high-class disco.

For good measure, he even tossed in a little anecdote about the off-site parking service offered to hotel guests. I think he told me the story as much to amuse me as to demonstrate his tough, hands-on management style. When Trump first bought the Plaza, he told me, guests' cars were being parked around the corner, at a separate facility. He was astonished to learn that the parking garage did not split its fee with the Plaza. "Imagine that," he said. So he marched over to the garage, introduced himself, and came away with a 50 percent split, which he claimed would improve the Plaza's profitability by more than $1 million a year. He really got a kick out of telling this story.

My next step after this first meeting was to pursue our other prospects and give Trump some time to think about the deal. Time, as I saw it, was working in our favor, at least at that point. The longer I held firm at $425 million, and the longer we actively courted other buyers, the longer he would have to stew over the deal. We began active discussions with several candidates in May, around a month after our first Plaza breakfast. The most promising of these discussions were with America West Airlines, a small Arizona-based airline not competitive with Eastern. Those negotiations were handled by my very able associate Kevin Moore, president of Jet Capital. Kevin and I had real doubts whether the aggressive America West team could secure the financing for the shuttle, but in the leveraged days of the 1980s, anything seemed possible. And because the airline had to go to the banks for financing, we were pretty sure Trump would hear about it. We needed America West's interest to play off against Trump's and others' interest.

Trump and I had another breakfast meeting around a month later, in mid-June, again at the Plaza. I told him that the Texas Air board had still not decided to pursue a sale but that I wanted to go ahead and bring them the best offer indication we could find. I told him we had other interest in the shuttle and that his initial price of $250 million was far too low. "You've got to do a whole lot better," I said. He came up to $325 million. I was surprised at the leap, but I still did not budge from my first figure. I told him I thought his offer was substantial but still short of what we felt the board would be expecting if indeed we decided to sell.

"So where are we, then?" he said.

"We're closer," I said, "but we're still not there in terms of price."

In truth, we were a lot closer than I was letting on. We were having some difficulty getting firm financed offers from our other prospective buyers. The marketplace was not as rich as I had thought or hoped. Besides, I thought a deal with Trump made the most sense because it did not bring the competitive problems that another airline would and because he was willing to live with a ten-year restriction on resale to another airline. Plus, I felt that Donald Trump had the ability to close the deal. This was a key element in his favor. Just about the last thing one wants in a deal like this is to do all the paperwork, gain government approval, and then have it all unravel six months later when the buyer can't come up with the money. That was always a possibility in a deal of this size and complexity. But Trump was in the best position to make the deal with the least hassle and the least risk—or so we thought.

In fact, at another breakfast, he showed me a financial statement to allay my concerns in this area before I even had a chance to express them. He simply reached into his inside jacket pocket and handed me a statement of his net worth while we were eating. I guess if you're Donald Trump, you always keep one of these things handy. The document was revealing, claiming net liquid assets of $934 million ($2.45 billion in 2024 dollars) and a total net worth, including his real estate holdings, of more than $3 billion after netting out the debt. Trump modestly and candidly pointed out that the number that counted was the net liquid assets figure, since his real estate holdings accounted for most of the rest and real estate prices were often quite subjective. Amusingly, the top of the net-worth statement was marked CONFIDENTIAL in bold letters, and then, right next to it, FOR USE BY HOWARD RUBENSTEIN & ASSOCIATES ONLY, also in big letters. Howard Rubenstein was Donald's public relations agent; I really got a kick out of that.

We also involved family in our back-and-forth. One day, at Sharon's suggestion, I invited Trump, along with Ivana and their children, to join us at the Tavern on the Green for dinner, an invitation he gladly accepted. There Ivana noted that Sharon had brought a number of toys for the children, theirs and ours. She remarked at how well prepared Sharon was for a night out with the kids, something new to her, and mentioned that she and Trump never took the kids out because they stayed with their nanny for dinners. At one point in the conversation, she mentioned that their son Eric was having an interview the next morning at Buckley, where they were eager for him to enroll. Sharon, upon asking if Ivana was taking him over for the interview, was told that their nanny would take him there; Ivana said she was tied up. Sharon told her she thought that was a mistake, and Ivana countered, half kidding, that they weren't worried at all because Donald would build the school a gym if necessary. Ultimately, Eric didn't get in and went to Trinity, another excellent K–12 school, instead.

At our next Plaza breakfast, in July, Trump raised his shuttle offer to $350 million. I had meanwhile come down to $400 million, so we were finally in the same ballpark. We had another meeting the following week, in his Trump Tower office, and for the first time, we had company for our conversation. I brought along Kevin Moore, who was by then working actively on this deal. Trump had his lawyer, Harvey Freeman, with him, and the four of us talked through the specifics of a potential deal. We were close on almost every important point. From time to time during the meeting, Trump would walk over to the window that looked down from his office to the Plaza Hotel, a few blocks away, and I took one of these opportunities to press my point on the shuttle's intangible value. It was a lifetime sale, I said, just like the hotel. I thought I could move him up in price a little bit, but he was not budging. I did not want to press too hard. After all, he had already gone from $250 million to $350 million, which was starting to look like the best he could do. So we let things rest at that point.

I also continued to have reservations about going forward. In the months since we had begun the Trump discussions, Eastern's business had brightened a bit, and there seemed to be some possibilities for labor peace. It no longer seemed certain to me that we had to do the shuttle deal. I thought perhaps we had a new window through which to maintain the shuttle or explore the best possible terms over a longer period of time.

---

Trump, perhaps sensing my continued uncertainty and wanting to move things along, extended our business relationship to include a family outing. He knew my family summered on Nantucket, where he was planning to join his family in late July 1988, so he graciously invited us for lunch on board the *Trump Princess* with Ivana and the children. Sharon and the kids were really looking forward to it. I was, too. We had all seen pictures of the yacht in the newspapers and on television, and we were curious to see what all the fuss was about.

Our initial weekend plans for the lunch were upset a bit, as it turned out, but not by much. Trump's ship captain called on Friday afternoon to tell us that he had decided not to chance bringing the ship into Nantucket Harbor. He was afraid he'd run aground, since the *Princess* drew eighteen feet and the harbor was dredged to only nineteen feet.

So he rerouted to Martha's Vineyard, where there was a deeper draw. Trump also called and suggested we meet them there. "Catch one of your flights to the Vineyard," he said, "and we'll have lunch there, as we'd planned in Nantucket."

So we did. It was a beautiful sunny Saturday in early August, and the change of venue was not really any big inconvenience. It was just a ten-minute ride to the airport and a short hop in a small airplane to the Vineyard airport. We dressed for a relaxing day on the boat. Sharon and the kids and I wore casual shirts and shorts. To say that we were underdressed would be a vast understatement. Trump was basically wearing the same outfit I had seen him wear in New York. He had slipped out of his suit jacket and wasn't wearing a tie, but he was still wearing what looked like suit pants along with a somewhat sportier shirt and business shoes. Ivana was dressed in a fancy outfit with short pants; it looked like she was going to a cocktail party. And their kids were decked out in the kinds of clothes most parents save for holidays and special occasions. Trump's parents and his sister joined us on board, along with his in-laws, and they also were dressed as if they were going to a serious lunch.

The formality did not end with the clothes. We ate in the ship's main dining room. It was beautiful on deck, with a nice breeze and a clear sky, but we stayed inside. We had a big, heavy meal, complete with a bottle of fine wine—which Trump didn't drink because he does not touch alcohol. Don't get me wrong: it was a wonderful meal, but it wasn't quite what we were expecting. Our kids were hoping for more summery fare—perhaps hamburgers, french fries, and the like. Nothing matched the interesting setting, however.

We were all seated at one end of a long, formal table, with the Trumps fanned out in one direction and the Lorenzos in the other. Donald and I sat at the head, and Ivana and Sharon were at our sides. I was not planning to discuss the shuttle, but Trump coyly brought it up anyway. He wanted to know where I stood with our board on pursuing a sale. Sharon told me later that she noticed Ivana stop their discussion when she heard the shuttle mentioned. They had been talking across the table about something else—something more appropriate to the occasion, I imagine—when Ivana just tuned Sharon out and tuned her husband in.

"Look, Don," I said, trying to shift the conversation to a more Saturday tone, "we're still looking at it; we're still talking about it. We're meeting in a few days, and I'll know more then. I was hoping to have a price that I know they will find hard to turn down if they decide to sell." But I also explained that selling the shuttle was not our first choice because of its symbolic and real importance to our employees and our public image.

Like our first breakfast at the Plaza, this meal also came with a tour and a story. The tour was extraordinary. The *Princess* was truly a masterpiece, although it was more than a little excessive, even for Donald Trump. The boat was basically in the same shape as it was when Trump bought it. The bathrooms were all done up with gold-plated fixtures. There was even a fully equipped hospital ward on board, although it wasn't staffed. Trump was particularly delighted with the Khashoggi-installed walls and ceilings, which were made of elephant skin. I had never seen anything like it. It must have cost a fortune. However, the real problem with elephant skin, I learned, was that it was impossible to clean. Trump seemed quite concerned about the kids and their messy hands. All you need is a room full of kids with jujubes or whatever, and there goes the elephant skin.

The story about the purchase of the yacht provided another chance for Trump to make a point about how tough he was in negotiations. According to him, Khashoggi had spent well over $100 million to build and decorate the yacht, but when hard times hit, it was put on the market for $100 million with no takers. Ultimately, Khashoggi accepted Trump's offer of $30 million, and while the papers were being drawn up, Trump managed to shave off another million by showing some chutzpah.

Clearly, the first thing he planned to do once the transaction was completed was put his own name on the vessel; I had never known him to build or purchase a high-profile property without putting his name on it. When Khashoggi called to confirm that the name on the yacht, *Nabila*—named for his daughter—would be taken off, Trump said he assumed the name was part of the package and that he liked the name. After some back-and-forth, Khashoggi consented to a $1 million discount on the price in exchange for which Trump agreed to drop the name to make room for his own, which was undoubtedly what he planned to do in the first place—hence his $29 million purchase price.

At our next meeting, at the Plaza, I came right out and told Trump his $350 million price would not do. This time, he quickly said he would go to $365 million. "That's progress," I said, trying to mask my pleasant surprise at the jump. "I'll have to go back and discuss it with our folks." While my tone was probably even and nonplussed, in truth I was delighted. It seemed we had finally reached Trump's bottom line, and it was pretty close to what we'd been hoping for.

---

Before we finalized the deal, however, I wanted to make one final pass at exploring the alternatives to a sale. During these protracted negotiations with Trump, I asked Kevin Moore and some of the Eastern guys to examine the feasibility of financing the shuttle ourselves. We could hock it, which was essentially what Trump was planning to do. Kevin had reported back that we could get a $200 million loan secured by the shuttle, which in many ways would be preferable to an outright sale to Trump at $365 million. The only hitch to this refinancing was that it required labor peace at Eastern, which we very clearly did not have, and if we had it, there would probably have been a restriction on asset sales.

Of course, that did not mean it couldn't be achieved, so I used the few days following Trump's last and best offer to meet with Jack Bavis, head of Eastern's pilots' union, on a hot August afternoon. We met at the University Club in New York, during which I laid out the situation. I told him we were close to a deal to sell the shuttle in order to fund Eastern's working capital, but that it might be preferable to keep the shuttle and borrow against it, provided we could reach some sort of workable agreement with the unions.

Bavis was a moderate union leader, unlike some of the hotheads who dominated the ALPA group, and he reacted very positively to our discussion. He did not want the shuttle sold and was willing to look with me at some of the alternatives, so we talked through what a labor deal might look like. When we came up with something we both could live with, he promised to go back to his master executive council to canvass the reaction there. I heard back from him a few days later, by phone, and the response was not what I was hoping for. Not only did the radicals on the council have no interest in a deal, a dejected Bavis informed me, they also wanted to toss Bavis from his leadership position for having talked with me without their approval.

By early September, it was apparent that our only viable option was to proceed with the sale. I called Trump and told him we had a deal, then instructed our attorneys to finalize the documents, which had already been prepared in draft form. Predictably, the finalization process had its share of snafus and misunderstandings, all of which were to be expected in a complicated deal of this type but none of which was insurmountable. The paperwork was completed within a month, and we made plans to sign and announce the deal on October 12, 1988, at a Plaza press conference.

The announcement was noteworthy for the way Trump pulled out all the stops. With Donald Trump, it was not enough to simply call the media and disclose the terms of the deal. He took over one of the hotel's function rooms and really dressed the place up. He placed a model 727 at the front of the room, which he had painted in Trump colors. He had not yet settled on a design for his new airline, but this served nicely for the time being. The room was jammed with reporters and some of his support personnel. He even tied the purchase in with his Atlantic City properties, suggesting that the shuttle could possibly fly in gamblers. "Flying people in would be an interesting concept," he said. Trump seemed to relish the noise and attention. It was his day, his glory, and it was clear he loved being at the center of it all.

Shaking hands at shuttle deal announcement in front of a Trump airplane model (1988).

A week after the sale, he was still flying high. "I like buying Mona Lisas; the shuttle is the single finest asset in the airline industry, the best," he was quoted as saying. "I like collecting works of art. This is a work of art."

Reaction to the sale was pretty much as expected. Of course, the unions were dead set against it. But it was clear to us that the unions, so intent on letting the airline bleed dry, were dead set against any move that would give the company some breathing room. The pilots' and the machinists' unions checked in with their loud disapproval. Moreover, the machinists tried to block the sale in court, claiming that we were prevented from making any material changes to the company structure while we were still at an impasse over a new contract. It was a preposterous legal position. We knew it. They knew it. It was just harassment and PR—a delaying tactic.

One of the amusing and unexpected reactions to the shuttle sale came from Carl Icahn, who had expressed his interest in buying Eastern in the weeks leading up to the Trump announcement. Icahn's pursuit had been contingent on the airline remaining intact, with important assets such as the shuttle unsold. In going forward with the shuttle sale, I fully believed that Icahn's interest (if it was indeed genuine, and I had my doubts) would be heightened by the shuttle sale, because now the buyer would be looking at an additional pocketful of cash. Happily, this prediction was right on the money. I spoke with Icahn shortly after the Plaza press conference, and he told me he liked the deal and he liked the company with all the extra cash.

Trump and I spoke from time to time over the following six months, by phone and at a couple of breakfasts, while he concluded the financing for the deal and recruited an experienced management team to head his new enterprise. He also asked us to make recommendations for new management.

Trump seems to be getting some advice (1989).

As we were approaching the Christmas holiday break, Trump invited us to ski with him one day in Aspen, since we were also planning to be there. We had built a log house in Snowmass, next to Aspen, because our children were enjoying skiing and because building a log house had been one of my longtime goals. I arranged with Trump's assistant that we would meet at the bottom of the Little Nell run, at the Little Nell lift, at 9:30 a.m. on the appointed day. Then Sharon and I waited for Trump and Ivana at the base of Little Nell, but nine thirty came and went without any sign of them.

We waited and waited on that chilly morning, and at around ten fifteen an employee of the Little Nell hotel approached us with a message from Trump. He apologized and said that he was sorry he'd gotten delayed and would have to meet us at the mountaintop restaurant at noon for a brief ski run; Ivana wouldn't be joining the group. Looking a bit haggard, he joined us shortly after noon, along with Arnold Schwarzenegger. We took one run together, noting that he was a pretty good skier. He and Schwarzenegger then took off.

On Monday, in the gossip columns, we learned what had probably caused his delay. It seems he had brought his then girlfriend, Marla Maples, and put her in another room at the Little Nell, where he and Ivana were staying. According to the gossip column, Ivana discovered this on the morning when we were supposed to meet. Needless to say, she wasn't happy and had a major argument with Trump over it.

We continued talks with Trump that winter as we awaited action from the government on our deal. In some of these talks, particularly as we got close to the March deadlines, we discussed some delicate and potentially troublesome matters, such as Eastern's fractured labor picture and the emerging possibility of a union strike.

"Don't worry," Trump said. "We'll be there, strike or no strike, ready to close the deal." He did seek at the time—and got—a breakup fee of $8 million in the event he was prevented from closing the deal.

Then, on March 4, 1989, the Eastern pilots struck in sympathy with the company's mechanics, almost shutting the airline down. Only Eastern's South American system and the shuttle operation were able to operate during this time. As a direct result, the shuttle's market share dropped precipitously. It had been consistently pulling between 50 and 55 percent of the market, but suddenly, it dipped to around 25 percent.

Some passengers were not sure it was still operating. Others simply refused to cross the picket lines. And others feared that the quality and safety of the service would be diminished. The dramatic decline threatened to kill the shuttle deal. Our lawyers advised us that Trump could opt out because of these drastic changes in market conditions.

---

On Wednesday, March 15, 1989, I called Trump on speakerphone. I was with Kevin Moore, who would add increased gravity to the call. I told Trump that my family and I were going skiing the following week in Utah. Since we knew that the Eastern strike could trigger the force majeure provision in the shuttle contract and allow him to walk away from the purchase, I wanted to know his intentions before we left, if possible, for obvious personal reasons. Trump assured me that he was fully committed to the deal and had no intention of walking away. We went ahead with our skiing plans.

On Friday, March 17, 1989, an article in the *Wall Street Journal* headlined "Shuttle Woes Bode Ill for Eastern—Ailing Carrier Faces Uphill Battle to Woo Back Shuttle Fliers" painted a very dismal picture of the strike's effect on Eastern's shuttle operations. On the following Monday, perhaps spurred by the article, Trump tried to change the terms of the deal.

I was out West with the family preparing to go skiing, and that morning I took an urgent phone call from Barry Simon. "You'll never guess what just crossed the newswire," he said incredulously. "Trump wants to redo the deal. He issued a press release saying that he wants a major price reduction, claiming that because of the strike the shuttle isn't worth what he originally agreed to pay. He's asking for a meeting with management." The next day, the *New York Times* reported that Trump said he wanted to cut the price by $125 million, to $240 million, because the shuttle's value had been severely hurt by the strike.

Our response was to try to put a fallback deal in place, since Trump's strategy was not much different from what businessmen generally would do: "No harm in trying," most would say. I did not think there was any point in negotiating with Trump without a reasonable alternative. I had our guys place calls to other potential buyers while I arranged for a flight back from ski country for the next day, Tuesday morning. Meanwhile, Trump's secretary called my longtime assistant, Millie Jones, to arrange a call and a meeting, but I thought a little coolness might go a long way at this stage. I figured Trump still wanted to do the deal, and I didn't want him to think we were nervous. I had Kevin Moore return the call, which I knew Trump would take as a snub, and he confirmed to Kevin that he was indeed interested in concluding our deal, but at a reduced price. Kevin told him that we were not prepared to cut the price, and that if Trump did not want to buy the shuttle now, at the agreed-upon figure, which we knew was his legal right, we were quite confident there were others who did.

Meanwhile, our talks with other potential buyers went into high gear. America West came on strong, with an allegedly Chase-financed offer of approximately $375 million. (The offer was for more, but it would have required Eastern to give up even more valuable aircraft.) Jack Kent Cooke, the Redskins owner, apparently wanted to sign a contract for $385 million. American Airlines and other prospective buyers were at various stages of evaluation. By Thursday, three days after Trump's press release, word had reached the marketplace that we had at least two other deals warming should the Trump deal fall apart.

Trump's secretary continued calling, attempting to set up a meeting. But I pointedly let Trump stew until Thursday, March 23 (a long time in the deal world), when I finally agreed to meet over breakfast the following morning—naturally, at the Plaza. I came armed with a compromise. We were not willing to reduce the price—he was now offering $350 million—but I did have a proposal that would offer him something of value. We had gotten into a very public dance, and I thought there was a meaningful chance that Trump would walk away from it, if only out of pride and to save face if we stonewalled his price-reduction attempt.

So I offered to throw in four more 727 aircraft of the type that the shuttle already flew. They were old, excess-to-our-needs airplanes that had been mothballed in the Arizona desert and were worth maybe $10 million in total, *if* you could find a buyer. Realistically, they were of little value to Eastern, but we had been told they would be of value to Trump. He had already made elaborate plans to refurbish his shuttle planes, a process that took several weeks per aircraft, and we knew he could well use several additional aircraft as backup. Fortunately, he accepted the proposal without much hesitation, and we shook hands on it. The next day, we put out a press release indicating that we had agreed to a major modification of the arrangement. The release was heavily designed to make Trump feel good and allow him to claim that he was successful in effectively getting the price lowered. We learned a lot about negotiation with Trump in the process: try to make sure the other side looks good. However, that is a good thing to remember in any negotiation and often forgotten.

The week of the renegotiation with Trump was also memorable for me in that on the Monday when Trump put out his renegotiation press release, Columbia University announced that it was temporarily withholding the John Jay Award from me, an award that was scheduled to be presented on the following Thursday, March 23. The university claimed that the machinists' union impasse provided a climate that "made it impossible to guarantee an atmosphere appropriate to such a celebratory event." In other words, this great university's leadership was afraid of union pickets. They went ahead and presented the award to me a year later, at the New York Public Library, a safe distance from the Columbia campus. (It was interesting to note that the tables were turned on Columbia during 2021–2022, when graduate student workers, including teaching assistants, joined a union and went on strike, inciting campus unrest.)

In any event, after our renegotiation with Trump, we moved expeditiously to close the shuttle deal, which we did on June 7, 1989. Trump sank a lot of money into the shuttle as soon as he took it over. He called the shuttle his "little diamond," and apparently that was all his people needed to hear to open the cash spigots wide. We had been operating the service with around eight hundred employees and employee equivalents, but Trump increased that number to 1,100 in short order, although part of that increase was the separate management layer he now had to add. Moreover, he gave his new fleet of planes a complete facelift. Each aircraft was redone at a cost of more than $1 million each ($2.5 million in 2024 dollars, roughly what it costs to reconfigure a 737 today from one operator to another)—a lot of money to put into a twenty-year-old airplane.

And he spent the money in very untraditional ways. All metal surfaces were changed to chrome, which gave the interior the desired glitzy look but was extremely labor-intensive, requiring a worker to polish the metal after everyday use. Even the bathrooms were elaborately made over, despite the strong reservations that his management apparently expressed to him about the impracticality of chrome surfaces, which they claimed would show fingerprints after just a few flights. When I heard this, I was reminded of Trump's tour of the expensive Plaza Hotel remodeling, with its gold-plated ceiling trim. But it was his airline and his choice now.

Shortly after the acquisition, the market share of the Trump Shuttle, as it was soon called, rose back up to around 45 percent. Trump was ecstatic, and the resulting press attention was great. Once again, it looked to all the world that the golden boy of New York real estate had not lost his golden touch. We had another of our Plaza breakfasts around a month after closing the deal, and Trump was positively exuberant over the shuttle's fortunes. He had heard that we were entertaining the idea of selling control of Texas Air, and we briefly aired the possibility of selling to him. We both mused over the kind of increase in market share the airline might realize with the Trump name behind it. We reckoned that even a 5 percent increase in Continental's sales could maybe mean $250 million more in the cash register each year.

However, Trump did not leave himself much time to fantasize about increasing Continental's market share through acquisition because he soon set his sights on bigger fish. In October 1989, he bid $120 per share for American Airlines—a potential deal worth more than $7 billion

($17.5 billion in 2024 dollars). The numbers were staggering. We spoke on the phone about his offer, because he wanted confirmation of the airline's value. But as it played out, Trump's offer did not get very far because the stock market went through an unrelated swoon, and airline stocks were particularly hard hit, making a deal more difficult. American's tough CEO, Bob Crandall, was not about to roll over, either. Dan Reed, a journalist at the Fort Worth *Star-Telegram*, reported that American had drafted a RICO lawsuit against Trump in anticipation of an unsolicited bid. But the change in the stock market killed Trump's effort before it got off the ground.[5]

---

Meanwhile, the Trump Shuttle profit-and-loss figures for the year were coming in, and they were awful. Although market share had gone up, it never budged above 45 percent. That, coupled with the expensive gold plating and chrome makeover, and the increased overhead, left plenty of red ink for Trump and his bankers to handle.

Soon the Trump Shuttle ranked as only one of Trump's troubles. In early 1990, cracks began to emerge in the rest of the Trump empire—and at home. Casino industry analysts were forecasting doom for his just-launched (and over-budget) Taj Mahal, in Atlantic City. His marital woes and extramarital affairs had moved off the gossip columns and onto the front pages. He was separating from Ivana, which became an even bigger story than his financial concerns. Trump and Ivana were divorced in 1990.

It was a public relations nightmare, and I think it really affected his shuttle business. The research showed that female commuters developed a distaste for Trump over what they saw as his shabby treatment of Ivana and switched their business to the Pan Am—formerly New York Air—shuttle. To stem the losses caused by the decline in ridership,

---

[5] Dan Reed's book, *The American Eagle* (New York: St. Martin's Press, 1993), page 246.

the one-way peak shuttle fare rose to more than $140, up from $99 at the time we bowed out. That chased away even more passengers, given the new competition that had emerged.

By midsummer 1990, things were very tough in the airline business for all carriers, not just the Trump Shuttle. With the invasion of Kuwait in early August, fuel prices spiraled up, nearly doubling by the end of the month. In the process, the Trump Shuttle losses increased markedly, as they did for most airlines. Trump's other businesses were not much help, either. In September, he missed a $1.1 million interest payment to the banks, and things began unraveling for him.

Soon after the default, the bank creditors took control of the shuttle away from Trump. After negotiations with a few airlines were attempted, the creditors reached agreement with USAir in December 1991. Soon the Trump name came down. The USAir arrangement provided for a lease, with an option to purchase, which it exercised in 1997, at a price of $285 million. Today, the original Eastern shuttle operates as the American Airlines Shuttle.

Trump was in the airline business for only a short while.

# CHAPTER TWELVE

# Making Continental Stronger

*Successful Strategies*
*1986–1990*

I N THE late 1980s, while we at Texas Air were dealing with issues related to the acquisition of Eastern Airlines, on the Continental side of our house we were also building and strengthening the company, taking advantage of opportunities as they appeared.

In those years, as part of our focus on Continental's hub structure, we continued our efforts to strengthen our Denver operation. And in the spring of 1986, having been outbid by People Express for the original Frontier Airlines, we purchased Rocky Mountain Airways, a small feeder airline in Denver. Its owners had decided that the time had come to back away from day-to-day operations and get some liquidity into their finances. They also were concerned about competition from Aspen Airways and its newly acquired commuter jets. As a consequence, we jumped at the opportunity for this relatively small but strategically attractive deal. Rocky Mountain flew to many of the principal ski areas from Denver and had been the foremost carrier in these markets for years.

Continental had been profitable in 1984 and 1985, with the operating and cost changes we had been able to make, and we expected that we would be able to emerge from bankruptcy protection by mid-1986. We did so that September, essentially paying creditors full value—one hundred cents on the dollar, in bankruptcy parlance. Because of this, Texas Air was able to retain all Continental's shares except those issued to employees and management, a very unusual outcome in bankruptcy. Our creditors were extremely pleased. Even American General Corporation, which had loaned us $50 million the year before the bankruptcy and might have been expected to be initially very unhappy, participated in the debtor-in-possession financing to aid us in going through the reorganization.

CAL also embarked on substantial fleet purchases to build the airline, including a major order for the then new Boeing 737-800s as well as additional Boeing 727-200s to augment our thriving domestic system. We also added DC-10s, enabling us to expand internationally with service between London and Houston after Pan Am left the route. Since serving London was a major first-time transatlantic milestone for Continental, I christened the first DC-10 to fly the route the *Robert Six*, in honor of the longtime chairman of the company, who had passed away shortly before. While Six disappointed us in the way he appeared to encourage attempts to stop our validly obtained controlling interest in the company, I nevertheless respected the role he had played in building the airline in its early days. I guess I have not been one to carry grudges.

During this time, we also kept a close watch on developments at People Express. In the spring of 1986, PEX (the airline's stock ticker symbol) appeared to be choking on its acquisition of Frontier and losing money in many of its basic markets. The airline was clearly facing difficult cash issues, and the potential of acquiring it and its Frontier subsidiary loomed large in our minds.

We believed strongly that the acquisition of People Express would open the door for us to build a major international hub at Newark Airport, which could be marketed as the gateway to New York City—perhaps the world's largest airline market. Less important, but still significant to us, was the acquisition of Frontier, which we expected would settle lingering concerns over competition from United in Denver. We also felt that the acquisition of PEX, whose low fares had been so destructive of Eastern's Florida markets, would give us more time to allow Eastern to become competitive—an elusive aim given the competitive landscape that developed.

We watched as PEX choked on the commitments and debt it had incurred from the decisions made by my old friend Donald Burr in his effort to build his airline unsustainably fast. After years of unprecedented growth, PEX was starting to report staggering losses and undertaking what appeared to be desperate measures to raise cash, such as the sale of equipment and the pending sale of the just-acquired Frontier Airlines. In many ways, People Express was a victim of its own success. Burr had always made much of the fact that his airline was the fastest-growing company in the history of American business, a distinction that some of the internet start-ups certainly hold today, but its rapid growth was also its undoing.

---

Burr and People Express seemed crazed with growth. I remember when we were discussing with Braniff a buy of a dozen or so of its used Boeing 727 airplanes. Braniff was being liquidated because of its own overly rapid growth. But we were told by our aircraft purchasing guys that People had just announced the purchase of sixty Braniff aircraft, most of the inventory that the airline had for sale, thus largely freezing us out.

We were a much bigger company, with far greater resources, but People Express seemed to be out there making significant aircraft acquisitions every month, even though it did not have the systems and management—or the balance sheet—to support the purchases. The airline had nowhere near the resources to match Burr's lofty ambitions. Its markets were undeveloped. It had no computer reservations system. It had no infrastructure. And it was loaded with debt, obtained in the days when PEX was a Wall Street darling. Perhaps worst of all, it had a very thin, inexperienced layer of management, with very few of the competent professionals who filled the ranks of other airlines. It had Burr and several executives largely untrained in the sophisticated systems that had engulfed the airline business in the 1980s in the wake of deregulation. These men and women certainly had enthusiasm—until they didn't.

Once the airline established its niche as a low-cost, no-frills East Coast carrier (not unlike the positions that Spirit Airlines in Florida and Ryanair in Europe have carved out for themselves today), Burr appeared to want to grab too much of a good thing too soon. It was as if he had done one thing well, then looked to milk it for all it was worth. There were continual announcements of new service—to Houston, Denver, West Coast points, and eventually even to London—and the quality of its service really began to suffer as its resources thinned. Burr's competitors all matched PEX in price but beat it strongly in service, which soon caught up with PEX. Without the price edge the airline had enjoyed in its early years and without the ability to match the yield management systems of the competition, and with its badly weakened finances, People Express seemed on its way into the history books.

In our advertising targeting People Express—which, particularly at Newark, competed extensively with us—we didn't make it easy, either, as we and others took advantage of the airline's compromised service reputation. In one ad, which got a lot of fanfare, we showed a People airplane and its stairway just next to a Continental airplane and its stairway. Passengers were shown marching off the People airplane and walking up the stairway of the Continental airplane. People's passengers came off as disheveled, sloppily dressed, and looking sad, while those going up the stairway to our airplane looked happy and smartly dressed. The message was unmistakable. We heard that Burr was not happy with it, but it was certainly effective for us.

There were other factors that contributed to the airline's downturn, and many of them were rooted in Burr's ballyhooed "people systems," the human relations management techniques that may have worked

Continental versus People Express ad (1985).

when PEX was a small company but were inappropriate when it grew substantially, particularly when the dramatic changes in the industry were taking place in the 1980s. One of Burr's mandates was that the airline fill its top spots by promoting from within. While this may have been a valuable recruitment tool and a noble attempt to boost employee confidence and morale during the early years, it acted as a restraint during the years of very rapid expansion. As the airline grew, for example, and its pricing needs became more sophisticated, Burr could not just pluck a pricing expert from another airline. He could not raid one of the majors for a top marketing or operations guy. He had to rely on his own people, who, while they had great enthusiasm, loyalty, and competence, nevertheless often lacked the expertise and training for positions requiring sophisticated technical knowledge. The airline suffered for it.

He also implemented a concept called cross-utilization, which required a certain amount of job-sharing at all levels of the company. Again, this may have been a reasonable concept on a small scale and a positive management tool, but it proved unwieldy and unproductive in the big company that People had become in later years. We heard stories that from time to time, the chief financial officer would be unavailable to an important caller because he was out flying on a shift as a flight attendant. Sure, this was different and newsworthy and very valuable, I'm sure, in giving executives some knowledge of the entry-level positions and how they worked, but in 1986 the bankers were calling with questions, and the CFO was not around. Not good during times of financial distress!

---

Whatever the reasons, Burr's woes stood as a potential boon for us. People, operating out of the old and original Newark terminal, pretty much owned Newark Airport. Newark had served as the PEX base of expanding operations long before anyone else recognized its strategic importance, to Burr's great credit. This dominant Newark position—and, most importantly, the new Terminal C that PEX controlled, which was slated for completion the following summer—was clearly very valuable to us, as it would have been for United and American, we thought. When we looked at the New York area, Newark stood out as the only immediate opportunity for growth and the chance to establish a major hub operation. LaGuardia had been capped in terms of landing slots and was geographically limited in terms of nonstop range; Kennedy was quite outdated and overdeveloped by international airlines, which had yet to find Newark. The only game in town, as we saw it, was across the Hudson River in New Jersey, and People Express, thanks to Burr, held the keys to that kingdom.

As we watched Burr's fortunes unravel, we considered several options. We could, along with everyone else, sit back and wait for the parent company to fold, then vie for its components during bankruptcy proceedings. The problem with this strategy was that asset sales in bankruptcy were a bidding contest, and I knew we would never prevail over deep-pocketed United and American and other carriers. On the other hand, we believed that the most viable alternative was to make a move for People Express while it was still intact. We held the advantage over other carriers in that our nonunionized employee environment would allow us to merge workforces, which would be difficult or impossible for the large, cash-rich, but heavily unionized carriers.

Since Burr and I were not particularly friendly in those days, I thought that the cleanest way to get to talk with People Express was through a PEX board member whom I knew well, John McArthur, the Harvard Business School dean, a very capable and experienced guy. I had gotten to know John during his deanship at HBS and quite admired him. In the spring of 1986, it was not clear to me that the company would be for sale. Nevertheless, I wanted to test the waters before contacting Burr.

Therefore, in May 1986 I arranged to meet McArthur at a downtown Boston hotel. He confided over drinks that the board had become increasingly nervous and concerned over the direction and financial condition of the company. He also said that Bill Hambrecht, whose banking firm in San Francisco provided the IPO for People when it first came on the market, was equally troubled. McArthur was uncertain what Burr, who clearly controlled the company and was very respected by the board, intended to do about PEX's financial position. He said he would talk to the other directors and to Burr about our interest.

Burr and I had a conversation as a result of my visit with McArthur, but he said they were considering other options to strengthen themselves financially. There had been reports in the press that in order to raise cash, the sale of Frontier and several aircraft was being pursued. In June 1986, PEX indeed announced the sale and leaseback of the Frontier Airlines fleet to United. But the deal raised major issues with the United pilots' union, which balked because of the significant labor concessions that had been accepted by its Frontier colleagues. The union leaders never liked to get too close to labor concessions for fear they would catch it like a virus, irrespective of how important they may have been to a carrier's survival after airline deregulation. Consequently, the deal was abandoned in July amid many rumors about People's urgent cash problems.

I didn't hear more from Burr until early August. As luck would have it, Sharon and I and our children were in the VIP lounge at Pan Am's JFK terminal awaiting a flight to Nice, France, when I was notified of a call from my faithful assistant, Millie, who said that Burr wanted to talk to me. We were headed for vacation and had arranged a house rental in Pégomas, a small town near Grasse, around twenty-five miles inland from Cannes and the French Riviera. I gave Burr a brief call and arranged to meet in ten days, when I would fly back from our long-planned vacation. Although some people may wonder why I just did not change my plans for this important meeting, I was not one to disappoint the whole family, who were eagerly awaiting this opportunity to live in another culture. And, of course, we were only minutes from boarding our flight.

In mid-August, when I arrived back to meet with Burr, PEX had already announced that it was putting Frontier Airlines into bankruptcy. With the deal to raise cash with United having fallen through, Burr simply shut Frontier down. He made no attempt to fly through bankruptcy. The airline was out of cash, and People Express, with mounting problems of its own, was no longer able to fund the bloodletting. In this environment, we began our discussions of a possible merger between CAL and PEX through the acquisition of People by Texas Air, our holding company. There was no longer any question about whether People Express was available. The only uncertainty was over price and conditions, but Burr seemed very amenable to a deal.

After my short interlude back in New York, I returned to the family in France and finished our French family vacation. However, this was not without excitement of its own: we were forced out of our house one night at 3:00 a.m. because of raging forest fires in the nearby woods, a phenomenon we could smell. I can still remember the bawling from our baby son, Timon, scared of the towering flames, which we could see when we stood on the high terrace we had in back. Not wanting to take any chances, we left our Pégomas house and checked in to the Grand-Hôtel du Cap, where my friend Saul Steinberg, who owned the property at the time, arranged a room for us, despite its being sold out. But the next day, the winds changed and the fires burned out, and we returned to our house and finished our stay there.

Back in the United States in late August, we accelerated our talks with PEX lawyers, bankers, and of course Burr himself. The terms that we were negotiating had to be carefully handled, because Burr was very sensitive about the treatment of his management and employees, more important to him in some respects than price. We also needed to find a graceful exit for my former associate. I feared that a straight deal, with no place in the merged entity for the People Express founder and spiritual leader, would be difficult for us to get done.

It's funny, but in all these talks and negotiations with Burr, he did not seem to resent having to come to Texas Air to bail him out, as he might have. There appeared to be no animosity between us, at least none that I could recognize. Sure, it was hard not to feel the weight of our early days together, many of them in the 1970s at Texas International, but at that point we shared only one common interest—trying to put together a deal that somehow managed to serve each other's interests. We did take one step that pleased Burr greatly and helped things along: we provided slightly better terms for shares held by the company's management, most of which were Burr's, than for the shares held by the general public—something, while not unheard of, is not generally done and was not a big deal in terms of shares. We also found Burr a graceful exit, naming him executive vice president and director of Texas Air, although that arrangement did not last very long. He left in early April 1987.

Finally, on Monday, September 15, 1986, we announced a merger transaction that would leave People Express a wholly owned subsidiary of Texas Air. We also agreed that Texas Air would purchase all the assets of Frontier, which we intended to operate as part of Continental. The cash component of the $300 million deal included roughly $50 million for People Express and $25 million for Frontier, with $10 million on signing and the balance to be paid in stock, notes, and note assumptions. The separate agreements were contingent on Burr's ability to trim People's debt load and win waivers from certain creditors, but we reserved the right to proceed with the Frontier purchase if for some reason the complicated People deal fell apart—subject, of course, to bankruptcy court approval.

One of the ironies of our People Express announcement on that September Monday was that a while later, Tom Plaskett, who had been executive vice president of American and had joined Continental as president, recounted being in Bob Crandall's Monday staff meeting and discussing the attractiveness to American of buying People to create a Newark hub. Halfway through the meeting, an assistant brought a note into the meeting saying that Burr and I were at that moment holding a press conference announcing Texas Air's purchase of People Express. We had always feared that the large carriers such as American might see the attractiveness of creating a Newark hub, amalgamating

Catching some photo frames at Houston walkathon (1985).

the traffic flows in one of the largest air travel markets in the world, New York City—a great location on the East Coast for connecting traffic to myriad viable transatlantic destinations. Had our deal been delayed a week, the airline hub structures that exist today in the United States might have looked very different.

On a personal note, that fall I kept up marathon training, and on November 2, 1986, I ran the New York City Marathon in three hours and fifty-six minutes. I had run four marathons before, three of them in New York, where my personal best, achieved on October 23, 1983, was three hours and thirty-eight minutes and my first run, in 1979, was four hours and five minutes. I also ran the Marine Corps Marathon in Washington, DC, in 1985. However, my 1986 run would turn out to be my last. At forty-six, I began to feel that marathons were more helpful to me psychologically than physically. My body paid a heavy toll in terms of wear and tear. So my marathon running came to an end, although I continued to run regularly, several times a week, for another fifteen years or so.

---

Having acquired People Express along with its Frontier assets, and still owning the remaining systems of New York Air after we had been forced to sell its shuttle business by the government, we faced the task of bringing together these disparate operations as smoothly as possible. We decided to merge them on February 1, 1987, after weighing our ability to get it done effectively against the benefits of getting this behind us. To accompany the operational merger, we developed and announced a new fare program that we called Max Saver, a sharply discounted coach-fare system with restrictions, also taking advantage of our lower cost structure. The other major airlines went along with these fares, albeit reluctantly, since they did not have the cost structures to support the lower fares. Continental was widely touted as the industry price leader.

For maximum impact at the press conference, our marketing and promotion genius, Jim O'Donnell, always up to something clever, arranged for $5 million in piles of bills to surround the podium—with appropriate guards, of course—signifying the savings to the public the fares provided. The sight of Tom Plaskett, Don Burr, Doug Birdsall (who was running New York Air), and me in front of these stacks of bills was one to behold. It served its purpose, however, and got us a lot of attention in newspapers and on TV from coast to coast. This was always a unique O'Donnell strength, implemented with the help of his very capable number two, Bruce Hicks. The strategy harked back to the Texas International days, when we staged elephant peanut parades and could not afford big-league advertising. But in this case, because of our size, we could afford it, and we accompanied the press conference with full-page ads in many newspapers.

$5 million dollar low-fare press conference (1987).

While we had a strong send-off from a marketing standpoint, the operational merger was something else. Some journalists called the merger—scheduled to take place on a single day—the Big Bang. The name, unfortunately, was prescient. It blew up in our faces and was plainly a disaster. There had not been sufficient time to properly train People employees in computer reservations and loading bridges and acquaint them with the many new cities that were part of Continental's vast system. In late February, our press was terrible, and we deserved much of it. There were pictures prominently placed in newspapers showing piles of luggage, many mis-tagged and lost. It took us several months to recover from this badly handled operational merger. In addition, these mishaps and the bad press caused our traffic to drop and Continental's financial hemorrhaging to increase.

While there were those who largely blamed Tom Plaskett, as our president, for the badly handled merger, I felt that was unfair. Only a miracle and a much longer time frame could have produced a smooth integration: the first element was out of his hands, and the second was not entirely up to him. I took part in many of the decisions, including the decision to hasten the merger. Many of our executives felt that we needed more time; others felt that we should acquire People and then shut it down, sidelining its employees until they could be properly trained. Under this strategy, the PEX operation would have been brought back piece by piece, and only those trained employees whom we wanted would be rehired. I was never in favor of this type of treatment; hence, we never did it. However, in retrospect this decision may well have been a mistake, and we would have been better off with the tougher shutdown option, although People employees would have been very unhappy.

During this period—early 1987—I was also focusing extensively on Eastern and the issues there. In addition, we sought to activate Jet Capital as a company making investments in situations other than those involving Texas Air. To that end, we invited Kevin Moore to join Jet as president. Kevin, thirty-two years old at the time, had been a deal guy for William Farley, the takeover activist in Chicago. One of the first deals Kevin attempted was the purchase of the Eastern shuttle along with an investor group—but of course, as I've related, that didn't get very far because of the strong union and Wall Street opposition.

During this period, with Plaskett at the controls at Continental in

Houston, I was spending increasing amounts of time in New York, usually at our Rockefeller Center offices, in the old Eastern Airlines building. It looked like my need to be in New York would increase as we went forward. With this as our new reality, Sharon and I decided to buy a home in Greenwich, Connecticut, and put the children in school there, because we both hated the thought of my being in New York while the rest of the family was in Houston. We closed on the Connecticut property in June 1987, and Sharon began the sizable task of making the necessary changes and renovations to the then eighty-year-old home, Altnacraig, which had originally been owned and built by the founder of the Singer sewing machine company around the turn of the century.

As we moved into summer, Continental operations improved to a great extent, but the bad start to the merger left a public relations and marketing hole for us to fill with our passengers and employees. The airline continued to lose a lot of money. Several of us, including most of our directors, began to feel that we had a leadership vacuum at Continental. On trips to Houston, I would be confronted by pleas from managers who claimed they could not get direction. When I was in the Continental office, I could see that there were frequently several frustrated executives waiting to get in to see Tom.

Tom had asked to bring his longtime secretary to Houston to work for him, which we allowed and which was probably a mistake. She acted as a sergeant at arms, making sure she cleared those who entered his office. This did not build morale, particularly in the entrepreneurial environment that had always prevailed at Continental. Even worse, it wasted a lot of executives' time. Managers who needed answers to various questions—sometimes quick answers—were left waiting. Note that in the days before email, much executive interface was handled in phone calls and in-person visits. We did not realize when he asked to hire his former assistant how difficult it would be for her to meld into the rhythm of the office and get along with the other assistants, not to mention the managers she kept waiting.

During the first two weeks of July, I was spending time with the family in Nantucket, where we had summered for many years, as well as going back and forth to Greenwich, where our recently bought home was being prepared for our move-in in September, just in time for the school year. However, these plans were interrupted on Sunday, July 19, when I traveled to Houston and was confronted with the company's continued losses in a meeting with our financial officers. We held our regularly scheduled board meeting on July 21 and discussed the company's situation. Unfortunately for me and our family plans, the unanimous opinion of our directors was that we needed to ask Tom Plaskett to resign and that I should return to run Continental directly. The airline was in an extreme position, as the directors saw it.

The hiring of presidents is not easy, and Tom was a seemingly very well-qualified person. He had been the much-lauded marketing head of American under Bob Crandall. He also was one of the fathers of some important marketing innovations, including the adaptation of the computer reservations system to compete with our competitors' low fares—so-called yield management. Tom was widely considered to be one of those in contention to succeed Bob when he retired. But Crandall would not do so until 1998, long after Tom joined Continental.

However, I also began to feel that despite his considerable marketing prowess and experience, Tom lacked leadership skills and, perhaps, sensitivity to what was needed at Continental. It seemed to all of us that he wasn't in control of the business. We had been through the hiring dance and realized there was no perfect person, and I realized that any new leader would bring change that not all executives would like. But the financial numbers were stark, and it seemed as though the management group was paralyzed and lacking options to plug up the company's cash drain. We appeared leaderless. Tom left Continental in July 1987.

This was an unattractive turn of events for me (and Sharon) personally. I realized that if I took back the reins at Continental, I had to commit to do it for some time, which would leave Sharon and the family in Connecticut and me in Houston—this was not an option for us, I thought, since I did not know how long the situation would last. As a result, the day after the board meeting, on July 20, I decided we all had to return to Houston full-time and give up our plans for Greenwich. My first call was to Glenn Ballard, the headmaster at the Kinkaid School, where the children had been studying, to see if we could get them reenrolled. This was before saying anything to the family, including Sharon, because I knew her first question rightfully would be "What about school for the children?" Glenn came back the following day with the good news that he could reenroll three of our children back at Kinkaid, even though they were full at this point in the summer, but he wasn't sure about the fourth. I told him I would wait to tell the family until I heard back from him later in the week. Promptly on Friday, Glenn called to say that all would be okay.

I also pursued a real estate change for the family during that momentous week. While in Houston, I revisited a house on Willowick Road, in the River Oaks neighborhood, that Sharon and I had eyed before. It was on a large, beautiful piece of land, with a swimming pool and a tennis court. Because it seemed very much available, I made arrangements to put in an offer on it after I had discussed it with Sharon and the family. We had lived in a cozy home near Kinkaid on Wickway Drive, near the intersection of Voss Road and Memorial Drive, but it was time to move on and be nearer downtown.

Later that week, I flew back to Nantucket for the weekend to break the news to the family. After hearing about the situation at Continental, and after thinking about it for only a few minutes, Sharon was in 100 percent agreement and was delighted with the thought of attempting to purchase the River Oaks home. She loved it when she toured it. While our children were happy with the thought of the new home, they were most unhappy with the decision to leave Greenwich, since they had had their goodbye parties in Houston and were enrolled in their new Connecticut schools, already making friends there. But they soon got over it, and we all returned to Houston full-time in August.

We then put the Greenwich house back on the market and purchased our soon-to-be River Oaks home.

Back in Houston, holding the reins at Continental, I pressed the executive team for an additional operational improvement program and a public relations campaign to back it up. The PR campaign led to the staging, at Houston's convention center, of the first Worldwide Performance Celebration, as we billed it. The very high-tech presentation, which I gave to several thousand employees at the convention center and which was broadcast to 20,000 or so employees at other Continental outposts around the world, ended with a performance by Gladys Knight and the Pips. My presentation outlined the steps we were taking to bring Continental up to our prior high standards. It was of course critical that our employees be on board not only with our goals but also with our approach to achieving them. We ran full-page ads in many newspapers, including the *New York Times* and the *Wall Street Journal*, using the phrase "Once people called us the Proud Bird; lately they have been calling us other names." We told the world that we were bringing back the Proud Bird.

We made a lot of marketing and operational progress in the fall, but we were also hit with one of the most distracting and disturbing events in my airline career: our first major accident. On Sunday, November 15, Continental Flight 1713, carrying eighty-three passengers and crew, crashed on takeoff from the Denver airport. The accident occurred around 2:20 p.m. Denver time in snowy weather and resulted in the deaths of twenty-five passengers and three crew members, including the pilot, first officer, and a flight attendant, and serious injuries to many more.

Sharon and I were driving home at around 4:00 p.m. from a museum visit that Sunday when I got a call on the car phone saying that Flight 1713 was down. This is the call that every airline executive dreads. Whenever I got a call from the system coordinator at flight control, I always held my breath. As soon as we got to our house, I told Sharon and the children that I was heading to Denver. I wasn't sure what I was going to do there and was advised against it, but I wanted to be with our people and the relatives of the deceased and injured passengers.

The following morning, I visited two of the hospitals and saw some of the people who were injured, a few of them badly disfigured. One was unconscious and so unrecognizable that his wife could not identify him. If I had any doubts about why safety is the number one consideration for an airline executive—and I didn't—this sight might well have dispelled it. On the Tuesday after the accident, we held a memorial service at a Denver church at which I spoke. I also issued a written statement to the press on the night of the accident, expressing deep condolences. But I did not hold a press conference, and I was criticized for it. At the time, though, we were not sure of the accident's cause. Still, I did visit and meet with our employees in Denver before returning to Houston.

Ultimately, the National Transportation Safety Board determined that the cause of the accident was the icing on the aircraft's wings, which accumulated during the too-long wait for takeoff (around twenty minutes after deicing). Naturally, ALPA, which formerly represented our pilots, claimed that the captain's inexperience caused the accident, because the wings should have been deiced again. The DC-9-10 involved in the accident had particularly sensitive wings because that type of aircraft isn't built with leading-edge slats, as many aircraft are. The DC-9-10 thus needs more liftoff speed than other types of aircraft. These facts were no consolation for the loss of life that Sunday. I did take some comfort, a few years after the accident, to receive a note from the wife of the man who initially could not be identified, whom I had met at the hospital, telling me that he had returned to a somewhat normal life and thanking me for caring.

------

As we moved into 1988, paying attention to the developments at Eastern from my position at Texas Air and Continental took a lot of my time and energy. Also, because many of the programs at Continental were interlaced with Eastern's in order to take advantage of the weight of the two companies together in the marketplace, major time constraints were placed on my Continental responsibilities. This required me to promote or bring in from the outside another executive to focus on the day-to-day affairs of Continental.

On February 2, 1988, we announced that Martin Shugrue, a forty-seven-year-old former commercial pilot, would join Continental as president, reporting to me. Marty, who had been vice chairman of Pan Am, had been dismissed by the airline two weeks before, along with Eddie Acker, its chairman, because of growing differences with the board over what had to be done to rescue the failing carrier. Ironically, they were replaced at Pan Am by Tom Plaskett, who had been brought in as chairman and CEO. The airline business was always well known for its musical chairs, but this maneuver really took the cake.

Tom became CEO of Pan Am on January 1, 1988, and was faced with the daunting task of trying to turn around the financially ailing airline. He seemed to be making progress when on December 21, 1988, Pan Am flight 103, a Boeing 747, was blown out of the sky by a terrorist bomb while climbing over Scotland en route from London to New York. The event was fatal to the 259 people on the airplane and eleven people on the ground. It was also fatal to Pan Am, starting a financial spiral that eventually ended in bankruptcy and, in 1991, liquidation. Tom made Herculean efforts to save the airline after the bombing, scouring the world for money or a merger partner. But the global economy, a recession, the run-up to the 1990–1991 Gulf War, and the postwar terrorism fears that followed ensured that there would be no reprieve. Pan Am ceased operations in December 1991.

---

A major event occurred for us in 1988: the opening of Terminal C at Newark International Airport on May 22—the long-awaited launch of Continental's major Newark hub. After all the difficulty we had in acquiring People Express, this was our reward. In addition to being the only airport in the New York area capable of providing the space for a hub, Newark served one of the world's largest air-travel markets, with many international destinations. Over the years, this hub has become vastly profitable and was one of the major inducements for United to merge with Continental in 2010.

One issue for us in opening Terminal C and establishing a new Eastern hub there was what to do with the space in Terminal B that had originally been occupied by Eastern when it dominated the terminal. We were concerned about the Port Authority forcing us to give up this space: we didn't want it to be used by one of our competitors for a competing hub. Our ingenious property team, helmed by Sam Ashmore, who had been with me from the start, came up with the idea of convincing the Port Authority that Newark needed an international terminal and that Terminal B was the ideal solution. This was even though there were only two international long-haul flights from Newark at the time—the former PEX London trip, now ours, and one Virgin Atlantic London flight. But it worked, and the Port Authority gladly saw it our way. Airport authorities are often giddy when you speak of international flights.

Thus we began attracting international carriers who would provide feed for us, and we would enjoy the strengthening of our connecting hub traffic while filling out the space at Terminal B. I must honestly admit that our creating the international Terminal B, which is now one of the largest international entries into the United States, was largely aimed at building a profitable Newark hub rather than delivering another international gateway to the New York area, although we knew it had that potential.

One of the trips I made in furthering this goal was to London during the summer of 1988. Sharon and I traveled there mostly so I could meet Richard Branson, principal owner of Virgin Atlantic, in order to encourage a major feed relationship with Continental, despite our being competitors on the London route. We met with Branson on his houseboat, the *Duende*, anchored in the Little Venice waterway. He was living there at the time with his girlfriend and a recently born baby. (He got married a few years later and moved off the boat to a town house, where some years later we also met.) Branson was quite intrigued by what we were building at Newark and indicated that he would follow up. He also was a very interesting guy. Not college educated, he was a poster child for the self-made entrepreneur and a classic nonconformist before it became cool in tech circles years later.

For our return to the United States on that London trip, Sharon and I decided to fly back on Branson's Virgin Atlantic to get a feel for the competition, and we were extremely impressed with the operation, particularly the Upper Class compartment. Virgin had chosen not to have a first-class service but rather to place a much greater emphasis on an expanded business class, which had many of the extras of first class. In those days, just about every transatlantic operator offered first class as well as business class. Upon my return, I requested a full review of our first-class and business-class services.

We knew we were not carrying a lot of paying first-class passengers, so dropping first class would not have affected us a great deal in terms of lost revenue. We also knew that our transatlantic competitors, unlike us, had significant numbers of first-class passengers and would consequently be reluctant to drop first-class service. Shortly thereafter, I introduced at an officers' meeting the idea of dropping first class and beefing up business class, as Virgin had done. Several officers voiced the view that we would be looked down on for not having first-class service; we wouldn't any longer be a "first-class" airline. But after substantial research, including focus-group testing, we decided to drop first-class service and put the first-class seats in a new, expanded business-class compartment, albeit with somewhat less legroom. We also toned down the first-class meal service somewhat.

Our new business class, branded Business First in later years, was an instant success. It gave us a very salable business product at what was an attractive fare for us, considering our low cost structure. In a sense, we were competing on price, but instead of lowering our price, we were vastly improving our business-class service. Our competitors fumed. But over the years, the improved business product was an important element of Continental's profitability. With an expanded business compartment, the airline could run a good load factor, even with no passengers in the main cabin, and still cover costs. Continental's move did force some competitors to gradually upgrade their business-class product over the years—often significantly—without dropping first-class service. Still others followed our lead and dropped first class altogether in favor of an improved business class.

---

In September 1988, at an outing of an aviation organization, I discussed the idea of Newark's potential for feed expansion with Jan Carlzon, CEO of the Scandinavian carrier SAS. We were riding horses near each other at the time when we got into the subject. SAS was operating two flights a day from JFK but did not have much feed traffic from around the United States to its Scandinavian destinations, which Continental could provide at Newark. As our discussions grew in intensity, both during and after the meeting, we seriously explored the idea of a larger joint agreement whereby SAS would have an equity participation in Continental as well as a close feed arrangement.

After much discussion, we finalized an equity-feed arrangement with SAS in early October 1988. The deal constituted the first major operating compact between a foreign carrier and a US airline. Under its provisions, SAS paid Texas Air $50 million and secured the right to buy up to 10 percent of TAC common stock on the open market and receive a seat on TAC's board of directors, which Carlzon himself filled. In addition, and most importantly, we entered into a major code-sharing and handling agreement at Newark. This allowed SAS to deemphasize JFK Airport because of the significant connecting traffic it was likely to receive from Continental directly in Newark. (Pan Am, with the largest domestic network at JFK at the time, jealously guarded its feed traffic.) In addition to the benefit of the feed traffic from SAS, Continental also gained the halo effect of a major partnership with one of the world's most respected airlines. The financial part of the deal was also unusual in that, because we didn't want the share dilution and didn't need the cash, we didn't receive the proceeds from the 10 percent equity position they secured, which would have been normal for a deal of this type.

We announced our arrangement with SAS at a press conference on October 4 at the Plaza Hotel. Carlzon brought twenty or so of SAS's most attractive female flight attendants—who, I'm sure, were not difficult to find, given what I had seen on my SAS flights—and placed them around the room. After the formal announcement, he walked over to each one and, bowing his head slightly, kissed her hand.

Jan was well known for his attention to employee attitudes. In 1987, he published a book titled *Moments of Truth*, in which he wrote that in talks with customer-contact employees he would say, "We have fifty thousand moments of truth every day," referring to the number of times an employee came into contact with a customer. He certainly demonstrated his philosophy and special "touch" that day.

While I admired Jan and the sensitivity he displayed toward his employees, I noted to myself what a luxury it must be to have the backing of three major governments, as SAS did. Not having to battle for his company's economic survival, as we had had to do, was a great luxury that enabled a CEO to focus his attention on employee attitudes and other "softer" items, which play an enormous role in the customer experience and an airline's reputation and image.

---

A very important area of our business that I also spent a lot of time on over the years was airport space planning, strategy, and negotiation. Premium close-in facilities were highly coveted, and we fought our competitors over airport space many times. One of the most important deals for us in this area was approaching culmination in November 1988: a major new airport in Denver that would replace the close-in Stapleton International Airport. Like many airport projects, this one, while attractive over the long term, was largely driven by the egos of city officials who wanted a huge, expensive airport to be built on their watch.

A new airport in Denver would give us an advantage in that our Stapleton space was nothing like the space enjoyed by United, our big competitor. United had been able to upgrade its space there some years earlier. But the cost of space in the new airport, more than double the cost at Stapleton, was very difficult for United and us to swallow. In addition, the fact that the site chosen by the city was much farther from downtown than Stapleton caused us to fear a significant loss of traffic on short-haul routes. For these reasons, we and United would not agree to sign up for the new airport, which had the effect of stalling the city's ability to finance the project. As a result, the city was very willing to negotiate a deal with United or Continental separately, which would allow the financing to get done.

As I've mentioned, one of the most important management assets we had at Continental (and, previously, at Texas International) was Sam Ashmore, the shrewd strategist who ran our properties team. He was the kind of manager whom you only wished you had many more of. I worked with Sam over my entire time in the airline business. Just as he had been on our other major projects, he was the point person on this critical Denver situation. He came to me in late 1987 and said he could envision a deal in which we, independent of United, could support the new airport—the establishment of which he strongly felt was inevitable—on a basis that would be quite attractive to Continental. He said that we might be able to get the first, most attractive terminal (Terminal A), leaving United farther away, in Terminal B or C, and that we could negotiate the building of a passenger bridge over to our terminal directly from the central check-in terminal, a significant passenger advantage. He also thought we could get some reduction of the costs of the airport itself as part of our support of the project.

To test Sam's theory, I arranged to have a run along Denver's waterways, followed by dinner with Denver's mayor, Federico Peña, whom I had gotten to know. Over our meal, I outlined our three-part plan to support the new airport on a napkin; Peña was very receptive. At this point, there began an extended period of back-and-forth, including involvement by United. By the fall of 1988, the pieces had largely fallen into place except for who would take financial responsibility for any overruns, which there almost always are. I flew to Denver and gave a speech on November 15, 1988, at the Mile High Club in which I pleaded our case to local businessmen: the city needed to bear some portion of the cost of any overruns, along with United and Continental, to ensure some checks and balances on the city's ambitions—a request to which the city eventually acceded.

At long last, Denver International Airport got built, and today when one walks over the passenger bridge to Terminal A, it is possible to appreciate the negotiations that resulted in its construction. Ironically, in later years, after the United and Continental merger, the combined airline was housed in Terminal B, since United was already there. Continental flights were moved from Terminal A so that they could be positioned next to United's larger network for connections and operating efficiency.

I have been involved in critical negotiations with several other airports over the years. In 1979, we at Texas International spent a lot of time in the office of the Houston mayor, Jim McConn, trying to get space in half of Terminal C at Houston's expanded airport, after the other half had been promised to our then competitor Continental. At the time, the city fathers seemed to want to give the other half to the more prestigious Pan Am. We won out, but—ironies of history—when Texas International took over the bigger Continental, in 1981, the Houston airport situation was perfect in that both airlines together occupied the full terminal.

---

One of the aspects of my executive career in which having a high batting average was tough was recruiting executives from the outside. As the CEO of a fast-growing company in a fast-changing industry, I felt it was important for some talent to come from outside and in the process bring in new ways of doing things and, perhaps, more sophistication.

While I do not think I had a great batting average in recruiting, my record needs to be viewed in the context of what we were dealing with. It is one thing to bring an executive into a company that is profitable and has a reasonably defined path. However, it is quite another matter when one views the post-deregulation environment in the United States and its very entrepreneurial nature. The dog-eat-dog atmosphere that we operated in dramatically affected our employee culture and made the assimilation of managers from the outside more difficult. Despite the difficulties of bringing people in, however, we did have our recruitment stars, Phil Bakes being at the top of the list. Unfortunately, though, we had far more failures. One occurred in late 1988.

Marty Shugrue seemed to be doing a reasonable job at Continental in the largely operational role he had, but it became clear to me and our directors that a stronger CEO at Continental was essential. This was a position that I had largely occupied, in addition to my Texas Air responsibilities, since we parted company with Tom Plaskett in July 1988. So to fill that post, we recruited Joseph Corr in early December 1988. Joe was a strong, confident guy, which we felt was needed. He also had considerable management experience as CEO of AMF (formerly American Machine and Foundry), an Icahn-controlled company. In addition, he had worked for a short while at TWA, also controlled by Icahn at that time. In our interviews with Joe, we made clear that the top management ranks at Continental, in particular Marty Shugrue, were not to be disturbed, because we believed we had some great management assets despite our need for a CEO from the outside. However, less than sixty days after he started, Joe put Marty out the door. He also threatened the jobs of several other senior executives. I had to step in and require Joe to attempt to work with them—at least give them a chance.

But as the year wore on, there were a number of instances of Joe's being unwilling to consider the views of his managers. Of course he didn't necessarily need to agree with his managers' recommendations, but it became clear that he was a very egotistical, dogmatic guy who thought he had all the answers for Continental, even though others had years of experience and were already putting effective changes into practice.

For example, although Joe had no prior experience in pricing and fares, he dogmatically believed that low fares were bad and all our fares should be raised. One month, for example, I noticed that Southwest Airlines traffic had increased very sharply, which was unusual for the gradually growing company. Later we found out that Joe had insisted that most all discount fares on Continental be eliminated all at once, even though it made no short-term or long-term economic sense. Inexperienced financially oriented guys frequently go after a quick fix in order to raise fares and yields. Southwest did not change its fare level, and it absorbed significant amounts of our traffic, in the process probably taking some of the shine off the hard-earned "first call" advantage that Continental enjoyed. By the fall of 1989, it was clear to me and our board that Joe had to go, and we worked out a severance package with him that allowed him to leave the company on his first anniversary, in December 1989.

But the good news was that we replaced Joe with Mickey Foret, who had been with us from our early Texas International days. It probably was a mistake on my part not to have made Mickey president sooner. He was a taciturn, hardworking, financially trained, loyal guy who worked his way up the management ranks and fully understood CAL's unique culture and economics. We announced Mickey's promotion in December 1989 and received many compliments for the choice from the inside and outside.

While Mickey was president, in January 1990, we discussed the colors and livery of Continental and the visual image we portrayed to the public. We had considered modernizing our image years earlier—getting rid of the orangey-red wave pattern that had been CAL's logo for ages. However, I believed that it was not a good thing to paper over a product that needed to improve just to get a different visual image. I felt that a company often gets only one chance to show off an improved product. But we had made great strides in those other ways, so I felt that the time had come to emphasize the change with a new look.

Our marketing folks hired a well-respected outside firm, Lippincott & Margulies, to develop a more international, worldlier style, given the growing importance of our Newark hub globally. I remembered that L&M was known for the many branding programs it had undertaken, including the one it did for Eastern Airlines while I was there in the early 1960s. The firm was headed up by the very capable Clive Chajet, who took a personal interest in our project and was present at all our meetings, as was I.

We decided we would incorporate a globe in our logo, not unlike the one used by Pan Am, which had long enjoyed an international image but was heading out of business fast, as we saw it, because of its inability to adapt to the deregulated airline environment. We ended up with a blue color scheme, including a stylized globe as part of the logo, and began the major task of repainting our airplanes. This provided the visual identity for Continental from early 1990 onward. I was pleased to note after Continental's merger with United in 2010 that although the United name was used for the combined company—for sensible reasons, given its worldwide reputation—the Continental color scheme we developed was chosen as the color scheme of the joined companies and remains largely so today.

At this point in my life, I was also feeling that a change was due for me and my family.

CHAPTER THIRTEEN

# Leaving Continental

*A Change of Course*
*1990*

THE LATE 1980s were years of reflection for me. My first business partner and close friend, Bob Carney, had sold his position
in Jet Capital in 1987, and I missed my longtime partner and
his sage advice. I also could see that my anti-union reputation, while,
of course, very unfair, could hurt the company. I would be turning fifty
shortly, and I began to think seriously about a life outside the airline
business. After all, I had spent twenty-five years in that sector, eighteen
of them as a CEO, and I knew how tough it was. Despite my love of it,
I imagined that there was a life beyond it.

Airlines had been in my DNA since I was a teenager. But I tried to
be honest with myself: I wanted a life away from the public eye and the
twenty-four-hour schedule that was the lot of any major airline CEO,
particularly one who had endured difficult financial situations and
many very bruising public fights with unions.

As a result, I mentioned to our directors in mid-1988 that I hoped
to be able to step away from running Texas Air and Continental before
I turned fifty, in 1990. Sharon and I also spent a lot of time discussing

this move. She was not particularly in favor of it, because she was concerned about the hole it would leave in our lives. On one flight back from Europe, I recall making a long list of the pluses and minuses of selling, which invariably involved both financial and personal considerations.

But before I could consider life after Continental, I had to develop a plan to sell Jet Capital's controlling stock position in the company, either indirectly by selling our holding of Continental's equity, or directly by a sale of Jet Capital. Unlike most CEOs, I could not just look for another opportunity or resign. Because we at Jet Capital were the major controlling shareholders, I did not want to leave the company with our stock position remaining behind—or remain at the company without our major position. So, in the summer of 1989, I hired Drexel Burnham to quietly work on a sale of Continental or Texas Air, with its controlling position in Continental. I also sought out some individuals who had expressed interest in acquiring the company or made sense as a possible acquirer, although these discussions were always handled in a low-key, highly discreet manner.

One of the most interesting discussions I had in this capacity was with Lee Iacocca, CEO of Chrysler. I had gotten to know Lee in Nantucket through a friendship with his daughter Kate, who vacationed there. We felt that Lee's strong image would be a major plus for Continental and provide it with a fresh image. He was also a man interested in new challenges. I even flew to Detroit and had a sit-down with him to discuss the idea. Lee was quite interested. He always had an attraction to airlines, he explained, but, as it turned out, he had several other major issues on his plate at the time and felt that he could not dilute those other efforts. We soon were forced to ask Drexel to cut short its search for a buyer—disappointing, since the transactions the firm envisioned would also have involved minority shareholders being bought out.

---

As 1990 came into focus, I began discussing with Jan Carlzon the long-term interest SAS had in Continental now that it was a 10 percent owner. Previously, in 1989, during lunch at the InterContinental Hotel in New York, which SAS owned at the time, Jan laid out his strategy for strengthening SAS internationally. He sketched out on a napkin how he planned to link up the traffic flows of several airlines, starting with British Midland Airways, which had a large, valuable hub at London's Heathrow Airport and in which SAS had already taken a sizable position. At the center of the napkin was Continental, with which SAS already had developed a strong traffic arrangement and, of course, in which it owned a 10 percent stake.

In addition to Continental and British Midland, Carlzon indicated that he valued the SAS position in LAN Chile. SAS acquired its LAN interest in the hopes of obtaining important traffic feed from South America to its system. But up to that point, LAN had been a disappointment, incurring substantial losses while providing only limited traffic feed to the SAS system. In a way, it seemed to me, Carlzon had been spoiled by SAS's arrangement with Continental, which was bringing major traffic feed to the SAS system and which provided other benefits, including a handling arrangement at Newark and important brand awareness throughout the United States. He probably assumed this was easily repeatable.

Carlzon had a seat on our board of directors and was an active and effective participant in our discussions. However, though he never said anything directly, I could tell he was frustrated that Continental and its partners were being hurt by the negative image and publicity stemming from Eastern—which of course was a frustration we all shared—including my personal reputation, developed by the unions, as the bad guy.

I decided to approach Carlzon with the idea, which I was sure he had thought of also, of buying Jet Capital's controlling position in Texas Air. While we both knew that a foreign carrier could not control a US carrier or own more than 25 percent of its equity, having a much larger stake than its current 10 percent could well be attractive to SAS. A deal to acquire Jet Capital would allow SAS and Carlzon to effectively direct the activities of the company. While Jet Capital voted more than 30 percent of the equity of Texas Air, the actual economic ownership was just under 10 percent. But a buyout of Jet Capital would leave a control vacuum on the CAL board that SAS could fill with US nationals.

On various occasions, I discussed the thought of selling our interests with Rob Snedeker, our chief financial executive. Rob had been a partner going all the way back to Lorenzo, Carney & Co. in the 1960s and was a substantial shareholder of Jet Capital. He was in full agreement with the idea of selling, since he was well aware of the difficulties we had encountered in trying to sell Continental in total and giving all shareholders a chance to participate in the sale. Rob was also intimately aware of the substantial debt repayment schedule that Texas Air and Continental faced beginning in 1992. It was clear to us that this debt position would limit our flexibility and put significant pressure on the company as time went on, particularly if we encountered difficult times and were finding our ability to refinance the debt very tenuous.

We were also noting the weakening of the economy and had the feeling that more weakness might well lie ahead. Coincidentally, when we were examining SAS boarding data on the flights we handled at Newark Airport in the spring of 1990, we could see significant weakness already showing up, a marker of what might lie ahead. We figured that if SAS encountered a substantial downturn in its results, it would be much less likely to be interested in investing further in Continental. I decided that this was the time to move and flew to Stockholm in May 1990 to present the Jet Capital buyout idea to Carlzon.

At that point, we had dropped the name Texas Air from our holding company and had renamed it Continental Airlines Corporation, while our fully owned airline was termed Continental Airlines, Inc. This reflected the fact that we no longer owned Eastern Airlines and that New York Air had merged into Continental. Clearly the most basic part of Texas Air, at that point, was Continental Airlines. In a way, this made it easier to talk with Carlzon, since he had always had little interest in Eastern. In presenting the buyout idea in Stockholm, I told him that I had already initiated a search for my replacement and that there were several airline executives who might be interested, including

Hollis Harris, who was president of Delta at the time. Hollis handled the operating functions under Ron Allen, Delta's CEO, and while he did not have any financial background or much experience outside of day-to-day operations, he carried a powerful title and was believed to be a reputable manager. Carlzon was very enthusiastic about the possibility of attracting Harris and said his interest would be even higher if we could get him.

On the question of price, I told Carlzon that we would not be interested in a deal that was solely based on the price of Continental's stock on any single day. I proposed that we use the average stock price over the previous year as the price of the deal, reflecting the fact that we were selling our position for the first time in eighteen years and it would not have been reasonable to pin the deal on one day's closing price. This was quite important to us, since our stock had fallen a lot after the announcement of the 1989 loss and the effects of the Eastern bankruptcy situation, which hopefully would be only a temporary stock weakness. Jan said he would study the prospective deal and get back in touch.

In June, Rob and I flew back across the Atlantic to meet again with Carlzon. Meetings with Jan were very interesting. His office was completely paperless—and this was before the age of computers. We would walk in, and after the customary small talk, he would contact his principal financial executive, who would join us and give a full report on where the Jet Capital analysis stood, displaying a number of papers. Eventually, after some back-and-forth, we arrived at an agreement on a price for our position that was developed in line with our averaging proposal and that, although considerably more than the current market price, we felt was reasonable under the circumstances. With this understanding in hand, Rob and I flew home to begin work on the sale with the lawyers.

---

From that point on, things moved quickly. I interviewed Hollis Harris in late June, and he indicated that he would accept the Continental position if it were offered. We also developed a timetable that would have us announcing the deal at the end of July. In addition, we had a holding company board meeting during which we set forth the deal. There was a lot of discussion at the meeting, and of course much of the focus was on the premium that we would be receiving over our current share price. We agreed to bring in unaffiliated investment bankers to evaluate the fairness of the plan to minority shareholders, and their report ultimately satisfied the directors.

The agreed-upon timetable had us signing the agreement on Wednesday, August 8, 1990, after a board meeting of our holding company the prior Monday and an SAS board meeting on Tuesday. Thanks to the miracle of the Concorde supersonic airliner, which crossed the Atlantic quickly in those days, Carlzon could move very speedily between meetings. The plan was that on Wednesday, after the signing, we would immediately inform the Department of Transportation by means of a senior Continental corporate officer who would travel to Washington early on Wednesday. The signing was scheduled for noon, and Carlzon's arrival was expected at around 11:00 a.m. in our Rockefeller Center office after his transatlantic journey to New York.

But things did not exactly go according to plan. On Thursday, August 2, the world saw the unexpected invasion of Kuwait by Iraqi forces. This attack had an immediate impact on the worldwide oil market, and for an airline, it was not a good impact. As planned, Carlzon flew over on Sunday, August 5, for some last-minute discussions with us and to attend the holding company board meeting on Monday morning at which the evaluation and fairness report was formally delivered by the independent investment bankers and the deal was approved. The nomination of Harris to succeed me as CEO was also approved. After the meeting, Carlzon flew back on the evening flight to Stockholm, and on Tuesday, as planned, he had his SAS board meeting at which the purchase was approved.

On Wednesday morning, signing day, we awoke to a major front-page story in the *Financial Times* claiming that the Kuwait invasion would hit airlines especially hard because of the skyrocketing price of fuel. We gulped and had great concern about the effect the story would have on Carlzon. We knew he was an avid *Financial Times* reader and would certainly see the article as he recrossed the Atlantic that Wednesday morning on his way to our deal signing at noon. Jan did not disappoint us.

At 10:30 a.m., while he was being driven in from the airport after his Concorde flight, Jan called to say that we should delay the signing of the deal for a week or two and let things in Kuwait settle out. I told Jan that there was no way we were prepared to do that. I explained that we had a corporate officer already at the DOT, and the press had been invited for an announcement in the afternoon. I told him that if we didn't sign now, we would terminate the deal—essentially saying it was now or never. He told me he would think about it and meet at our office as planned.

I also put in a call to Carl Pohlad and brought him up to date on my conversation with Jan. I explained that it was my feeling that when a deal like this gets postponed, it never gets done. Carl agreed and said he would give Carlzon a call, which he did. When Carlzon arrived at our office, he could see the elaborate preparations that had been made for the signing and the follow-on press conference. For example, we had written a letter to employees explaining the transaction and included a statement from me about the sale and a welcome to Hollis. By noon, Carlzon had acquiesced, agreeing to go ahead, and we held our signing. After that, everything went according to plan, with the announcement to the secretary of transportation and to our employees followed immediately by the press conference, which Carlzon enjoyed. This was a big deal for the employees. The response to the deal was predictable: unions invariably said good riddance to Lorenzo, but the media, by and large, viewed it favorably. A number of newspaper editorials published a salute to my days in the business.

The following Monday, August 13, I was back in Houston, introducing the executive group to Hollis. I also moved out of my airline office. Up to that point, I had maintained two offices in Houston—one at Continental, in the American General Building, and the other at the holding company, in Allen Center on Allen Parkway in the downtown area. Hollis was still finishing his time at Delta, which meant he didn't really need his airline office, but I wanted to send a very clear signal to our people that Hollis was now in charge. Two days later, on Wednesday, August 15, Continental held a major goodbye-to-Frank event at the George R. Brown Convention Center in Houston for more than three thousand employees. We showed a video that had been prepared by our marketing team describing the major progress that had been made at Continental under my tenure.

On September 12, 1990, the deal was formally closed with SAS, and my days of Continental ownership and executive leadership ended. It was a bittersweet time for me. While I was glad that our family now had sharply increased liquidity and that I would have the freedom and time to invest our resources, I was very sorry to leave behind a company and an employee group that had meant so much to me. I knew I would miss the many great friends I had gotten to know over the years. I was a very full-time guy, and I only knew how to do things with all my energy. Now it was time to move those energies elsewhere.

As I prepared to leave Continental, James Ott, a writer for *Aviation Week*, summed up my legacy in an August 1990 article titled "Lorenzo, Peanuts Fare Creator, Furloughs Himself from the Airline Business." Ott wrote, "Frank Lorenzo has etched an indelible mark on the U.S. airline business. Whether he is a union buster, an opportunist, or keen businessman depends on one's perspective, but his mark has been deep and may be lasting."

Ott continued, "For an executive with two airline bankruptcies on his record and a permanent place on the union hate list, it may come as a surprise that Lorenzo has some loyal coworkers and former colleagues. He is a private man with an awful public persona. People who have worked with him say that the public image is false, a grotesque creation of the union propaganda machine."

The *New York Times* wrote, "Both despised by unions and admired by airline strategists, Mr. Lorenzo epitomized the industry during the freewheeling days of merger mania and brutal fare wars that followed deregulation twelve years before. His tough bargaining stance with unions and use of bankruptcy protection rules to break up high-cost contracts made him, more than any other executive, a target of fierce union attacks."

Many other news reports of my departure were similar. I think these are fair summaries of my legacy. But they were written at the 35,000-foot level. Closer to the ground, my legacy is really that of the hardworking executives, managers, and frontline people up and down our ranks who, with me, led the way.

---

My involvement with Continental didn't completely end on September 12, 1990. As part of our sale of Jet Capital's stock interest to SAS, I committed to a no-compete agreement and to remain as a director of the company, both for two years in order to be available during the transition. But as it turned out, I was no help to Harris. In fact, I never received as much as a call from him, although I attended almost all board meetings and witnessed the Greek tragedy that was to unfold. I'll get to that shortly.

In late September, Sharon and I took part in Continental's inaugural trip to Japan, which we had planned earlier in the year. The previous March, CAL had embarked on a major route expansion, adding one hundred daily departures and seven new cities. It also received new route authority from Houston nonstop to Tokyo. This expansion to Tokyo from our major hub was a big victory for us. Although domestic operating authorities had been deregulated, the government still called the shots on international routes, and the grant process was very political—so we were pleased to see the success of our pleadings in Washington and the help we received from Texas legislators. But even though we had scheduled the Houston–Tokyo service to start early in July, a strong season for the service, summer was not generally a good time for inaugural flights from a business point of view. So we waited until September for the "official" inaugural flight, which took place just after the SAS closing. Sharon and I went along on the trip with Hollis, a group of Houston city officials, and a couple of other CAL executives.

The trip to Japan was a beautiful one, well arranged by our Japanese staff, led by Jun Mokudai, whom we had recruited to CAL from Northwest the year before. We spent some time in Tokyo and the rest of our time in the countryside and in Kyoto. Japan always impressed me—the people were so friendly, and everything seemed so perfect. Unfortunately, on the trip, I was able to detect an aloofness on Harris's part toward the city officials and the other CAL executives making the trip. CAL had always been a village, relying on an immense amount of teamwork, and to my mind, Harris's attitude didn't augur well.

In September, I set up a new firm, Savoy Capital, as an investment advisory concern. Initially, it was with Rob Snedeker, but he shortly thereafter told me that he had lost interest in business. He seemed burned out to me, which was understandable, given the tough and dispiriting days he had lived through. I wanted to establish a business through which we would invest our own capital along with capital from outside investors, enabling us to do things away from the airline business. For office space, we bought the former Texas Air space at Allen Center from Continental, which became the home base for Savoy Capital. My longtime loyal assistant, Millie, did not even have to move: when she switched from the holding company's payroll to that of Savoy Capital, she kept the same desk. Yvonne Hiller, our longtime accountant at CAL, also did not move far.

Sharon and I were able to plan some personal travel as well, a great luxury for us that we would now be able to enjoy. In early October, we traveled to Russia and Spain for two weeks with Team 100, a Republican contributors' group, to celebrate my new freedom. We had never been to Russia, and because those were still the Soviet days, the trip turned out to be very enlightening. We stayed at one of the few nice hotels in Moscow in those days, the October Hotel, normally only available to Communist Party officials and their guests. While this hotel was reasonably nice, particularly compared to the alternatives, guests were unable to place or receive international calls, so we were out of touch for several days, since this was well before the existence of the internet and cell phones.

In mid-October, as we made our way to Spain and the last portion of our trip, the ability to communicate with our office returned, and I got an urgent message from Clark Onstad—CAL's very capable government affairs person. Clark wanted me to know that he had learned that the CAL board was going to hold an emergency meeting the following week to discuss the possibility of filing for bankruptcy. Clark also told me that Mickey Foret, who had continued under Hollis as president, had been terminated.

As one might expect, I was shocked by this news and made immediate plans to drop our planned sojourn in Spain and return to Houston. Mickey had been one of the rocks of the organization, and I could not believe that Hollis would fire him—unless he just didn't want someone telling him the truth. Naturally, I also realized that Hollis had the right to choose his own team. And choose he did: many loyal and very capable Continental managers such as Jim Arpey, the first officer I had hired at Texas International in the early 1970s, Neal Meehan, and later even Clark were told to leave.

The board meeting was indeed held in late October. It was my first after the stock sale and my first without an executive role. It turned out to be a very sad meeting. Filing for bankruptcy was indeed considered. Fuel prices had doubled since July because of the Kuwait invasion, and what was projected to be a normal offseason loss for October of around $20 million was turning into a more than $80 million loss—almost entirely because of fuel. Fuel costs had risen from approximately $40 million in July to double that, more than $80 million in October, and were projected to continue at these high levels—although fuel prices were always anyone's guess. When management extended the elevated prices in its forecasts, with no assumption of fare increases, certainly an unreasonably conservative assumption given the circumstances, it would only be several months before the company ran out of cash.

Needless to say, Jan Carlzon was shocked and very upset about this. He argued against the projection of fuel costs staying abnormally high for so long. Management assumed the enormous rise in fuel costs would continue indefinitely, without anything else happening. It was also unreasonable on management's part to assume that no action was necessary in response to the situation in their forecasts. Cuts in flying, cost cutbacks, fare increases, some moderation in fuel prices—these were all things are that could and should have been considered and built conservatively in their forecasts.

Under most bankruptcies, the shareholders are wiped out, so it was no surprise that Carlzon was feverishly opposed. However, management personnel who do not have a major stock position are often in favor of filing, if only because bankruptcy provides a clean slate and new low-priced stock options that they can ride up from their previous lows. Bankruptcy also takes the owner out from direct management and substitutes a bankruptcy judge in his place. Therefore, while the board decided to hold off at the October meeting, it was no great surprise to me that Harris was back at it in the December meeting, recommending that the board authorize a bankruptcy filing. This time, the board voted to do so.

Because of my contract, I had to stay on the board and witness this unfolding Greek tragedy. And tragedy it was, particularly for SAS and other shareholders. Over a two-year period after the filing, as conditions improved, the airline and its creditors sought other investors who could provide a capital infusion and acquire control in a plan to emerge from bankruptcy. SAS also entered a rough period during which Carlzon left SAS, and the company subsequently declined to provide more capital to Continental and support its major position.

A couple of friends from Houston discussed with me the possibility of becoming part of a deal to reacquire control, but I had moved on in my thinking and did not want to return to the airline wars. It was a "been there, done that" moment for me. As it turned out, the board (which included me) sold the airline to Texas Pacific Group, a new private equity firm founded by David Bonderman from Dallas and a West Coast partner, James Coulter. The Continental transaction went on to be hugely profitable for them, and the deal put Texas Pacific, later called simply TPG, squarely on the private equity map. At my last meeting as a member of the CAL board, we voted to sell the airline to TPG, and all the directors resigned to make way for new ones.

At that time, I was very busy with activities at Savoy Capital and with a lawsuit brought by some of CAL's subordinated creditors against Rob Snedeker and me. They sued us for a major portion of the sale proceeds, claiming that we had been unjustly enriched by the CAL sale. They tried to use the transaction structure—wherein CAL, funded by SAS, bought stock options from us for tax purposes—as a hook, claiming that for an instant, CAL had the option proceeds and should have kept it. They sought to bring the case, which was, obviously, totally without merit, before a jury. However, since we did not want to go through a long jury trial, we ended up settling the case after a year of back-and-forth.

The meritless creditor litigation was extremely time-consuming and frustrating for us. I learned after many sessions with our lawyers that jury decisions are all too often driven by emotion, not facts. They can be dangerous in situations like ours, particularly given the publicity that had been generated and despite the fact that all the evidence was on our side. The CAL sale was a relatively straightforward transaction, and the creditors' counsel clearly knew this, but there was always the possibility that the jury, infected by union propaganda, would take sides.

---

We were also occupied at Savoy in early 1992 by a start-up airline deal. I had promised myself when we set up Savoy that I would not get directly involved in airline start-ups, which were very popular at the time. Such an endeavor would distract us from the diversified business we were creating and require me to devote much too much of my time and focus to it. But I broke my promise by agreeing to partly finance and work on a start-up on the East Coast, because the need and opportunity were so obvious and because the management team, whom I knew well and who had brought the idea to us at Savoy, was so capable.

The business plan for the airline, initially to be called Friendship Airlines, called for developing a DC-9 aircraft hub in Baltimore, whose airport was then called Friendship International Airport and had no major hub operation. There were also many DC-9 aircraft on the market, in good shape, including quite a few from the liquidation of Eastern. The CEO of the airline was to be Steve Kolski, whom I knew well from Texas International days. He had been extensively involved with our start-up, New York Air. Dave Hackett, a great partner of mine who at the time was with Savoy, also played a major role with the new airline. Dave had airlines in his DNA—his father was a longtime senior captain for United.

Savoy agreed to provide the initial capital for the venture and assume the risk of financing and government certification. Financing proved to be a long, drawn-out process, since we were the first major start-up in the 1990s after a number of old-line airline failures. Both Eastern and Pan Am were wound down, not surviving their bankruptcies, and times were difficult for all airlines, including Continental. However, in the end we raised more than $100 million (around $221 million in 2024 dollars) from private investors and institutions for our venture, which was a tidy sum with which to start an airline in those days.

We did a lot of research into the viability of our investment thesis—the Baltimore hub—in an effort to determine whether any major airlines had the same idea in their near-term plans. The last thing we wanted was to start a new carrier that would be in the crosshairs of a carrier with a major Baltimore strategy and significant resources. One carrier that certainly could have been a possibility was Southwest. To get a feel for this, one morning at the Metropolitan Club in Washington I had a visit with Herb Kelleher, the longtime CEO of Southwest and a good friend. I often told Herb that in many ways, we owed much of our success to Southwest, both in the transaction in acquiring TIA in 1972 and in what Southwest taught us. Herb let on that he could see a significant Baltimore operation in the future, but not over the near term.

Another carrier that might well have had plans to bolster its Baltimore operation was USAir. However, it had strategic issues that kind of boxed it in. On the one hand, it was very big at close-in National Airport, and on the other, it seemed to want to build up its presence in Philadelphia to the north. But it was a competitor that was preferable to others, because unlike Southwest, it was a high-cost operator and a bit sleepy—or so it seemed from the outside. Consequently, we didn't worry about USAir.

We also studied the aircraft market and the likely availability of trained pilots. On both counts, we were quite reassured. Plenty of quality DC-9 aircraft were available, even in addition to those at Eastern, and there were many pilots just looking for our kind of opportunity. As we worked on finalizing the business plan and the financing, several eventful things occurred. The first was that folks at United Airlines let us know that they were unhappy with our using the name Friendship, since they used the word in a copyrighted nickname for the airline. Not wanting to chance a lawsuit, we changed our name to ATX Airlines because businesses that used letters as names were becoming very popular.

In addition, the Baltimore airport authorities decided not to support our application because of union objections. So we decided to move our main hub to Philadelphia, which at the time did not have a major hub airline. There, the unions had no success, because the airport authority and the capable Democratic mayor, Ed Rendell, were committed to what made the most sense for the airport and for area residents—unlike Baltimore.

Much more union opposition was to come. In fact, the major national labor unions joined the pilots' and the machinists' unions and took up the fight against us. They consistently found us a convenient hook for stirring up their constituents, since they had done a pretty good job of muddying my name in the past. Because of their PR investment, everything negative became "Frank Lorenzo" this or "Lorenzo" that.

A prime example of the union's opposition was that in February 1993, the AFL-CIO, at its annual executive council meeting in Bal Harbour, Florida, came away with six goals for the year. The first was predictable—stopping NAFTA, the trade agreement with Mexico and Canada. NAFTA had become a major issue for unions in their opposition to the newly arrived Clinton administration, which was striving to get the trade agreement approved. There were other goals that required fighting the new administration, too, the most important of which was welfare reform, also a Clinton priority. But the fifth AFL-CIO goal, as stated in a PR release and on a sign board in the hotel auditorium, was "keeping Frank Lorenzo from returning to the airline business." The unions put a lot behind this goal, making it a rallying cry for their members.

We filed our application with the DOT in January 1993. Normally, this application is almost automatically granted unless the principals have a criminal record—although even then they get a clean DOT slate after ten years! It was unheard of and unprecedented for a group like ours to be questioned, let alone made to endure a time-consuming, expensive hearing, since we had long, successful operating records. In fact, the DOT up to this point had been encouraging groups with financing to file, suggesting that it had a special desk for processing new carrier applications and that the process did not even require a lawyer. We were told this in November 1992, near the end of the Bush administration. However, we were set for a hearing in early 1993, after the new Democratic administration took over and the new regulatory world set in.

We tried to stop the hearing, since we knew it would mean a very public, expensive, and unnecessary union fight, but to no avail. It was becoming increasingly clear that the fix was in and that an administrative law judge—essentially an individual largely unaccountable externally—would set the stage for the DOT decision. Predictably, the hearing was in effect a public referendum on Frank Lorenzo's suitability for a major role in an airline, despite his having built one and a major airline for eighteen years and having been previously investigated by the DOT at the unions' urging and found to have a clean safety and maintenance record.

During the hearing, the well-respected Washington lawyer Thomas Hale Boggs Jr., who happened to be a friend, testified on our behalf as to our fitness. I had gotten to know Tommy, as he was called, when we purchased Eastern in 1986, because he was a representative of administrative employees and because he was a director who had been placed on the board by the pilots' union. At the time, we decided to keep a few former Eastern directors on our new board, even after we bought the company and could choose all its directors, in order to provide some important continuity and public credibility. Many wondered at the time why I would select a former ALPA nominee to stay on. Despite his union ties, I was impressed by Boggs's perspective and, given his strong Washington Democratic leanings, felt that he would add a lot of balance and credibility with unions. It was also clear that he was good at arithmetic and could add up Eastern's numbers and understand that something had to change.

There was great irony in the attack Boggs took from the ALPA attorneys at the ATX hearing. ALPA concluded its arguments before the law judge by saying that Boggs's testimony was biased and should be disregarded. A former ALPA representative was now biased and should be ignored! Who would have imagined this scenario?

Our arguments and witnesses were to no avail, and the law judge presiding over the case recommended that our application be rejected, quoting a litany of union complaints. He cited among many "facts" that I was chairman of Eastern at a time when the company had paid the biggest maintenance fine in airline history. Wow! Not mentioned, conveniently, was that while we did pay the fine—the biggest up to that point, at some $9 million—it had accumulated over the course of many years prior to our acquisition of Eastern and had been a disputed sore point between the airline and the FAA for years. We decided to clear up this old problem and simply pay it, since we were eager to have a clean slate with the FAA and it was an emotional issue with the airline's maintenance management, which wasn't helpful.

The DOT followed up shortly after the judge's decision with its formal rejection of our ATX application. We learned afterward from our Washington friends that for the Clinton White House, we were a very convenient "fish" to throw to the unions, since the new administration had other battles to wage with them and did not want this to be one of them. The AFL-CIO's fifth goal was an easy victory for the administration to let them have. We went to court afterward, since the case was an obvious distortion of the regulatory process, but as we knew beforehand, federal courts do not generally second-guess regulatory decisions unless fraud, collusion, or something similar can be proved—the unions were too experienced for that.

Another irony was that a month after our turndown, Sharon and I were seated in mezzanine box seats at the Kennedy Center for a concert when we were asked by an attendant to join the president and his guests during intermission. They were nearby, in the presential suite. We indeed went into the suite and met President Clinton and the First Lady. The president was very friendly but said nothing of consequence. Afterward, we asked one of the attendants how it was that we were selected to come over at intermission and were told that Mr. Clinton received the list of box attendees beforehand and chose a few names to invite. We figured that Clinton probably did not associate my name with the ATX case, since it was no doubt handled by his underlings.

Regardless, if there were doubts in our minds about whether an administration, supposedly guided by principles of independence and fairness, can influence a regulatory issue, they vanished. After the DOT's decision, Bob Crandall of American Airlines, a strong competitor of Continental during my ownership, said the DOT was clearly wrong to have denied our application. Crandall always had a sense of decency and had his own battles with American's unions.

Following the ATX affair, we continued the process of developing Savoy's business, generally undistracted by airline deals. Well, almost undistracted.

Later in 1993, we received a call from a successful Chilean businessman, Enrique Cueto, who was putting together a group to acquire control of LAN Chile and wanted to meet with us at Savoy. LAN had been owned by SAS and constituted the southern part of its new intercontinental connecting strategy. (CAL was intended to be the US and transatlantic part.) However, with control of CAL and Carlzon gone, SAS was not interested in retaining its LAN ownership—hence the call.

Dave Hackett, who remained at Savoy after the ATX deal fell through, set up the meeting; I was able to attend only part of it. Cueto laid out the group's plan to acquire control of LAN from SAS and build the company as a premier Latin American airline. At the time, there were not any profitable, successful airline operations in South America, so the opportunity seemed very promising. Cueto, having had experience with South American carriers, planned to become the company's CEO and lead the effort. He proposed that we become a partner in the deal with them.

Cueto was accompanied at the Houston meeting by two other proposed investors, one of whom was Sebastián Piñera, who was at the time a successful Chilean businessman, well known for introducing credit cards to Chile—an initiative from which he profited significantly. Aside from being an investor, Piñera was also interested in politics and would go on to become president of Chile from 2010 to 2014 and again from 2018 to 2022. We turned the LAN investment down, largely because we weren't very confident of investments in South America and Chile at the time and were concerned about the probability of a profitable South American carrier turnaround.

The Cueto-Piñera group, which would go on to great success with the LAN investment, turned the losing air carrier into a highly successful company a decade later, partnering with American Airlines. On assuming the Chilean presidency in 2010, Piñera sold his 26 percent interest in the company for well over $1 billion. We would go on to other investments in South America and would most likely have come to a different decision on the LAN investment in later years. Ironically, I bumped into Piñera between his presidencies in 2015 at a luncheon hosted by an old Argentine friend, Santiago Soldati, in his José Ignacio, Uruguay, home. Piñera reminded me that we had met at our office in Houston, although he didn't remind me of how successful the deal ended up being. We have turned down a lot of eventually successful deals over the years, as well as many turkeys, but I suspect this was the most ultimately profitable one we left on the table.

In the mid-1990s, even though we were determined to stay away from airline start-ups, we were receiving a number of calls from airline entrepreneurs looking to raise capital. We were not eager to repeat the ATX experience, with its frustrations and expenses, anytime soon and were committed to the diversified investment route that Savoy had been pursuing with some success.

In 1995, however, I received a call from Abe Claude, a former J.P. Morgan banker who had become a headhunter at Russell Reynolds Associates, asking whether I would take a call from a Spanish partner of his, acting as go-between for Javier Salas, then the CEO of SEPI, the Spanish holding company controlling Iberia airline. SEPI also owned and directed many important Spanish government companies. I ended up having a pleasant lunch with Salas, whom I had flown to Madrid on Iberia, their airline, especially to see. He offered me one of the first of three nongovernmental seats on Iberia's board. Privatization of government-controlled properties was in the air then, and adding three nongovernment voices to Iberia's board was planned as a first step. But apparently, someone leaked the names of the proposed board changes to the press, and ALPA in Washington, learning of this, went to Spain to convince the Iberia pilot union that I was a terrible guy and should be fought.

When I heard about this, I went to Spain and again lunched with Javier and told him that I did not want to get into another public union fight and that we could handle matters through a private advisory contract. As a result of this association, Savoy went on to spend two very interesting years advising the government, principally through Salas and the CEO of Iberia, Juan Saez. Our work provided the initial stage of a tie-up with American Airlines, which also brought in British Airways as well as a strategy to deal with Iberia's South American airline investments—Aerolíneas Argentinas in Argentina, VIASA in Venezuela, and Ladeco in Chile. Our work with Iberia and a later attempt to purchase Aerolíneas Argentinas, then owned by Iberia, with a group largely from Spain and Argentina, introduced me to a world of opportunities in Spain that affected many of my undertakings for years afterward, both in and out of business.

Later in the 1990s, Savoy partnered with a Spanish investment banking firm on a private equity fund for investment in the Iberian Peninsula. Savoy also maintained an investment office in Spain until 2004, closing it only when the anti-American Zapatero government was elected, at the time of the terrible terrorist-inspired Atocha train station bombings.

Presenting an award to Leopoldo Rodes from Spain, at the Hispanic Society Gala (2012).

On the cultural side, I became directly involved with Madrid's Prado museum in 2006 as a member of its international advisory board. I have found this association, which gave me an insider's view of the museum's major financial turnaround, very interesting as well as culturally stimulating. Sharon and I have made many great friends within the group, and it continues to be an important activity of ours.

Also important to me has been my association with Spanish cultural organizations in the United States. I served for a number of years as a director of the Queen Sofia Spanish Institute in New York, which offers Spanish lessons and hosts myriad cultural, medical, and humanitarian events. My association with the organization led me to put together a successful exhibition of Spanish artworks in 2004 at the institute's former building on Park Avenue, principally sponsored by Boeing. The art came from the Hispanic Society of America, which was celebrating its one hundredth anniversary in 2004. The following year, I was elected one of five trustees of the Hispanic Society. Its museum building, renamed the Hispanic Society Museum and Library in 2015, houses one of the most amazing collections of Spanish art objects and books and manuscripts outside Spain.

I've also been actively involved with a number of charitable organizations as trustee or director, such as the Boys & Girls Clubs of America and the Woodrow Wilson National Fellowship Foundation, which has

With Denzel Washington at Boys and Girls Club of Houston (1991).

since been renamed the Institute for Citizens & Scholars. In addition, I've been a member of the Nutrition Council at the Harvard T.H. Chan School of Public Health, Department of Nutrition, given my passion for good nutrition and making nutrition education accessible to K–12 schools in lower income areas.

My interest in the art world has also been nurtured by Sharon's activities in the field. After graduating from Mount Holyoke, she went on to receive a master's in art and education at Columbia University as well as a JD and MBA in Houston. She also studied at the City University of New York, receiving an additional master's degree (in the history of art of Spain and Latin America) and nearly completing her doctorate, lacking only the approval of her thesis. It has been enjoyable to see her recognized as an authority on a range of art-related subjects. Among her many activities has been teaching a seminar in art law at the University of Pennsylvania law school, writing art criticism for the lifestyle blog *A Sharp Eye*, and lecturing on a variety of art subjects

Sharon and I are never too far from an airplane, because we love to travel. Both of us got the bug at an early age. I took my first flight when I was fifteen, as I've recounted. Sharon took her first trip when she was seventeen and went to Paris by herself for a summer, polishing her French at L'École Française. We have visited my parents' hometown in Spain on numerous occasions and have dug up the birth records of Sharon's ancestors in their hometowns in Scotland and Denmark.

Without question, travel has been a rich source of fulfillment in my life, both on land, in numerous car trips that Sharon and I have done through our lives, and in the skies. Not least important, sharing these special destinations with family is one of life's greatest pleasures.

# Postscript

I AM often asked about the major changes have taken place in the airline industry since my days in the field. There certainly are almost too many to list. We all know that airports and airplanes are more crowded. But behind the scenes, much has also changed.

The influence of technology on the industry has been nothing short of profound. When I left the business, I didn't even have a computer on my desk. Now passengers at airports are going through new boarding procedures made possible by automation, and in many cases, artificial intelligence. The government now uses facial recognition to eliminate the time and manpower consuming passport control. We just show our face and then get waved into the country under some border entry facilities.

In addition, many airlines follow checked baggage electronically, which vastly improves recovery when needed. Now you can buy an AirTag from Apple or something similar and follow your own bag. When it doesn't show up in baggage claim—and the airline doesn't know where it is—you can simply point to your phone screen and tell the airline, "Here's my bag—go get it."

But perhaps the most obvious changes for passengers have taken place in the area of marketing and sales. In my day, a passenger could call an airline and make a reservation without showing up for their flights. The no-show problem—passengers not showing up for their reservations—was a big one. This led to the low load factors that were commonplace and affected the seat cost. We used to think of 60–65 percent load factors as normal. Today, as travelers know, it's much higher, in the 80 percent range at a minimum. No longer do we just make reservations; now we buy tickets that are usually nonrefundable.

In addition, technology has greatly changed airline operations, especially takeoffs and landings. All a pilot sees today in a modern cockpit are glass screens. GPS and automated navigation approaches to airports are common. But much more needs to be done and researched in terms of air traffic control to take advantage of new technology. Maintenance recordkeeping has been vastly streamlined as well. Computers follow an aircraft's operation throughout its journey now. This "health monitoring" can often pinpoint a failing part before it dies so that a mechanic can meet the plane at the gate and fix or replace the part on the spot without the need to troubleshoot from scratch. This reduces or eliminates delays and helps keep the plane and its passengers on schedule.

But while the effect of technology has been enormous, in many ways I believe that a less obvious yet equally far-reaching change has taken place in the area of leadership. There are many more entrepreneurial types of individuals leading airlines these days in the competitive, less regulated environment made possible by deregulation. Many of them, of course, have started new airlines, like Wizz Air and Volotea in Europe, Breeze Airways and Avelo Airlines in the United States, and lots of others throughout the world.

However, this entrepreneurial focus has not been limited to start-ups. I don't think that the airline business under government regulation would have attracted many of the leaders of today—although there are exceptions, such as Fred Smith, who started Federal Express in 1971, years before deregulation, and is probably the most respected transportation entrepreneur. One example of an entrepreneurial manager currently is Scott Kirby, the CEO of United, who is leading the way in a number of new areas for his airline. He has been strongly encouraging the development of SAF (sustainable aviation fuel), now increasingly seen as a reality down the road. He has also been pushing for the use of battery-powered aircraft on short flights and has led the way in financing with the establishment of a venture capital arm to invest in these areas.

American, Alaska Airlines, and many others also have entrepreneurial leaders and new venture capital arms. They have placed orders for battery-powered eVTOLs (electric vertical takeoff and landing vehicles), battery- and hydrogen-powered aircraft, and hybrids. Manufacturers have also been very active in these areas. Boeing invested in and is developing Wisk, an electric autonomous advanced air mobility (AAM) aircraft, and is placing big bets on SAF.

Another major effort in the area of alternative energy involves hydrogen. While Boeing apparently doesn't believe a hydrogen-powered aircraft is achievable until at least 2040, Airbus has a 2035 target date for a hydrogen-fueled aircraft in the one-hundred-seat sector. (It should be noted that in 2023, its executives began hinting that this target date could very well slip by years.) It uses four propeller-driven motors, and its range is more suitable for the regional market than for mainline airlines. But hydrogen requires a massive investment in production and distribution infrastructure. It will be, I think, decades before mainline hydrogen aircraft are feasible.

In addition, there are a host of technical challenges for a sustainable battery-powered aircraft to overcome. For example, the weight of an airplane goes down in flight as fuel is used. But the weight of batteries stays the same, cutting into range. So the technology must make huge advances before even medium-range aircraft are possible. These and similar aircraft will have a minuscule effect on the commercial airline industry. Commuter aircraft constitute a low-single-digit fraction of the total number of aircraft in service, and it will take decades to turn over the fleet with these and superseding larger designs. But this doesn't mean that small steps won't be pursued. It's an important start.

Major airlines are undertaking other entrepreneurial pursuits in addition to the development of new aircraft. Delta's purchase and operation of a refinery come to mind. The eVTOL start-ups intend to create an entirely new air taxi industry—tiny flying machines that allow passengers to overfly congested highways between airports and downtowns or between downtowns and suburbs. However, an entirely new certification system will be required across the globe, and new air traffic management systems must be created to control the plethora of "bumblebees" buzzing around the cities and in and out of commercial airports, below controlled airspace.

------

I have been asked a number of times: What became of the great old airlines like Pan Am, TWA, and the like? Many other airlines disappeared through mergers or acquisitions, including Western, Northwest, Braniff, Allegheny, and Piedmont, to name a few. Each carries its own story.

In the case of the well-known Pan Am, the company's leaders never developed a strategy to deal with deregulation. The airline was viewed as the US flag carrier and pioneered many famous new services, going back to the days of the Clipper—a flying boat—and, in recent years, the double-decker Boeing 747. After deregulation, however, its management was focused on route expansion, mainly to China as well as domestically, when it should have focused on its cost structure and the likelihood that it would be running up against low-cost competition. Buying National Airlines largely for the route structure and domestic mass it provided, then agreeing to raise National's labor costs to those of Pan Am, made no sense and was certainly a nearsighted management decision in a deregulated environment. After many unsuccessful attempts in the 1980s to reinvent itself, the company sold assets such as the famous Pan Am Building in New York to raise needed cash rather than take steps to be more competitive. Pan Am finally declared bankruptcy and ceased operation in 1991. Most of its route assets were bought by Delta.

TWA had much the same issue as Pan Am. Its management never developed a strategy to deal with deregulation. The airline, founded in 1930, had been owned by Howard Hughes since 1939. In 1960, Hughes was forced to put his stock into a trust at the insistence of banks before they would finance the jets TWA needed to compete. By 1966, Hughes had had enough of dealing with the banks, and despite the trust, nothing prevented him from selling his stock. The rest of the story is told in chapter 9. It was an unfortunate ending to a great airline.

Another question I've been asked concerns the influence of airline deregulation on the airlines I've been involved with. It is impossible to overstate its influence, initially on our efforts to merely survive and in later years on our efforts to sustain ourselves as a successful carrier.

Although deregulation was not approved until 1978, TIA got a taste of what it meant in 1971 when a start-up, Southwest Airlines, received approval from the Texas Aeronautics Commission to begin operations and compete with us. Operating wholly within Texas, Southwest was out of the jurisdiction of Washington and not regulated by the Civil Aeronautics Board. The Texas commission liberally approved Southwest's low fares and market entries while TIA was governed by the lethargic CAB from Washington. Southwest, as a new airline, employed new workers at entry-level wages and instituted liberal work rules. TIA's wages were the product of many years of union negotiations, going back to 1947, and were much higher and contained many expensive work rules as a result.

Southwest executives publicly vowed to put TIA out of business. We had to drastically adapt, or we would die. This led to renegotiating labor contracts and our experiments with Peanuts Fares. When deregulation was approved on the national level, in 1978, not only could Southwest expand beyond its traditional borders into the rest of the United States, the legacy major and local-service airlines could also expand at will into TIA markets and set prices we needed to meet in order to compete. New entrants popped up all over the country. Many of them were potential threats to TIA. In response, and taking our own advantage of deregulation, we expanded TIA's routes and marketing, launched New York Air, and embarked on growth through mergers and acquisitions. We had to gain infrastructure and slots at airports, and we needed a sophisticated computer reservations system. Our efforts to acquire National, TWA, Continental, Eastern, and others were driven by these realities. Some were successful. Some were not.

Our teams led the way on many fronts. Perhaps the most important was to show airline management, as of course many have done since, that price is an extremely critical factor for most airline passengers—just as it is in many businesses. We take this for granted today, particularly with computerization, which puts price first and foremost on flight reservation sites. But during the days when I was active in the industry, the importance of price was only beginning to be understood. Perhaps because most airline management personnel were able to fly for free or close to it, they never felt what consumers felt.

Today, carriers and the entrepreneurs who lead them have taken various approaches to the cost equation. There are carriers that "spend" some of their cost advantage by providing slightly better service, such as an improved seat pitch. There are also scheduled services provided by tiny airlines, such as Tradewind Aviation, which operates from small, convenient New York–area airports, and JSX, operating out of close-in Love Field in Dallas. Both airlines use small aircraft and emphasize their convenience. Of course, there are also many larger airline start-ups in the United States and abroad—the so-called LCCs and ULCCs (low-cost and ultra-low-cost carriers)—offering, as their names imply, even lower prices. These carriers provide bare-bones service, which passengers are willing to tolerate in exchange for the much lower prices. Carrier executives certainly understand price these days.

TIA did not invent cut-rate fares. Sharply discounted fares were in existence long before us, but there were major restrictions on their use. TIA, however, was the first airline to offer the *unrestricted* sharply discounted fares that today are common across the globe. We launched this fare promotion—Peanuts Fares—just before deregulation legislation was approved and began making record profits with them. Later aided by the freedom under deregulation to make creative marketing decisions without governmental economic oversight, we began internally considering "unbundling" services from fares in the late 1970s. Unbundling is common today and taken for granted. In earlier days, charging for checked bags and even food was unheard of. We didn't go forward with much of this at the time at our airline, although Donald Burr, after he left TIA in 1980 to start People Express, did use the unbundling concept quite effectively. Today, all airlines have some form of unbundled service, often to the great annoyance of the traveling public.

Many old-timers in the 1970s and 1980s resented me for taking an aggressive approach to our problems and challenges, several times in the feared arena of ownership and control. We were the first to resort to the stock market to solve our strategic needs. We were the first airline to launch a bidding war for a carrier and the first (and, to date, the only) airline to successfully acquire another carrier by appealing to its shareholders through the tender-offer route. These moves, of course, were made possible by the elimination of the economic regulation of the industry. Consequently, I was never a member of the "club." I was kind of feared by other members, perhaps largely because of these unfriendly deals and my willingness to take risks. I always sat at the end of the table during industry association meetings while the more established, more tenured, and older members sat toward the other end. They didn't want to sit near me.

---

Another question I'm often asked is whether airline deregulation has gone too far and whether some economic regulation should be brought back. This question brings to mind the famous comment by the dean of airline deregulation and chairman of the CAB during its dismantling, Alfred Kahn, who noted that with the legislation, the egg had been broken and was not capable of being put back together.

Some argue that airline deregulation has brought a progressive consolidation of the industry. However, it would be a mistake not to look at the industry before deregulation, when there were many mergers and acquisitions. Today, around 80 percent of US domestic passenger traffic is carried by four airlines: American, Delta, United, and Southwest. But there is no reason to believe it would have been different without deregulation. In fact, there might be even fewer dominant carriers, since Southwest was essentially a product of deregulation and is today one of the largest carriers. Also, Alaska Airlines bought Virgin America in order to gain assets and critical routes in San Francisco, Los Angeles, and elsewhere, and Alaska and JetBlue have attempted mergers with Hawaiian and Spirit, respectively, but been rebuffed by a very active FTC. As we did at TIA and Continental, these carriers have concluded that mergers and outright acquisitions are needed to gain critical mass, although the government had different ideas It should be noted that this need would still be present in the absence of deregulation.

Under regulation, the CAB protected existing airlines from all types of new competition, both from entrepreneurs and from one another. Applications for new routes often took years to process through the CAB. Changes to fares had to be approved. So did other changes, such as adding coach class to airplanes, lowering fares, adding liquor to in-flight service, and, as we found out, prohibiting cigar and pipe smoking.

Today there are efforts in political circles to reregulate the airline industry and occasional op-eds advocating the move. The theory is that airport congestion, crowded planes, ancillary fees, and pretty much all air transportation ills are the fault of deregulation. For example, in response to airlines squeezing in an increasing number of seats, the federal government is considering requiring a minimum seat pitch. In response to airlines installing lavatories that a small adult can barely fit into, the government is considering requiring potties that can accommodate wheelchairs and people with disabilities. In response to extended delays, the Department of Transportation now requires compensation to be paid under certain circumstances.

Yes, there's no doubt that the freedom to set fares, fees, and airplane configurations are rooted in deregulation, but this is what competing in a free market and its benefits are all about. As for crowded airports, this is a problem rooted in the historical lack of adequate funding by Congress. Fortunately, these calls for reregulation have been made in the wilderness, and I hope they stay there.

This trend, if that is a fair word, toward reregulation isn't happening in a vacuum. Today, airline labor unions are seeing a resurgence, alongside the resurgence of unions generally. Pilots won big, big wage hikes at American, Delta, and United. Later, Southwest and Alaska followed with hikes not as large but still quite substantial. Airline unions are doing fine in today's deregulated environment, but we can only assume they would be delighted to see a return to the regulated days—if the egg could somehow be put back together.

---

I have also been questioned about the legacy I left in the industry after my Continental days. Certainly, I have left more than just a lesson in how to reduce labor costs in a deregulated industry. I have no special secrets for that. In fact, Frank Hulse, the founder of Southern Airways, faced off with his ALPA pilots by hiring nonunion pilots during a strike long before I arrived on the scene. A long pilot strike doomed Mohawk Airlines, leading to its acquisition by Allegheny. Despite the reputation and unreasonable vilification received for being anti-labor, I feel that a larger price is often paid over time if the problem is just kicked down the road. I also feel that confronting the obvious issue up front allows a company to be honest with its employees about their futures and to move on to other critical areas. For example, we were able to build two new major strategic hubs, Houston and Newark, after we got our difficult times behind us, opportunities that other carriers would have jumped on had they been able to.

As I reflect on my airline career, I remember wanting to get involved with airlines even when I was a teen. Not aviation generally, mind you, but airlines. Perhaps it all got started when I planned and bought tickets for—with Dad's cash, of course—the trip to Europe I took with my family the summer after I turned fifteen and we went to see my brother, stationed in Germany, and explore the Continent. That was my—and my parents'—first experience on an airplane. For the following three summers, I sought a job with TWA, the airline we had flown to Europe on, and each year I was politely rejected by its personnel office until finally, when I was eighteen, TWA asked me to come in for an interview. I had been bitten by the airline bug, it would seem.

When I was in my early twenties, I tried other types of businesses—working for a brokerage firm, L. F. Rothschild & Co., during the summer of my junior year in college and applying to and being interviewed by American Can Company. I also interviewed with the auditing firm Haskins & Sells after college so I could consider the field of accounting while I was waiting for my hoped-for Harvard Business School acceptance. As a student at HBS, during the summer, I went to work for Kaiser Aluminum in California, but I realized there what it was that I really wanted to do. I only liked aluminum when it was part of an airplane. Hence my first job at TWA—but even that was after I turned down a Boeing offer following a trip to Seattle upon my HBS graduation.

If anything, my experience shows the value of pursuing your calling. My goal was building airlines. Most days for me did not seem like work—and I believe everyone should do what they love so they can feel this way. I always encourage young people heading out into their careers to follow their passion.

Later, when I was fifty, I also found pleasure in a field far removed from the airline business—the world of investing, which since then has also become a passion. I was exposed to investing at an early age. I can still picture my dad listing his stock purchases in a book each day, and I even recall some of the stocks he owned. When we were teenagers, he would ask my brother Val or me to walk down to the subway station on 63rd Drive in Rego Park after 6:00 p.m. and pick him up a copy of the closing edition of the *New York World-Telegram and Sun*, which listed the day's stock market prices. Sometimes it's easy to know where your passion comes from—all you have to do is remember what you love.

# Acknowledgments

THIS BOOK, a long time in coming, is a look at my upbringing and my career in the airline business and the strategies my colleagues and I adopted to deal with massive changes in the industry. Except for a few passing mentions, I have not attempted to detail my life after my airline days except to say that I did find great satisfaction in the world of investing and charitable organizations.

In developing and writing this book, I have been fortunate to have had tremendous encouragement and help from many gifted and accomplished individuals. I am grateful to one and all for their emotional and intellectual support as we gathered and organized the details of a long saga with many twists and turns.

This book would not have come to fruition without the support of my family, to whom I owe an enormous debt. From my parents, I learned patience and to never give up. They also taught me—and demonstrated by their example—how to succeed when you don't have much to start with, the real entrepreneurial spirit. From my brothers, Val and Larry, I learned tolerance. From my children, Nicole, Mercedes, Carolina, and Timon, I received loving reminders to persist, even when the going got tough. A special thank-you is due to Mercedes, who suggested the title of this book, *Flying for Peanuts*, as it combined our successful peanuts fares program and aviation, during her read of an early draft. Timon, in addition to his assistance with social media, helped me a lot with matters related to the computer and Microsoft Word and was enormously helpful at many points in the process.

Most important, from my loving wife, Sharon, to whom I owe so much for her caring, I learned to keep my head down and my feet on the ground no matter how complex the journey. I would not have made it without her efforts, pertinent suggestions, curiosity about how the project was coming along and, importantly, the reading of drafts.

I started putting *Flying for Peanuts* together around twenty years ago, a long time for a single book. Unfortunately, I too often thought of the project as *mañana*—i.e., I have other priorities today. I also found it difficult to spend time looking back because, after all, I had moved on. Initially, the project started with substantial research and writing assistance from Gordon Bock, a resident of Vermont. Gordon, who began the process with interviews, many with my now deceased mother, and days of lengthy research and writing, was followed by several writers, most prominently Peter Hochstein, who brought the project back to center stage in 2020 and whom I was very sorry to lose in 2022, when his life tragically ended during the COVID-19 pandemic.

This book then was shepherded by Scott Hamilton, an aviation writer and expert who helped me move forward to the end. Scott is an author in his own right whose books include *Air Wars*, a study of the competition between Airbus and Boeing. Scott has been of great assistance conveying to readers the breadth and depth of the profound changes in the field of commercial aviation during my active tenure in the business.

The editor of *Flying for Peanuts* was bestselling author Glenn Plaskin. I want to thank Glenn for his editing and his insightful review of the book and advice. His work was most important to me and to this project. (I appreciated being introduced to Glenn by my Nantucket neighbor and colleague, and now author himself, Ed Hajim.)

Also, I want to acknowledge the help of Justin Cummings from Savoy Capital, who saved me from computer disaster at various points. Eric Maniez, also at Savoy, handled the photos and illustrations; I would have been lost without his assistance.

In getting me to focus on completing this book, Ken Roman, formerly the CEO of Ogilvy & Mather and the writer of several award-winning books himself, offered invaluable support, especially by providing introductions and reading various drafts. I owe much to Ken.

There are so many things, beginning with the formation of Lorenzo, Carney & Co., for which I owe Robert J. Carney a lifetime of gratitude. Bob and I started out with an "office" in the public library when we were twenty-six years old, certainly with more chutzpah than experience, and went together from there. Bob continues to be a good friend today. I also must give an enormous nod of thanks to our first partners at Lorenzo, Carney, Robert D. Snedeker and Andrew Feuerstein. Rob continued as a valuable financial partner in all our airline properties until we sold control of Texas Air in 1990. Andy, after some years away from the business, returned as general counsel of New York Air, always keeping us out of trouble there.

As we moved forward with the acquisition of Texas International Airlines, there were countless others who led the effort and who helped this small airline become the legend it did. Robert D. Gallaway and James Arpey were the first to come on board, even before we had gotten CAB approval, and did a great job for us for many years.

In addition, Sam Ashmore, Jim O'Donnell, Jim Cassidy, John Adams, Sam Coates, Bruce Hicks, and Drake Hiller all played a major role throughout the TIA days and in some cases many years later as well. John Adams, after expertly negotiating so many of the exasperating labor confrontations we had at Continental, went on to have a career advising foreign car manufacturers that wanted to establish a presence in the United States, almost always in right-to-work states in the South

During the National Airlines period, and, later, at Texas Air and New York Air, Charles Goolsbee and Barry Simon were vital to our efforts, as was Phil Bakes, who joined us during this period, having been deputy counsel on the Senate airline deregulation committee. Phil went on to serve us in many leadership positions—at Continental as president, and at Eastern as CEO—until we lost control in 1990.

I also appreciated the work of Neal Meehan and the team he rapidly put together at New York Air with Stephen Kolski, Ken Carlson, Michael E. Levine, Larry Twill, and Doug Birdsall, among others, also quite important to our efforts. At Savoy Capital and TAC, I want to make special mention of Greg Aretakis and Dave Hackett, who were intimately involved in our airline investment activities. I also want to note the invaluable work of our outside counsel for most of my airline days—Tom Schueller of Hughes Hubbard & Reid. Tom continued to aid us for many years after TAC.

If I have accidentally missed mentioning others on our team who made it all work, I hope they will forgive me—their help was and is very much appreciated.

In addition, there there were many outside gifted advisers who served us admirably as board directors at Continental: John Robson and Alfred Kahn, both former CAB chairmen; Lindsay Fox, from Australia, who attended almost all meetings; and Thomas Boggs, of Washington, DC. Tommy continued to be my close friend for many years until his untimely passing in 2015. Lindsay continues as my close friend to the present day. I also want to give thanks to Robert Garrett, who played a major role on our board in later years and, in earlier years, as our banker, providing much of our securities financing and sage advice. Doug Tansill and Mike Milken were also of great help on the outside financing front. I got many ideas and contacts at Mike's "predators' balls." Carl Pohlad, from the start of our involvement, provided good counsel as director and adviser and never seemed bothered by the fact that his firm had previously controlled TIA. Other Texas friends who were of help were Jim Wilson, who served admirably on our board and provided wise counsel, and Ben Barnes, who continues as a good friend and counselor today.

Very importantly, I owe a big debt of gratitude to Millie Jones, my assistant for twenty-four years, first at Continental and later at Savoy Capital. Millie's ability to sense my needs, often before I did, was of enormous value to me. Millie, a good friend today, would be embarrassed if she knew how many times I have said, "That would not have happened if Millie were still with us."

Most important, there are the tens of thousands of employees of all the companies we built who combined to make our growth possible. Despite all the labor wars, thousands of employees were loyal to

Texas Air and its airlines. Some have been mentioned by name in this story. Others include the pilots who bucked the picket lines to establish the New Continental and ensure our survival. All were giving up their union position because of a belief in what we were doing. Some even write me today, which is inspirational.

I must also thank my many mentors, including professors at both Columbia College and Harvard Business School. At Columbia, the name that will always stand out to me is that of Professor Richard Neustadt, who insisted that I move on to Harvard Business School despite my grave doubts as to whether I could make it. At HBS, the two names that stand out are those of Jim McKenney, a great counselor, who many years later served on the board of New York Air, and C. Roland Christensen, whose lessons about strategy and subsequent encouragement served me well. I also must give a shout-out to Michael Porter, whose advice about competitive strategies was helpful to us, as was his advisory work on airline pricing.

I am hopeful that this account of my successes and failures will provide people in the aviation field with an awareness of how much work has been done to produce the amazing product we have today—safe domestic and international air travel. It is a story with many facets and layers, and I am enormously grateful for the assistance of the many people who helped us all produce it. The freedoms and responsibilities of the United States corporate and political environment, along with aviation technical research, will determine how the industry evolves in the days ahead.